STUDIES IN ECONOMIC HISTORY AND POLICY:
THE UNITED STATES IN THE TWENTIETH CENTURY

Drastic measures
A history of wage and price controls in the United States

STUDIES IN ECONOMIC HISTORY AND POLICY:
THE UNITED STATES IN THE TWENTIETH CENTURY

Edited by
Louis Galambos and Robert Gallmam

Other books in the series:

Peter D. McClelland and Alan L. Magdovitz *Crisis in the making: the political economy of New York State since 1945*

Drastic measures

A history of wage and price controls in the United States

Hugh Rockoff

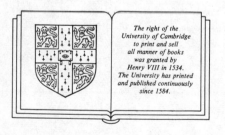

The right of the
University of Cambridge
to print and sell
all manner of books
was granted by
Henry VIII in 1534.
The University has printed
and published continuously
since 1584.

Cambridge University Press

Cambridge
London   New York   New Rochelle
Melbourne   Sydney

Published by the Press Syndicate of the University of Cambridge
The Pitt Building, Trumpington Street, Cambridge CB2 IRP
32 East 57th Street, New York, NY 10022, USA
10 Stamford Road, Oakleigh, Melbourne 3166, Australia

First published 1984
Reprinted 1985

Printed in the United States of America

Library of Congress Cataloging in Publication Data
Rockoff, Hugh.
Drastic measures.
(Studies in economic history and policy: the United
States in the twentieth century)
Bibliography: p.
Includes index.
1. Wage-price policy – United States – History. I. Title.
II. Series: Studies in economic history and policy.
HC110.W24R6 1984   331.2′973   83–21019
ISBN 0 521 24496 X

Contents

Editors' preface

The problem of inflation in America has been recurrent since early colonial days, and the history of governmental attempts to cope with this problem by imposing direct controls is equally long. Today, as this is being written, our most recent inflation is abating, each month bringing news that the rate of price increase is still lower than that of the month before. But it is too much to hope that the problem has permanently receded. We will encounter inflationary pressures again and again in the years ahead, and during the current interval of relative price stability it behooves us to learn as much as possible about the nature of inflation and the devices for keeping it under control.

Hugh Rockoff's book is thus timely and important. The author tells the story of American price controls from colonial times up to the Nixon price freeze. He describes the systems of control, placing each in its special historical setting. He appraises carefully the degree of success attained in bringing prices under control and weighs the benefits of each experience against the probable costs. Rockoff includes the direct and obvious costs, such as those associated with the government's administrative apparatus and private compliance; the less obvious costs, such as those incurred in the policing of the laws and in handling the added judicial burdens generated by noncompliance; and the indirect and pervasive costs of the misallocation of resources arising out of the suppression of the normal operations of the price system. His treatment of these issues is lucid and analytically rigorous. He provides us with a balanced rendition, free of the ideological commitment that characterizes much of the writing on this important subject.

Rockoff's book has lessons for today and tomorrow. We, the editors, are pleased that it has taken its place as the second volume in the series Studies in Economic History and Policy: The United States in the Twentieth Century.

LOUIS GALAMBOS   ROBERT GALLMAN
Professor of History   *Kenan Professor of Economics and History*
The Johns Hopkins University *University of North Carolina at Chapel Hill*

Preface

This book began with a conversation I had some years ago with the distinguished social psychologist Solomon Asch. His classic experiments on the response of individuals to group pressure flowed directly, or so I interpreted his remarks, from his attempt to resolve a crucial debate within his discipline. Economic historians, it seemed to me, also worked with experimental data, although in our case the data came from "natural experiments" – episodes of rapid and extensive change that threw the operation of economic principles into sharp relief. But too often we concentrated on minor problems suggested by fashion or the availability of data. The right thing to do, it seemed to me, was to follow Solomon Asch's example and search for the natural experiments that were relevant to the crucial issues. This line of thought led me to the decision to explore the effects of wartime price controls. For within the discussion of macroeconomic policy, the main alternative to current reliance on monetary and fiscal policy appears to be some form of controls. The judgment shared by many economists, moreover, that controls would always do more harm than good, derives in part from the proposition, properly qualified, which still lies at the heart of modern economics: Unfettered competition will produce maximum economic efficiency. Clearly, the wartime experiences provide evidence on a crucial debate.

The judgment that controls will always fail also derives from the erroneous belief that economic historians have exhaustively examined past experiments with controls and pronounced them a universal failure. Perhaps the importance of the issue has led people to assume that the work has been done and that the results support their preconceptions. In fact, these episodes have not received the attention they deserve.

The complete analysis of these episodes will be the work of many scholars over many years. Here I have taken the first two steps. First, I have tried to construct narratives of America's experiments with controls that pull together the available statistical and qualitative evidence, narratives that can serve as a starting point for others, as well as myself, for pursuing more specialized lines of inquiry. For the general reader, however, my second purpose is more important. I have also tried to form a tentative judgment concerning the typical costs and benefits of controls, and the circumstances that affect the ultimate balance of costs and benefits.

The voyage launched in response to Asch's remarks did not lead to the point I had expected. I began with the conviction that a close reading of the historical record would show what people thought it showed: that controls were always harmful. My intention was to place conventional opinion on a firmer basis and to convince the minority who still advocated controls (perhaps in the hope that future experiences will be different) to give greater weight to the lessons of history. But what I found made me more sympathetic to controls. I did not reverse my attitude toward controls 180 degrees; but I did come to the conclusion that there is a role for controls in certain inflationary emergencies. At times it becomes obvious that restrictive monetary and fiscal policies are necessary to bring inflation down to a tolerable level. But restrictive policies imply high rates of unemployment and reduced output – costs that often force us to abandon resrictive policies before they have worked a permanent cure. This was obvious even before our most recent attempt to control inflation, despite the claim in some quarters that if only the government could be sufficiently resolute in its adherence to its anti-inflationary policy, excessive costs might be avoided. In these circumstances temporary controls, if properly managed, can speed up the process of adjusting prices and wages to the restrictive policy, and so can reduce the pain associated with disinflation to bearable levels. In the chapters that follow I lay out the evidence that leads to this conclusion. Any sort of medicine may be abused, but the point is that this fact should not blind us to the potential benefits of a medicine when used in the proper circumstances.

The bulk of this manuscript was written in the academic year 1977–8 when, through the graciousness of Robert Fogel, I was on sabbatical at Harvard University. Although I have incorporated the results of more recent work in the narrative at various points, it has proved impossible to take account of all of the work bearing on these episodes published since then. My impression is that if the book were to be rewritten today, I would have to change many of the particulars, but that I would not be forced to alter the general thrust.

To many of my colleagues in economic history the methods employed in this book will appear to be something of a departure from current fashions. While there are some regressions hidden away here and there, the main emphasis has been on simpler forms of inference. This departure was dictated by the belief that these episodes can be viewed as natural experiments. If things change a lot in a short period of time, we can hope to understand the major consequences of those changes without recourse to econometric methods designed to deal with the essentially ambiguous messages of calmer periods. The hope, in other words, is that by choosing the right body of data we can avoid what appears to be the sterile path of repeating the same intellectual wars over the postwar experience with increasingly sophisticated econometric weapons.

I have incurred a heavy debt in writing this book that can be discharged only to a small extent by merely listing names. Stanley Engerman read the entire manuscript, including multiple drafts of certain chapters, and several related papers. His numerous suggestions have substantially improved the final product. A number of colleagues read the whole manuscript or at least several chapters and gave me many useful suggestions, which I have generally taken to heart. This group includes Peter Asch, Hope Corman, Stuart Bruchey, Robert Fogel, Claudia Goldin, Ian Hirst, John James, Geofrey Mills, Maury Randall, Richard Sylla, and Michael Taussig. They cannot be held responsible for the quality of the final manuscript – I did not always take their advice – but with their help the end result has become far better.

Several people made special contributions. Jeffrey Morse read several chapters from the point of view of the "intelligent layman" and forced me to dispense with much unnecessary jargon. John J. McCusker read the chapter on colonial and revolutionary controls. His great knowledge of these periods saved me from several mistakes. John Kenneth Galbraith took time out from a busy schedule to discuss his unique perspective on controls. Finally, my editors Robert Gallman and Louis Galambos did a superb job. The reader has much for which to thank them.

Librarians at Harvard, the National Archives (especially John Howlerton), the New York Public Library, Princeton, and Rutgers (especially Leslie Ota) gave generously of their time. Three graduate students, Robert Henninger, Steven Shilling, and Paulette Straum, did much of the computational work. The Rutgers University Research Council provided financial assistance for which I am extremely grateful.

HUGH ROCKOFF

New Brunswick

1. The debate over controls

The seemingly obvious remedy for the wage–price spiral is to regulate prices and wages by public authority. In World War II and the Korean War in the United States demand pressed strongly the capacity of the labor force as well as that of the industrial plant. . . . During both conflicts the wage–price spiral was successfully contained by controls.

John Kenneth Galbraith, 1967

Price and wage controls waste labor, both because of the distortions in the price structure and because of the immense amount of labor that goes into constructing, enforcing, and evading the price and wage controls. These effects are the same whether controls are compulsory or are labeled "voluntary."

Milton Friedman, 1979

The challenge of inflation

One of the most important debates on economic policy in recent years has concerned wage and price controls. For over a decade, the non-communist world has suffered a chronic inflation which has disordered economic life and crippled attacks on unemployment and poverty. Traditional remedies have proved costly when not ineffective, and there are few observers who would dare predict that the problem will abate soon. Inevitably, the hope emerges that order might be restored by bringing the power of the state to bear on wage and price decisions. But just as inevitably, warnings arise that the cure will be worse than the disease. Bureaucracy, inefficiency, evasion, and corruption, it is said, will become the identifying features of the controlled economy. Clearly, if the participants in the debate are correct, the stakes are high.

Right now, of course, the focus of public debate is on other means of dealing with inflation. Decreasing the rate of growth of the money supply – the conservative approach to monetary policy – may have some impact on the rate of inflation and the level of unemployment,

1

but it will not alter our economic and social structure in a fundamental way. Similarly, the debates on fiscal policy, whether, for example, to decrease the level of government spending and whether to do so by decreasing the government's deficit or the level of taxation, ultimately concern marginal changes in the structure of our economy.

But this is not so with wage and price controls. Introducing controls would profoundly alter the relationship between the government and the private sector, producing far-reaching changes in the economic and political life of the nation. While the current debate is not centered on these controls, they are likely to emerge as a major consideration in the years ahead. In the past twenty-five years controls have remained consistently popular with the general public, and when inflation has accelerated they have become popular with government officials as well. In 1971 these pressures caused an administration to impose controls that was, on purely ideological grounds, strongly opposed to them.

The term *wage and price controls* covers a broad group of policies, only some of which will be considered here. Sometimes the term refers to the control of a price in a single market or sector – in medieval times, for example, the price of bread. This type of control has important consequences, but it is generally not aimed at controlling inflation, the upward movement of the general level of prices. Nor is it likely that individual controls could provide this effect. Controls on prices in individual markets, if successful, are likely to divert purchasing power to other markets, and cause prices in those markets to rise somewhat faster. For this reason controls of this sort are not discussed in the following chapters.

The term *controls* is also used on occasion to refer to a variety of measures that seek to control the general level of prices, but that rely on moral suasion, or other limited forms of enforcement. An example is the guidelines for wage and price increases employed by the Kennedy administration, or the similar policies attempted by the Carter administration.[1] These measures were aimed at controlling the general level of prices, and might legitimately be included in a history of controls. I have chosen to exclude them largely because in retrospect they seem to have been relatively ineffective. Closely related to these measures are the proposals made by a number of economists for penalizing wage and price increases or rewarding restraint. This set includes the Tax Based Incomes Policy proposed by Wallich and Weintraub, which would penalize firms which granted wage increases above a guideline, and the numerous offshoots and descendants of this proposal.[2] This class of policies is not treated at length in the narratives simply because there are few historical precedents. Although some of the episodes discussed – for example, the period of selective controls at the beginning of World War II, and the period after VJ day – will be of interest to students of these policies.

Beyond these limited forms of controls are temporary wage and price controls applied over a wide range of goods and services, backed by the judicial power of the state, and aimed at combating inflation in an emergency. There are several examples of this sort of control in the American experience, and it remains in the public mind as one of the key alternatives to current policies. Focusing the historical narratives on these cases enables us to examine in some depth a series of highly varied episodes. To take one example, in some cases controls began with an across-the-board freeze covering virtually all prices. In others, controls began with a program aimed at a large subset of "strategic" prices. This is an important difference and represents a choice which will probably be faced if controls are again adopted.

At the other extreme lies a permanent system of controls and rationing. This policy, too, lies outside the American experience, and in any case, would have few adherents as a potential cure for inflation. Few Americans would be willing to stand indefinitely the reduction in economic freedom that is implicit in such a policy.

When Americans debate the need for controls, their discourse can be likened to that over some new and potent drug. Advocates of the drug generally have the simpler case. They tend to emphasize the ability of the drug to alleviate an important symptom of the disease. The case for a new narcotic, for example, will emphasize the drug's ability to alleviate pain, and perhaps the corresponding freedom to employ drastic means of treatment. The critics of the drug, on the other hand, tend to emphasize long-term and indirect effects. The new narcotic might produce a dependency. When its use was stopped, the patient's suffering would actually be worse than before, and the narcotic might produce harmful side effects.

In the same way, the advocates of controls tend to emphasize the direct effects on current prices, while the critics emphasize the potential for a price explosion when controls are removed and such side effects as the development of black markets. In the debate over a new drug the issue is seldom whether the benefits or the side effects exist in the first place, but rather over the extent of the benefits and the seriousness of the side effects. It is the same in the debate over controls. Few economists would deny, for example, that controls are likely to create some black markets. What separates the advocates from the critics of controls is a different intuition about the potential extent of these effects.

The parallel between the debate over a new drug and over controls weakens when one examines the processes through which the debates are resolved. The medical profession can rely on scientific experiments to delineate with some precision the dimensions of the benefits, costs, and risks associated with a particular drug. This may not end the controversy completely – physicians may evaluate benefits and costs differently – but the likelihood of a genuine consensus is real. Economists, however, cannot experiment. The best they can do is to turn to the economic historian for an account of "natural experiments" with controls. For this reason phrases like "controls have never worked" and "we did it in World War II, and we could do it again" recur again and again in the ongoing debate over controls. Yet, surprisingly, few economic historians have addressed themselves to the history of price controls and even fewer have done so from the vantage point provided us by modern tools of economic analysis. With a few exceptions, the "natural experiments" with controls in American history have not been subjected to careful, critical examinations. It is the purpose of this book to fill this gap in our knowledge.

The case for temporary controls

Despite widespread opposition to permanent wage and price controls, a consensus exists among mainstream economists that in the right circumstances temporary controls can make a positive contribution to the fight against inflation.[3] This possibility exists because of the role of expectations in the inflationary process. Suppose that after a long period of expansionary monetary policy, with prices rising at ten percent per year, a new policy of slow monetary growth is adopted. Inflation would not stop instantaneously. Instead, because decision makers still *expect* inflation, they would continue to raise prices. Labor unions would seek contracts containing wage increases to cover the inflation they expect, and businessmen would raise their prices spurred by the fear of rising costs and confident that their rivals were taking similar actions. The result, in the short run, would probably be a severe recession. Eventually, rising inventories and falling sales would persuade businesses to reduce their price increases, and the economy would return to full employment with a slower rate of inflation. But in the interim the costs would be heavy. It is unlikely, moreover, that a democratic government would be able to stay the course. The more likely result would be the abandonment of the restrictive monetary policy.

In the situation described above, temporary wage and price controls could have a therapeutic effect. By persuading businesses to act in a manner consistent with the more restrictive monetary policy, controls would reduce the costs of transition and increase the credibility of the new policy.[4]

Even such a staunch advocate of the free market as Milton Friedman has spotted one case in which he believes that temporary controls served this purpose:

I know of one empirical case in which it did work – the case of Argentina. One year back in the 1960's a government was determined to end an inflation – a rare event in Argentina! It was very substantial, not your moderate kind of inflation. . . . They announced a new monetary policy which was going to be very strict and they accompanied it by a temporary fixing of prices and wages. By altering people's expectations, and cutting off the tendency for wages to rise in line with anticipated inflation, they did succeed in rather substantially reducing the rate of inflation with relatively little cost in the way of unemployment. Needless to say, this was a temporary success.[5]

Temporary controls of this sort, to put the matter differently, communicate useful information to decision makers in the private sector. If total demand per unit of output were being increased at only five percent per year, while decision makers were raising costs and prices by ten percent, it would be important for decision makers to be aware of these relationships. But few businessmen would really understand or care about a statement to this effect. An equivalent statement that prices can (should or must depending on the law) rise at only five percent per year would be widely understood and would be acted upon by the private sector's decision makers.

The special conditions underlying this case can be seen in Figure 1.1. Here the path of the fundamental determinant of the price level, money per unit of real output, is shown by the bottom line. The break at time t_0 shows the adoption of a restrictive monetary policy. In the absence of controls prices would follow the path shown by the topmost line. The break in this line at t_1 reflects the onset of a recession, the result of prices and wages being carried by momentum to a point inconsistent

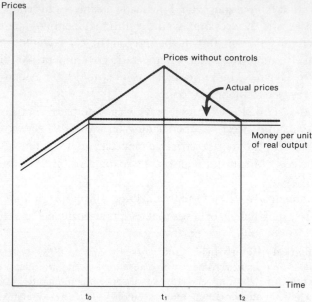

Figure 1.1. Price controls with monetary restraint.

with the fundamental conditions of demand. With controls, on the other hand, the price level would follow the middle line, thus minimizing the costs of transition to the final equilibrium at t_2 when controls are removed.

The scenario sketched in Figure 1.1, however, is only one side of the coin. If controls are not used in conjunction with a restrictive monetary policy the result could be a price explosion when controls were removed. This possibility is sketched in Figure 1.2. In this figure controls are imposed at t_0 but money per unit of output, shown by the middle line, continues to rise rapidly. In the absence of controls prices would follow the topmost line, but with controls they follow the bottom line. Thus, when controls are removed at t_1 prices rise more rapidly for a time until they return to the new equilibrium.

In this latter scenario the sole effect of controls has been to convert a relatively constant rate of inflation into a variable one. One of the basic assertions in the case against controls is that political considerations make this scenario inevitable. The imposition of controls, it is argued, frees the monetary authority to increase the money supply, perhaps even faster than before, in order to satisfy critics concerned with high

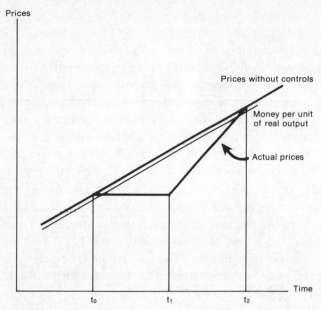

Figure 1.2. Price controls without monetary restraint.

interest rates or unemployment. Thus, one of the central questions in the following narratives is whether the price explosion model of temporary controls is as inevitable a picture of reality as the critics of controls claim it is.

The costs of controls

What dissuades most economists – even those who accept the first scenario as possible – from advocating temporary controls, is the belief that the costs of controls will be so great that even a substantial reduction in inflation could not justify their use. The most obvious of these costs is the large government bureaucracy required to administer and enforce controls. References to huge bureaucracies abound in the writings critical of controls, but no attempts to measure with accuracy the bureaucracies that have administered controls, or to forecast the bureaucracies needed in the future, accompany the arguments. In the following narratives, I will provide the reader with a description of the bureaucracies that have, in the past, administered controls so that he or she can decide whether the governmental apparatus would indeed be too costly.

This question is more complex than it appears to be on the surface. For one thing, the task of administering and enforcing controls was often divided among a number of agencies. Indeed, the question of which administrative tasks flowed from the attempt to control prices and which resulted from other constraints imposed simultaneously is often a difficult one to answer without an appeal to economic theory. Not all of the bureaucrats who administered controls, moreover, were government employees. Controls created bureaucracies internal to the business sector, which interpreted and applied the rules and responded to the government's demands for information. In wartime, the typical case, volunteers were used to help enforce the rules. The size of the bureaucracies cannot be appreciated, moreover, unless they are understood within the context of the economies in which they worked. The size of those economies, the extent of the inflationary pressures, and the degree of patriotic compliance all must be considered before a judgment can be reached about the bureaucratization likely to flow from a new attempt to impose controls.

Even if this bureaucracy were very small, however, the critics of controls would argue that they prevent the price mechanism from allocating resources efficiently. Demand and supply, they contend, are in constant flux. If there exists a surplus of one commodity and a shortage of another, then the price of the good in short supply will rise relative to the other. Resources will be attracted to the production of the good in short supply and demand for it will be choked off. Controls prevent this adjustment process from working automatically, thus lowering the real income of the community. This proposition, that a free price system allocates resources with maximum efficiency, is in fact the central proposition of modern economics. The work of most economists specializing in microeconomic theory could be described as specifying the conditions under which this proposition holds, or fails to hold.

As usual, Professor Friedman has put this point with the greatest force.

The reason suppressed inflation is so disastrous, . . . is that the price system is the only technique that has so far been discovered or invented for efficiently allocating resources. If that is prevented from operating, something else must be substituted. What do we substitute? It is always some kind of clumsy physical control.[6]

Given that this argument is central to the debate, it is surprising that the discussion has been carried on in terms of anecdotal evidence. It is not hard to find cases during periods of price controls in which controls clearly interfered with the efficient allocation of resources. I will examine many of them in the narratives that follow. But a long list of these cases is not likely to convince the skeptic. Allocative mistakes are also constantly being made in a free price system simply because businessmen must predict the future, and they can do so only imperfectly. The real question, the skeptic will say, is whether the volume of mis-allocations is greater under controls than under free markets – and if it is greater, how much greater. This question cannot be answered without recourse to an examination of aggregate statistics. The skeptic wants to know how large total output was in relation to total inputs under controls. Did this ratio rise or fall? Were other things happening in the economy that might have influenced this ratio? These are difficult questions to answer and this perhaps explains why so few advocates or critics of controls have plunged into the aggregate data. It is almost as if the participants in the debate have been afraid to put their cherished beliefs to the acid test.

Lest the reader think, however, that I intend to offer merely another dull recitation of statistics, let me explain now that I will also examine the black market. You should now be imagining otherwise law-abiding citizens slinking off to some deserted part of the city to buy goods at prices above those fixed by law; goods that cannot be had at the official price change hands in a dark alley, providing a script that holds equal fascination for the layman and the economic historian. This image also constitutes a major theme of the case against controls. What good are price controls that hold down an official index of prices if the "real price," meaning the black market price, is rising even faster than before? Indeed, even if inflation correctly measured is slowed by controls, is it worth the destruction of the social fabric implicit in the creation of a large black market? This fear is separate and distinct from the fear that controls will reduce economic efficiency. To the contrary, black markets may offset the negative impact of controls on productive efficiency. Suppose that the controllers have set the relative price of some good too low and that production has been curtailed as a result. One remedy is for the controllers to recognize their mistake and raise the price. An alternative, albeit a less efficient one, is for the producers to supply their product to the black market.

Although the term *black market* usually conjures up the sort of midnight transaction described above, this sort of thing has actually been less important than more mundane ways of evading controls. Some examples will provide a sense of the range of potential evasions. A simple one is the elimination of sales. If the price controllers attempt to freeze price tags as of a certain date, and demand continues to rise, the natural reaction of sellers will be to eliminate traditional discounts or regular sales. This action effectively raises the price to buyers that had previously taken advantage of sales or discounts. More irritating, and more significant, is the reduction of quality. There are two ways to raise the price of a candy bar, to take an example from World War II: either raise the price of the bar, or reduce its size or use inferior materials. In either case, the amount of money the consumer must pay for a standard amount of candy will go up. Under controls there is a tendency for increases to take the second, hidden form. These examples convey some sense of the enormous possibilities for evasion, and in the narratives to come these examples will be multiplied many times over.

Stories about black markets, even carefully verified stories, and even lists of dozens of stories, will not, of course, provide a sufficient reason for rejecting controls. Shoddy business practices occur under free markets, and most laws are evaded to some extent. The question at issue is whether evasion is likely to occur on such a scale as to make controls an unattractive alternative. In the case of black markets, however, the problems involved with measuring and assessing the effects of controls are magnified by the clandestine nature of the black market. Transactions that stand outside the law seldom find their way into official statistics. The one type of quantitative evidence which is available is the number of violations brought before the courts. This type of evidence will be explored at length. But frequently we can only guess at the relationship between the number of violators charged with illegal activity and the true volume of such activity.

Suppression of the black market is likely to require rationing, some form of quantitative allocation imposed by the government. If rationing is widespread, consumers are likely to find the constraints on their economic freedom irritating. This cost of controls, although not measurable in dollars and cents, has often been cited. The extent to which controls require rationing is thus also a major concern of the following narratives.

The imposition of controls means that considerable power is shifted to the government, either to the controllers themselves or to the legislature which sets the guidelines under which the controllers work. Ultimately, it is this shift of power which raises the most serious questions about controls. How will legislatures respond to their new powers? Will they set reasonable guidelines that permit the controllers to discharge their duties in an equitable way, or will they respond to the overtures of special interest groups by providing privileges and exemptions? The dangers, moreover, go beyond the corruption of the legislature to political freedom itself. Will the media be free to attack the government when the prices they receive and the costs and supplies of the resources they use are under government control? Indeed, will anyone feel free to oppose a government when the price and wage authorities determine his or her income? In effect, it is this danger to political freedom, I believe, which leads most economists to oppose permanent wage and price controls. Since I share their concern, I am pleased to report here that while the following narratives do raise serious questions about the legislative response to controls, they fortunately do not provide examples in which our basic political freedoms have been violated.

The uses of historical experience

While I have laid out the arguments over controls in terms of benefits and costs, it is clear by now that these cannot be reduced to strict numerical sums and added up to determine whether the net effect was positive or negative. The costs and benefits lie on different dimensions, so evaluations and comparisons require value judgments. There is not even agreement over how important it is to reduce inflation itself. The advocates of controls take it for granted that inflation is a destructive force worth going to great lengths to stop. The critics of controls tend to emphasize that once inflation is fully anticipated, people can protect themselves from its undesirable effects. Labor unions can negotiate higher wages or cost-of-living adjustments; lenders can protect themselves by charging higher interest rates. These and similar measures, the opponents of controls maintain, prevent the arbitrary redistributions of income which result when inflation is not anticipated.

The role of value judgments is even greater when comparing benefits with costs. Suppose that we knew that the rate of inflation could be cut from 10 to 5 percent at the cost of reducing aggregate productivity by two percent. Is that a fair bargain? People with different values would come to different conclusions. What a study of the historical experience can do is clarify the nature and extent of the costs and benefits. When, however, the historian weighs these costs and benefits, as I do in the following chapters, he must invoke his own set of priorities. That is why I have tried throughout to separate evidence from conclusions, so that readers can reach conclusions consistent with their own systems of values.

In reaching these conclusions, I think you will benefit from a careful study of the historical record. That record can do much to clarify the debate over controls because their history is surprisingly rich. Attempts to control wages and prices can be found in almost every epoch of recorded history. In ancient Babylonia the Code of Hammurabi fixed wages and prices in magisterial detail. In ancient Rome the most ambitious attempt was the Edict of the Emperor Diocletian issued in A.D. 301. This law specified maximum prices for a wide range of goods and services and provided the death penalty for violators. Severe as it was the Edict apparently failed, and became, so to speak, a dead letter (at least with the abdication of Diocletian four years later, if not before). Many centuries later, the revolutionary government of France tried repeatedly to maintain the value of its own rapidly depreciating paper money, the famous assignats, by fixing maximum prices. This experiment also failed, but this did not prevent other governments in other places from mounting similar attempts.[7]

Controls were also used in virtually every epoch of American history. They were frequently resorted to during the Colonial period and during the Revolutionary War. The Civil War, an episode in which one might have expected controls because of the severity of the inflation, was notably free of them. The exceptions were a few isolated attempts in the South. The absence of controls during the Civil War can be accounted for most easily by the ideological temper of the times. The prevailing economic philosophy was that of laissez-faire. In the North, particularly, the public and the administration looked on price increases as the inevitable cost of the war, a burden the public had to bear just like the far greater burdens on the men in uniform.[8] In later wars, however, America returned to wage and price controls to fight inflation. Democratic administrations during the World Wars and during the Korean War had little compunction about government interference with the market. During the Vietnam War the Nixon administration, which did have ideological reservations, resisted the call for controls for a long time, but eventually succumbed in August 1971.

These cases provide the substance of the following chapters. At first glance the association of each of these episodes with war might suggest that their relevance to the debate over peacetime controls is limited. We are inclined to dismiss wartime experiences as untypical, and hence irrelevant. But in several ways the wartime experiments with controls are ideal "natural experiments" with the type of controls that plausibly might be used in peacetime. For example, the wartime inflations were exacerbated by strong expectations of further inflation and by disturbances on the supply side – both of which are important aspects of the current inflation.

In describing these historical episodes I have tried to present a broad picture of controls and have relied on a wide variety of sources: traditional statistical series, numerous accounts written by former administrators of controls after their term of service, documents produced by the agencies controlling prices, newspaper and magazine accounts, court records and other official materials. In spite of this, I have undoubtedly made mistakes. My hope is that the gains in viewing the effects of controls in numerous circumstances, and in numerous forms, outweigh the cost of errors on details. Perhaps too, my broad-brush approach will stimulate my fellow economic historians to refine and correct the picture I have drawn. Even if it accomplishes nothing more, this book will have served a useful purpose.

2. Forgotten experiments

The attempt of New England to regulate prices is extremely popular in Congress, who will recommend an imitation of it to the other States. For my own part I expect only a partial and a temporary relief from it, and I fear that, after a time, the evils will break out with greater violence. The water will flow with greater rapidity for having been dammed up for a time. The only radical cure will be to stop the emission of more paper, and to draw in some that is already out, and devise means effectually to support the rest.

John Adams to Abigail, February 7, 1777

It is frequently said that opponents of price controls are preaching that "old time religion," faith in laissez-faire. By contrast, presumably, controls represent something new. To the historian of price controls this sort of statement must be considered simply as a symptom of historical myopia; government regulation of economic life was more the rule than the exception in colonial America. The rate of interest, the weight and price of bread, the fees of lawyers and physicians, and the wages of numerous workers such as carters, porters, and gravediggers were all subject to regulation at one time or another.[1] More to the point, a number of colonies also experimented with comprehensive controls over wages and prices. Let us review briefly the experience in two colonies, Virginia and Massachusetts Bay: Virginia because it witnessed both the first settlement and the first experiment with comprehensive wage and price controls; Massachusetts Bay because the Puritans were the most persistent about controls. For a time in the eighteenth century, interest in such experiments seems to have waned. But during the "hyperinflation" that marked the Revolutionary War, renewed attempts were made, and I will discuss these as well.

The modern fashion is to ignore experiments such as these on the grounds that since institutions have changed the experiments are irrelevant. To be sure, it would be foolish to jump to conclusions on the basis of experiments conducted in a very different economic and social environment. But it is also true that it is necessary to observe the effects of similar policies under alternative institutional arrangements in order to determine which features of our current setting are crucial. In the particular cases I will examine there are enough similarities between the purposes and policies of colonial times and those of our century to justify a measure of attention.

Virginia

Virginia, the first English settlement in North America, gave birth to the first comprehensive wage and price controls.[2] Virtually from its start, Virginia imposed a variety of price regulations on its citizens. In 1619 the export price of tobacco was fixed by the Virginia Company. The planters complained bitterly, and used the excuse that their tobacco was being resold with huge profits in Britain to justify passing bad tobacco. This is our first example of quality deterioration, a means of evading price controls that will recur in other contexts.[3] In 1621 the Governor and Council of Virginia laid down the first schedule of maximum wages. The schedule set the daily payment, typically four shillings or three shillings plus meat and drink, for various master craftsmen. Servants were entitled to one-fourth less.

These are examples of what might be termed "micro controls," attempts to control prices in one or more markets while other prices are left free to fluctuate. Such controls are usually not intended to control the general level of prices. Nor is it likely that they could do so if inflationary pressures were strong, because purchasing power diverted from controlled markets would add to inflationary pressure elsewhere. Control of the general price level requires "macro controls" – controls that are comprehensive in the sense that they cover most of the commodities traded in any economy. In any particular case, the distinction between micro and macro controls is a matter of judgment, because some markets or parts of markets are almost always left uncontrolled. But Virginia soon witnessed an experiment with what were clearly intended as macro controls.

During 1622 the colonists were attacked by Powhattan's tribe under the leadership of Opechancanough. The losses in men and material from the attacks, and from disease, were severe. Prices no doubt increased drastically. The upshot was that in 1623 the Governor issued a proclamation fixing prices and profit rates. Since this was the first comprehensive set of price controls issued in English-speaking America and since the circumstances and logic of it adumbrate many subsequent experiments, the proclamation and the associated price schedule are reproduced here in full.

A Proclamation touching the rates of commodities By the Governor and Captain general of Virginia

Whereas the rates and prizes [i.e., prices] of commodities here in Virginia, have of late and by degrees growen to a most excessive and unconscionable height, not only in Tobacco, but in ready money, to the great greevance of this state and commonwealth, the greatest abuse wherein hath risen by sacks, strong waters and other such drinks, especially from the common sort of people, who will give any rate, rather then want them: Which mischief being lately to grow and encrease daily (to the great weakning and impoverishing of this Colony) if some course be not taken for the present remedy, and future prevention therof. The Governor therefore (with the advise of the counsiel of estate) hath ordered and appointed, and by these presents doth straightly charge and command, that no person or persons whatsoever here in Virginia either adventurer or Planter, shall vent utter, barter or sell any of these commodities following, for above the prizes hereafter in these presents mentioned, viz.

		In Ready Money £ s d	In Tobacco £ s d
Sherry sacke	(per gallon)	0-4-0	0-9-0
Canary and Malaga	"	0-6-0	0-9-0
Alegant and Tent	"	0-6-0	0-9-0
Muscadell and Bastard	"	0-6-0	0-9-0
Aquavitae	(per gallon)	0-4-0	0-6-0
Sallet oyle	"	0-6-0	0-9-0
Wine Vinegar	"	0-3-0	0-4-6
Beere Vinegar and Sider	"	0-2-0	0-3-0
Loafe sugar	(per pound)	0-2-0	0-3-0
Powder Sugar	"	0-1-8	0-2-6
Butter and cheese	"	0-0-8	0-1-0
Newfoundland fish	(per centum)	0-15-0	1-4-0
Canada fish	"	2-0-0	3-10-0

And because it is impossible for them to sett particular and certain rates and prizes upon all sorts of goods wares and commodities by reason of the difference of kinds, and degrees in goodness: It is further ordered and appointed, that no person whatsoever wither adventurer or planter shall vent utter, barter, or sell, any goods wares or commodities of what kind or condicion soever for more profitt and advantage then (sic) ten shillings in the pound in meny [money] and twenty shillings in Tobacco, according as the said commodities are worth the first penny in England. Upon paine of forfeiture and confiscation of all such money and Tobacco received or due for commodities so sold (contrary to the aforesaid orders) the one half to the informer, the other halfe to the State. And if any shall buy any goods or commodities above the aforesaid rates and prizes, and shall not within ten dayes after such sale (or sooner if such goods were bought of any Ship, which is sooner to depart) informe the Governor, or some one of the Consiel of estate thereof: that then the said buyer shall forfeit the value of the said goods, the one halfe to the informer, and the other half to the State. And it is further ordered and appointed, that if any marchant or other, having sold his goods, shall dislike his Tobacco, and (upon triall by sufficient men upon their oathes) the said Tobacco shalbe found not marchantable, then it shallbe brought into the markett places of James Citty and there burnt. Given at James citty the 31th day of August 1623.

Francis Wyatt[4]

This set of controls illustrates a common feature of later regulations: the association of controls with war. War, through the destruction of goods and services and, in later episodes, through the emission of currency, tends to produce a sudden inflationary psychology and devastating increase in prices. Both political pressures, and as I will try to show, economic logic, combine to produce controls in these circumstances.

There appears to be little evidence on how well this first experiment in comprehensive price fixing worked. Two years later a renewed fear of shortages led Wyatt and his Council to issue a revised schedule. But in 1632 Virginia eliminated a law that fixed the price of corn, and in 1641 a royal ordinance, inspired by English merchants, eliminated these price-fixing statutes. Still later, in 1655, the limitation on the rate of markup to 50 percent was repealed. Little can be deduced from the legislative record about the impact of these controls during the emergency, but we can conclude that the results were not favorable enough to persuade the colony to use peacetime price controls.

Virginia did not attempt to fix the general level of prices and wages again during the colonial period. She did, however, legislate in selected markets. In 1639 she became the first colony to regulate physicians' fees. This statute was repeatedly reenacted and in 1736 fees were set for several health-related professions (with allowance for the distance traveled by the physician being taken into account). In short, there are clear precedents for some of the most controversial regulatory legislation now being considered in the history of seventeenth-century Virginia. At least in economic policy, there is nothing new under the sun.

Massachusetts Bay

Wage and price fixing were both familiar and congenial to the founders of Massachusetts Bay. In England during the Elizabethan period, price-fixing orders were frequently employed in periods of agricultural scarcity, and these were later codified in the Book of Orders issued in 1630 – just about when the Puritans began one of their most active periods of price fixing. Wage fixing, too, was familiar; its English history extending back centuries before the Puritans arrived in New England. Indeed, it is likely that some of the early leaders of Massachusetts Bay had firsthand experience with the provisions of the English codes.[5] The notion that the state should control the morals and behavior of individuals, moreover, was as accepted by the early Puritans as the commitment to liberty was by later New Englanders.

Although the prices of corn and beaver, two of the key commodities dealt with by the colonists, were set earlier, the first detailed attempt to interfere with the price-making process occurred in August 1630 when a scale of wages was set for the building trades. Wages for carpenters, joiners, bricklayers, sawyers, and thatchers were limited to two shillings per day. For piecework, sawyers were limited to 4s 6d per hundred for boards cut from felled and squared logs, and 5s 6d if they did the latter work themselves. A penalty of 10s was to be imposed both on the employer and the employee in case of violation. About a month later the rate for builders who received meat and drink was set at 16d per day and workers of the "second sort" in similar circumstances were set at 12d.[6] There was no attempt, at this time, to fix prices, although in some cases the distinction between wages and prices was a fine one. For example, fixing the piece rate of sawyers was virtually equivalent to fixing the price of boards.

Six months later the attempt was abandoned. But in 1633 another scale was fixed. The rates were similar to those of 1630 with skilled laborers again being allowed two shillings per day. These rates, apparently, were well below the current market, because Governor Winthrop, in his journal, reported that carpenters were demanding three shillings per day and unskilled labor 2s 6d.[7] Morris has argued that the high land-to-labor ratio in the colonies doomed wage control.[8] But this was only part of the story. Surely what doomed the schedule was the failure of the Puritans to realize that the wages they felt were appropriate were well below the prevailing market. Would wage control have been any more effective in the old world (with its lower land-to-labor ratio) if an attempt had been made to keep wages so far below the market equilibrium?

To balance the wage-fixing law the General Court also fixed the markup on imported commodities. The basic markup was to be 33⅓ percent, four pence in the shilling. But cheese, because of the risk of spoilage, and liquids (wine, oil, vinegar, and "strong waters") because of leakage, could be sold at any mutually agreeable price provided it was "moderate." Linen and other low-risk, easy-to-transport items were also free to seek their own level. But the General Court warned that "if any man shall exceed the bounds of moderation wee shall punish them severely."[9] A few days earlier the General Court had fixed the price of corn at 6s per bushel and had provided for a primitive kind of rationing: only corn that was unfit to be eaten by human beings was to be fed to hogs, and the number of hogs a person might keep was to be limited by agreement of the community.[10]

In all, this appears to be an example of macro controls. The Puritans were not merely trying to prevent certain prices or wages from rising relative to others. They also appear to have entertained hopes of holding down the general level of prices in the face of strong inflationary pressures.

The legislation of 1633 represents perhaps the only example in our history of wage and price controls being imposed in peacetime. But the situation in Massachusetts Bay in the 1630s was quite similar to a wartime economy. In 1630 the great Puritan migration had begun with an expedition of seventeen ships and 1,000 people, the largest such expedition in the seventeenth century. The Puritans arrived with a good deal of wealth, including cash, and pressing needs for housing, food, and so forth. Inevitably, the prices of these commodities and of the resources that produced them rose dramatically. Thus, although the source of demand was somewhat different, the rulers of Massachusetts Bay faced the same problem of how to cope with excess demands that normally face the authorities only in a wartime economy.

It is interesting to note, by the way, that the price regulations passed in 1633 were similar in several ways to those employed in World War I. In both periods the attempt to control the absolute level of agricultural prices was limited to key commodities. In both, rationing was done indirectly. In both, there were broader efforts to control profits in distribution without interfering with general upward changes. The emergence of similar codes in similar economic circumstances, but at widely separated points in time, suggests the fundamental moral appeal of controls in emergency situations and suggests that we may well see their use again.[11]

The policies of 1633 were, however, soon abandoned. In 1635 the wage and price laws were replaced by a general prohibition against "excessive" wages or prices. These laws do not seem to have been much enforced. But there were a few interesting cases. One was that of Edward Palmer who, in 1639, was accused of charging too much for the wood used to construct the Boston stocks. He was found guilty and as punishment was ordered to pay a fine and to sit in the stocks built from his own wood![12] In 1636 the regulation of wages was turned over to the towns. Apparently, this approach was plagued by competition among the towns for labor. In 1641 the General Court reentered the wage-fixing process, ordering workers to cut back their wages in proportion to the fall of commodity prices that had taken place.[13] This law is strikingly similar to the "Little Steel Formula" that was used in World War II. This formula, which was first applied to the steel industry, limited wage increases to amounts matching the increases which had occurred in the consumer price index. Again, it appears that in wage and price policy there is little that is new, and little that we might not witness again. With the exception of this 1641 law, however, wage control in Massachusetts Bay was left to local authorities during the forties, fifties, and early sixties.

John Winthrop's contemporary evaluation of the effects of the early Massachusetts wage laws has generally been taken, with good reason, as definitive.

The Court having found by experience, that it would not avail by any law to redress the excessive rates of laborers' and workmen's wages, etc. (for being restrained, they would either remove to other places where they might have more, or else being able to live by planting and other employments of their own, they would not be hired at all,) it was therefore referred to the several towns to set down rates among themselves. This took better effect, so that in a voluntary way, by the counsel and persuasion of the elders, and example of some who led the way, they were brought to more moderation than they could be by compulsion. But it held not long.[14]

It would be hard to find a clearer statement of the effects to be expected if the government fixes a maximum wage below the equilibrium, and then fails to ration available supplies.

There were a considerable number of subsequent attempts to regulate prices or wages in the Bay colony.[15] But, with the possible exception of the laws passed during King Philip's war, to be discussed below, these regulations appear to have been aimed at preventing individual sales at disequilibrium prices (sales influenced by fraud, ignorance, or short-run monopolies), rather than at lowering the equilibrium price in a particular market, or lowering the general level of prices. This distinction is illustrated clearly in the celebrated case of Robert Keayne.

In 1639, Keayne was accused of charging an extortionate markup on British goods. To be sure, Keayne's case occurred toward the end of the inflation caused by the Puritan influx, so it might have been motivated by general feelings against high prices. But the case was argued in terms of disequilibrium trades; Keayne had charged more than the market price. It was not held against him that the market price was high, although this could have been the real complaint.

Keayne was disciplined although not excommunicated, and the case led the Reverend John Cotton to discuss the ethics of pricing from his pulpit. According to Winthrop's journal, Cotton laid down the following "false" principles:

1. That a man might sell as dear as he can, and buy as cheap as he can.
2. If a man lose by casualty of sea, etc., in some of his commodities, he may raise the price of the rest.
3. That he may sell as he bought, though he paid too dear, etc., and though the commodity be fallen, etc.
4. That as a man may take the advantage of his own skill or ability, so he may of another's ignorance or necessity.
5. Where one gives time for payment, he is to take like recompense or one as of another.

and the following "true" principles:

1. A man may not sell above the current price, i.e., such a price as is usual in the time and place, and as another (who knows the worth of the commodity) would give for it, if he had occasion to use it; as that is called current money, which every man will take, etc.
2. When a man loseth in his commodity for want of skill, etc., he must look at it as his own fault or cross, and therefore must not lay it upon another.
3. Where a man loseth by casualty of sea, or etc., it is a loss cast upon himself by providence, and he may not ease himself of it by casting it upon another; for so a man should seem to provide against all providences, etc., that he should never lose; but where there is a scarcity of the commodity, there

men may raise their price; for now it is a hand of God upon the commodity, and not the person.

4. A man may not ask any more for his commodity than his selling price, as Ephron to Abraham, the land is worth thus much.[16]

What Cotton is saying, to use modern terms, is that the just price is the equilibrium price that would prevail in a world of perfect competition. What he seeks to prohibit are "disequilibrium trades," those that occur at some other price due to the ignorance or necessity of the buyer, or the monopoly of the seller. Point 3 under the true principles is especially clear. If an individual merchant suffers a loss, he may not take advantage of the ignorance of the buyer or a temporary monopoly to make up on his other stocks what he lost. But if losses are general, so that a competitively determined price would rise, then the merchant may raise his price.

The General Court used the implicit competitive price in 1641 when it laid down a rule for appraising cattle. The correct price was not to be determined by what someone was forced to take due to their "urgent necessity" to sell, but rather the price was to be determined by the value of the milk and offspring of a cow, the cost of hay, and so forth.[17] In a smoothly functioning competitive market it would be precisely the latter factors, rather than the former, that would determine the price.

The sensitivity of the Puritans to the potential for disequilibrium trades suggests an intriguing hypothesis: Regulation was needed in the early days of the colony because markets were "thin"; with only a few buyers and sellers, competition could not be relied upon to regulate prices and protect consumers. If this were so, one would expect that as markets grew, producing a smoother flow of information, the frequency of disequilibrium sales and the need for regulation would have decreased. Indeed, that seems to have happened. In the late seventeenth and eighteenth centuries interest in regulation, in Massachusetts Bay and other colonies, waned. In Massachusetts Bay this outcome was influenced by the increasing cultural identification of Massachusetts merchants with the mainstream of English society and consequent waning influence of the church, as well as the decrease in the need for regulation.[18] In this case, social, political, and economic factors were working together to persuade the colonists that a smoothly functioning market could now protect consumers more efficiently than could the Puritan fathers.[19]

When the market was disrupted, however, new controls were considered. Absolute wage scales were proposed in the General Court in

1670 and 1672, but on these occasions no legislation was passed. But the outbreak of King Philip's War in 1675, a bloody three-year war between the colonists and an alliance of Indian tribes on the frontier, led to the passage of new wage and price legislation. It was incorporated in an omnibus set of laws for the reformation of "Provoking Evils," meaning behavior that provoked the wrath of God. Specific wages and prices were not set. Anyone who felt they had been charged too high a price could, however, complain to the grand jurors or the County Court. The accused merchant was to be sent for and, if found guilty, he had to return twice the overcharge, or more than the price, as well as pay a discretionary fine. Allegations of excessive wages were to be taken to the town selectmen. If guilty, the worker was forced to refund twice the excess and to pay a fine of that amount. Thus, all judgments were to be left to the discretion of the authorities.[20]

The price and wage section of the laws against Provoking Evils does not seem to have given rise to a flurry of enforcement. Morris, who combed the records assiduously, found only a few cases.[21] The case of Richard Scammon, for example, who was presented in the Essex County Court for charging too much for the repair of a pistol lock, was the only case in this court during the years of King Philip's War (and for some years after). It is not possible in the present state of our knowledge, moreover, to draw any conclusion about the effects of this experiment, or the earlier one, on the general level of prices in the colony: The statistical record is, alas, too thin.[22]

We can speak with more assurance about the most celebrated sections of the laws against Provoking Evils, that is, the sumptuary provisions that banned excesses in dress and conduct. These were the best enforced sections of the new codes. It is tempting to view them as a manifestation of a religious spirit alien to our own. But during World Wars I and II we returned to sumptuary legislation to aid the enforcement of price controls, to conserve raw materials, and perhaps also to salve the fear that our personal excesses were in some way the cause of our national calamities. Robert Brookings, who attempted to simplify shoe production during World War I, and Stanley Marcus of Neiman-Marcus in Dallas, who devised simplified dress styles during World War II, were merely following a precedent laid down two and one-half centuries earlier. It seems likely also that the violent World War II reaction to the Zoot-suiters with their long coats and slacks and long hair can in part be explained by the same thinking which guided the Puritans.[23]

The laws against Provoking Evils marked the end of attempts to control the general level of wages and prices in Massachusetts Bay, although they stayed on the books for many years. Although repeated efforts were made to fix individual prices and wages, it was not until the Revolutionary War that similar attempts were made to impose comprehensive controls.

The Revolutionary War

America financed the Revolutionary War to a great extent through the issue of paper money. The alternatives such as borrowing could not be relied on as the sole means of finance, or so it seemed, in the early years of the war. While foreign borrowing, particularly from the French, was important as a source of foreign exchange, there were obviously few parties who would lend at reasonable rates to a government with such an uncertain future. Taxation was also of limited value. The division of power between the Continental Congress and the states inhibited action. Perhaps more important, the collection of taxes requires a well developed and expensive administrative network, one that was impossible to create in the midst of a revolution. The government did of course acquire resources through more direct channels. The soldiers who made up the Revolutionary army and the militias made perhaps the greatest sacrifice both in the risks they took and the income they sacrificed. Even the families who brought food and other supplies to their sons in the army made a measurable contribution. Nor should we leave out the supplies confiscated from alleged Tory sympathizers and others. But there was still an unremitting need for cash, and this was filled by the Continental currency.

Considerable criticism has been leveled at this means of finance. The inflation was severe and many suffered as a result. It bore heavily on those on fixed incomes or those who, for other reasons, could not increase their incomes to keep pace with rising prices. But one thing should not be forgotten: The Continental currency paid the army, if just barely, and purchased the arms and supplies that secured independence.

Table 2.1 gives indexes of prices and the money supply during the Revolutionary inflation. The money supply index was computed in a conceptually straightforward way, but the details are somewhat complex, and have been relegated to the bottom of the table. It is, as far as I

Table 2.1. *Indexes of prices and money during the Revolution*

Date	Prices (Philadelphia)	Stock of paper money (millions of dollars)	Total stock of money (millions of dollars)
December 1774	100	22	30
December 1775	90	31	35
December 1776	194	55	65
December 1777	521	72	96
December 1778	1,139	141	180
December 1779	8,454	286	559
December 1780	15,661	331	893
April 1781	21,046	378	1217

Note: The total stock of money consists of the stock of paper money plus an estimate of the stock of specie valued in terms of continental dollars.

Sources and methods: Prices: Bezanson (1951B, Appendix Table 3, weighted average, p. 334). Paper money, 1774: Hamilton (1851B, p. 228); Schuckers (1874B, pp. 9–10), seems to prefer a smaller prewar estimate, but Hamilton's seems more consistent with the price movements. Paper money, 1775–80: Schuckers (1874B, pp. 125, 127). I used the authorized Continental issues rather than Jefferson's estimate of issues emitted because the former is larger and therefore probably closer to the truth. No attempt was made to adjust the Continental issue for certain authorized withdrawals or the issue of new tenors in 1780. Schuckers gives only total issues for Massachusetts and South Carolina. I distributed these across years on the basis of the proportion of the issues of other states emitted in each year. Specie: Hamilton (1851B, pp. 228, 238). Hamilton's estimates, 8,000,000 "before the war" and 6,000,000 "now," were given in his celebrated letter to Robert Morris in April 1781 advocating a national bank. To interpolate between the estimates, I simply decreased the stock of specie in equal steps from 1774 to 1778 and then held it constant at 6,000,000 thereafter. Presumably, after 1778 French assistance of various kinds was sufficient to prevent net outflows. I then multiplied the stock of specie by its price in Continental dollars: Bezanson (1951B, Table 3, p. 65). In 1774, I used the specie ratio and in later years, the commodity ratio.

know, the first index of the Revolutionary money supply calculated on lines analogous to modern estimates, and it could be much refined. It should be regarded as a lower bound estimate of the true money supply, although it omits both flows into and out of the money supply. There are four main sources of downward bias. The estimate probably omits some of the state issues of paper money. It counts only authorized Continental issues, and the patriots who ran the Continental printing presses probably produced more currency than had been authorized by the Congress. It omits, moreover, a considerable volume of coun-terfeits. Partly these were the work of colonials, but the British also appear to have counterfeited the currency, with the idea of simultaneously defraying their own expenses and further weakening confidence in the Revolutionary government. Finally, it omits some private issues of currency. Against these sources of underestimate one can set the small volume of redemptions undertaken by the Congress and the states. Nevertheless, the basic feature of the money index, the tremendous increase from 1775 to 1780, correctly reveals what was happening in the Revolutionary economy.

The price index was computed with considerable care by Bezanson.[24] Mostly traded commodities are covered and so the index may be more affected by the disruption of trade than would an index that gave the appropriate weight to local services. On the other hand, the index seems especially well matched to the money index since it refers to Philadelphia, the seat of the Continental Congress; it is likely that in distant colonies the money supply was influenced more by local issues and less by the Continental currency.

Initially, the percentage increase in the money stock outran the price level, but eventually the increase in the money stock fell behind that in prices. The latter feature of the inflation was well understood by the colonials, and has been shown to be a common feature of "hyper-inflations." The closest American analogy occurred in the Confederacy during the Civil War. Between January 1861 and January 1864 the Southern stock of money increased by a factor of 11.59 while the price level increased by a factor of 27.76.[25] The explanation is that inflation tends to raise the cost of holding money, causing people to spend even faster, and thus further increasing prices. In addition, in the period preceding the monetary reforms of 1781 rumors were circulating (although vigorously denied by the Congress) that the currency was about to be repudiated. Such rumors tended to increase the velocity with which money was spent and so tended to increase the price level.

April 1781 marks the end of the inflation. In that month Congress virtually repudiated its own currency, and the continentals ceased to circulate as money. The country returned to its prewar system of a specie-based currency, completing a process that had been building for some months. Celebrations marked the death of the paper currency; the former colonists danced around bonfires in which they burned the Continental dollars.

The use of the printing press to finance the war has, of course, been criticized, but it has also been defended from time to time on the grounds of expediency. The most sophisticated defense (both at the time and since) was given by Benjamin Franklin. Even during the Colonial period Franklin was an advocate of paper money. Moderate issues, he had argued (along surprisingly modern lines), would stimulate trade and not produce inflation in periods when trade was stagnating. In the case of his personal economy the evidence was clear; Franklin won a contract for printing Pennsylvania's paper money![26] When the Continental Congress first issued paper money Franklin was concerned that the issues might depreciate and he urged that the currency bear interest as a way of preventing depreciation. Given the expansion that was to follow, this expedient would have had a relatively minor effect. But Franklin's logic was sound. By giving people an additional incentive for holding money, interest would have slowed the increase in the rate of spending that created the "artificial depreciation."

Later, however, Franklin came to view the depreciation in a more favorable light.[27] It was, he saw, a tax, and a not particularly inequitable one. In a brief history of the Continental currency written in about 1784 Franklin put the matter this way:

The general Effect of the Depreciation among the Inhabitants of the States has been this, that it has operated as a *gradual Tax* upon them. Their Business has been done and paid for by the Paper Money, and every Man has paid his Share of the Tax according to the Time he retain'd any of the Money in his Hands, and to the Depreciation within that Time. Thus it has proved a Tax on Money, a kind of Property very difficult to be taxed in any other Mode; and it has fallen more equally than many other Taxes, as those People paid most, who, being richest, had most Money passing thro' their Hands.[28]

Franklin notwithstanding, however, the inflationary pressures were sufficiently severe to prompt repeated efforts during the Revolution to control prices. Even before the battles at Lexington and Concord, the Association of 1774 (in which the Continental Congress proclaimed nonintercourse with Britain) contained two clauses calling for price ceilings. In one, merchants were urged to keep their prices at the level that had prevailed during the previous 12 months. Violators were to be cut off from commercial intercourse with their fellow citizens. A second clause simply called for reasonable prices on manufactured articles.[29]

The Continental Congress, however, had little power to enforce such resolves, and the more important attempts to control prices were carried out at the state and local levels, although efforts were made to coordinate the statewide controls at regional conferences. These are listed in Table 2.2, which gives the dates, locations, and participants. The number of

Table 2.2. *State conventions for controlling prices during the Revolution*

First day of meeting	Place of meeting	States represented
December 25, 1776	Providence, RI	NH, MA, CT, and RI
March 26, 1777	York, PA	NY, NJ, PA, DE, MD, and VA
July 30, 1777	Springfield, MA	NH, MA, CT, RI, and NY
January 15, 1778	New Haven, CT	NH, MA, RI, CT, NY, NJ, and PA[a]
October 20, 1779	Hartford, CT	NH, MA, CT, RI, and NY
January 29, 1780	Philadelphia, PA	NH, MA, RI, CT, NJ, PA, DE, and MD[b]

[a] DE was invited but did not attend.
[b] NY and VA were invited but did not attend.
Source: Baldwin (1882J, pp. 37–8). Baldwin lists two later conventions, but they seem to have been concerned with other matters.

conferences is testimony to the severity of the inflation and the division of opinion concerning the efficacy of controls.

The Providence Convention was called at the request of Massachusetts. This convention recommended, as would some of the later ones, a policy of monetary and fiscal restraint and legal price maximums to control inflation. A basic summertime wage rate for farm labor of 3s 4d per day was suggested. Prices for a list of crucial commodities such as wheat, sugar, and beef were also listed. Prices of imported goods at wholesale were not to be marked up more than 250 percent, except for a select list that could be marked up 275 percent. At most an additional 20 percent was to be added when imported goods were retailed. The prices of other goods and services were to be set by the legislatures of the states. The markup on imported goods reflected a substantial allowance for the risks of war at sea.[30] In modern wars these costs have been subsidized through special insurance plans in order to keep retail prices of imported goods in line with other prices. The most likely explanation for the modern practice is that it represents an attempt to achieve a kind of equity. The burdens of war are to be shared equally; they are not to fall more heavily on those who from reasons of taste or necessity tend to consume unusually large proportions of imported goods. But the colonial governments did not have the resources with which to pursue a policy of subsidies.

Connecticut, New Hampshire, Massachusetts, and Rhode Island quickly passed legislation putting the recommendations of the Providence

Convention into effect. There were strong penalties for those who broke the laws. Soon after, Massachusetts supplemented the price legislation with a "Land Embargo" prohibiting the export of certain key commodities from the state by land or sea.

Congress debated an endorsement of the recommendations of the Providence Convention at length. The debate is worth considering in detail because it illustrates again how little the public discourse on these issues has changed in the last 200 years. Our record of the debate is from the diary of Benjamin Rush, who naturally reports his own views at greater length and with greater cogency than he does those of his opponents.[31] Rush argued against price controls. His first point was that it had been tried before in England in the reign of Edward II without success. He quotes Hume approvingly to the effect that the attempt was a "monument to human folly." (Parliament attempted to fix prices on foodstuffs in 1315 during a famine; the attempt was abandoned the following year.) His second argument drew on more recent experience. Congress, he reminded his listeners, had attempted to fix the price of tea, but they could see for themselves that it now sold for a price far above the ceiling. In addition, even when ceilings had been nominally obeyed they had been evaded.

The Committee of Philada limited the price of West India goods about a year ago. But what was the consequence? The merchants it is true sold their rum, sugar and molasses at the price limited by the committee, but they charged a heavy profit upon the barrel, or the paper which contained the rum or sugar.

The inflation was not caused, Rush explained, by the rapacity of businessmen. Instead, "the extortion we complain of arises only from the excessive quantity of our money." To blame it on some weakness in the American character only provided the enemies of independence with an argument. Rush, who was an eminent physician, concluded by likening price controls to an opiate. "It may compose the Continent for a night, but She will soon awaken again to a fresh sense of her pain and misery."

Richard Henry Lee argued for price controls. Previous failures, he explained, were due to lack of regular governments in the early days of the Revolution. He could also not help pointing out that the "learned Doctor has mistook the disorder." What the continent labored under was a "Spasm" and spasms required "palliative remedies." Samuel Adams also argued for controls. But he had his own theory about why controls had failed in Philadelphia. The city "abounded with Tories." In Maryland, he asserted, the experiment had been a success.

Witherspoon sided with Rush against controls, advancing two interesting arguments. He claimed that controls had actually raised prices. His evidence was that in Pennsylvania salt was limited to fifteen shillings but was sold for sixty shillings per bushel, while at the same time it was sold in Virginia, where there was no limitation, for ten shillings a bushel. This phenomenon is theoretically possible. If the price controls were enforced vigorously at the wholesale level, but evaded at the retail level, then controls would have diverted salt from Philadelphia to Virginia, raising the price to consumers in the Philadelphia market and lowering it in Virginia. The remaining five-shilling gap between the fixed price in Philadelphia and the free-market price in Virginia could be explained by transportation costs or the risks of shipping to an area closer to the war zone. Witherspoon wound up his argument with a familiar part of the case against controls: "If we limit *one* article, we must limit *every* thing, and this is impossible." John Adams was also opposed to price controls, as the extract at the beginning of the chapter shows. In the debate he emphasized, as James Wilson had earlier, that price controls would curtail imports.

Dr. Rush had the last word, at least according to the extract from his diary. One can detect a certain irritation at the point scored by Lee. Rush returned to his medical analogy determined, we can imagine, to parry Lee's neat thrust.

The gentleman from Virginia has miscalled the malady of the continent. It is not a spasm, but a dropsy. I beg leave to prescribe two remedies for it. 1 Raising the interest of the money we borrow to 6 per cent. This like a cold bath will give an immediate *Spring* to our affairs – and 2 *taxation*. This like *tapping*, will diminish the Quantity of our Money, and give a proper value to what remains.

Thus, the modern debate over controls was anticipated almost in full, two centuries ago. What modern historians can add is more information, a more sophisticated array of statistical techniques, and a body of theory that helps us specify the relationship between these several factors. But the basic issues remain the same.

The result of the debate was a compromise. Congress did not endorse the recommendations of the Providence Convention, but referred them to the other colonies for consideration. It recommended a meeting of the middle states, which was held at York, and a meeting of the southern states at Charlestown, which was never brought off.[32] Opposition to the recommendations of the Providence Convention and the regulating acts based on them was not confined to the Congress. The York Convention ended divided. It merely sent copies of its proceedings to the states which attended, and to the Continental Congress.[33]

The next convention, at Springfield, was apparently held in response to the opposition to controls, heightened by some of the negative consequences. The town of Providence described the effects of Rhode Island's price-fixing law in the following paragraph addressed to the legislature:

[The price-fixing act is] so intricate, variable, and complicated, that it cannot remain any time equitable. . . . It was made to cheapen the articles of life, but it has in fact raised their prices, by producing an artificial and in some articles a real scarcity. It was made to unite us in good agreement respecting prices; but hath produced animosity, and ill will between town and country, and between buyers and sellers in general. It was made to bring us up to some equitable standard of honesty . . . but hath produced a sharping set of mushroom peddlars, who adulterate their commodities, and take every advantage to evade the . . . act, by quibbles and lies. It was done to give credit to our currency; . . . but it tends to introduce bartering and make a currency of almost everything but money.[34]

The recommendations of the Springfield Convention, given this view of the results of controls, were conservative. The states were urged "to make provision for drawing in and sinking the bills of credit which are not upon interest, by them respectively emitted, (small change less than a dollar only excepted,) by the first day of November next, ..." All clauses in the regulating acts "so far as they relate to affixing the prices at which the articles therein enumerated shall be sold, . . ." were to be repealed. The main concession to the advocates of controls was a resolution urging the legislatures to force the sale of articles that were "ingrossed or withheld . . . at reasonable prices for the use of the inhabitants."[35]

The official proceedings of the Springfield Convention provide little additional evidence on its reasons for opposing direct controls. The preamble to the resolution refers only to the antimonopoly acts being "attended with inconveniences. . . ."[36] The letter which accompanied the resolutions when they were sent to Congress contained a more explicit argument:

The first four of those states named [NH, MA, RI, and CT] the last winter passed acts to prevent monopoly and oppression in order to support the credit of their paper currency, but the other United States not judging it expedient to enact similar laws hath in great measure prevented their answering the good purposes for which they were intended, and has rendered very difficult, if not impracticable, fully to execute the same.[37]

The problem, of course, was that supplies were diverted to markets where prices were not controlled. But whether the Convention had solid evidence that this was happening, or whether it simply used this argument as an excuse for the failure of controls, cannot be inferred from the proceedings of the Convention. The necessity of maintaining controls across the board reemerged in World Wars I and II. In the latter case, in particular, there was a long experiment with controls over selected strategic prices, a policy that was undermined by inflation in the uncontrolled sectors. To be sure, in the Revolution the problem was geographical areas left free of controls, while in the twentieth century the problem has been uncontrolled commodities, but the principle is similar. In both cases purchasing power and resources are likely to be diverted to uncontrolled markets. Whatever the initial hopes of price controllers, they all learn sooner or later that the regulations must be applied across the board.

The recommendations of the Springfield Convention regarding price fixing were soon adopted. Indeed, the states involved went further than the Convention, and eliminated the entire regulating acts, including the provisions against engrossing and forestalling, that the Convention wanted retained.[38]

Sentiment for controls did not, however, die with the Springfield Convention. The inflation was growing worse, and the Continental Congress and the states had no alternative to still larger emissions of paper money. The proponents of controls saw quite clearly by this time that the past attempts at direct control had created a reservoir of skepticism. But they remained convinced that sufficiently general controls could work. In November 1777 Richard Henry Lee wrote to Samuel Adams in part as follows:

I know my friend Mr. John Adams will say the regulation of prices wont do. I agree it will not singly answer, and I know that taxation with Oeconomy are the radical cures. But I also know that the best Physicians sometimes attend to symptoms, apply palliatives and under favor of the Truce thus obtained, introduce cause removing medicines. Let us for a moment check the enormity of the evil by this method, whilst the other more sure, but more slow methods secure us against a return of the mischief. The middle and southern States (particularly the insatiable avarice of Pennsylvania) having refused to join in the plan formerly, rendered the experiment on your part inconclusive and partial; therefore I do not think Mr. Adams's argument drawn from that trial quite decisive against the measure. I incline to think that the necessity of the case will now procure its adoption universally, and then we shall see what great things may be effected by common consent.[39]

As a landlord, incidentally, Lee knew the dangers of inflation firsthand. He defended his personal economy by converting from rents in money to rents in kind, an action which raised a storm of protest.[40]

A new convention was called to meet at New Haven in January 1778. As Table 2.2 shows, this convention included representatives of the middle states, and so remedied, to some extent, the lack of coverage that Lee and others had blamed for the failure of the Providence convention. New Haven, like the others before it, urged the reduction of the stock of paper money as the fundamental cure for the inflation. But it made an impassioned plea for renewed controls. In a famous passage the Convention returned to the medical analogy that had wended its way through the Congressional debate.

Why do we complain of a partial infringement of liberty manifestly tending to the preservation of the whole? Must the lunatick run uncontrouled to the destruction of himself and neighbours merely because he is under the operation of medicines which may in time work his cure? and indeed without the use of those medicines will the confinement cure him? Must we be suffered to continue the exaction of such high prices to the destruction of the common cause, and of ourselves with it, merely because the reduction of the quantity of our currency may in time redress the evil; and because any other method may be complained of as an infringement of liberty?[41]

New Haven offered a detailed plan for regulating prices. Certain imports vital to the war effort were to be exempt from controls. But specific ceilings were to be applied to another list of commodities critical to the cost of living. Roughly a year had passed since the Providence Convention, and the maximum prices were considerably higher in the New Haven list. "Good merchantable wheat," which according to the Providence scale should sell in Massachusetts for no more than 7s 6d per bushel, was fixed in the New Haven list at 12s per bushel. Rye for Massachusetts had gone from 4s 6d to 7s; pork, from a medium-sized animal, had gone from 4¼d per pound to 7½d per pound. Other prices were set on the basis of fixed markups over their cost in 1774. Most prices of domestic products which were not set in terms of specific amounts were to be advanced no more than 75 percent above their level in 1774. The exceptions to be regulated by the states were a group that included salt, cordwood, vegetables, and other items subject to local variation, and a group, primarily clothing items, which were to be allowed a 100 percent advance over 1774 levels. A formula was also given for the markup on imports: No more than one Continental dollar per shilling sterling at wholesale and no more than 25 percent above that plus a transport allowance at retail. The rate charged for land transport was limited to 5/12 Continental dollars per 20 hundredweight per mile.[42] Innkeepers were singled out for special attention; they were allowed 50 percent over wholesale on liquor and other imported goods, while other prices could be increased 75 percent over their level in 1774.

Wages, according to the New Haven plan, were to be increased no more than 75 percent above their level in 1774. Thus, the plan again was similar to the Little Steel Formula of World War II, in which wages were allowed to advance 15 percent because that had been the increase in the cost-of-living index. But since some items were allowed to advance 100 percent in the New Haven list, and since it is likely that some of the items fixed explicitly in shillings and pence were more than 75 percent above the 1774 level – they were nearly that much above the levels fixed at Providence – the Convention appears to have accepted some decline in real wages as unavoidable.

The recommendations of the New Haven Convention met with a mixed reaction. Massachusetts, Rhode Island, and New Hampshire refused to enact legislation incorporating the proposals, while Connecticut, New York, New Jersey, and Pennsylvania did so. Feelings were bitter. When Rhode Island requested troops, Connecticut refused to send them because Rhode Island had rejected the New Haven plan.[43] But when the Congress, which had called the New Haven Convention, reversed itself and asked the states to repeal their price-fixing laws, they did so. Playing a small role, perhaps, in pushing the Congress toward this recommendation was a letter from Washington expressing his fear that the proposals of the New Haven Convention would have a "disagreeable effect upon our supplies of meat."[44]

The problem would not go away, however, and still another Convention met at Hartford in October 1779. This meeting adopted a somewhat simpler pricing formula than had the New Haven Convention. Most prices and wages were to be advanced to a level twenty times that of 1774. The contrast with the factor most often used in the New Haven proposals, 1.75, is dramatic testimony to the inflation in the intervening twenty-one months. But the recommendations of this Convention met an even cooler reception in the state legislatures. New York and Connecticut adopted price-fixing laws, but these were contingent on other states taking similar actions; since none did, the laws did not go into effect.

The final price-fixing convention was convened at Philadelphia in January 1780. Neither New York nor Virginia was represented, and the delegates from Massachusetts operated under instructions that emphasized the calamities that had attended earlier price-fixing schemes. This convention apparently adjourned without agreeing on any sort of recommendation for new controls.

So ended the attempt to control prices at the state level. From a practical point of view, this experiment was a failure. But as evidence for the futility of controls, it has only a limited application. Nationwide control, the only kind with a high probability of success, had never been tried. The Providence Convention had recommended legislation only for the New England states. The New Haven and Hartford Conventions had broader representation, but their recommendations were never enacted by all of the attending states. And the southern states were never brought into the price-fixing process.

The failure of the states or the Congress to slow the inflation led to similar efforts by local governments. In New Hampshire, Rhode Island, New York, New Jersey, Pennsylvania, and Delaware (and perhaps in other states), local committees tried to fix prices. Two of these attempts, by committees meeting at Philadelphia and Concord, are worth considering because of the importance of the towns involved and also because we have some quantitative information on the effects of the experiments. Bezanson's carefully constructed price indexes in particular make the attempt to control prices in Philadelphia worthy of special attention. The most important experiment in Philadelphia, the culmination of a series of such efforts, began in May 1779. On the 24th, Daniel St. Thomas Jennifer, one of Maryland's representatives in the Continental Congress, wrote to his governor as follows:

Speculation here has arrived to such a height and prices in three weeks increased 100 per ct. This has made those Vermins the Speculators become the object of resentment, and a Mob has assembled to regulate prices. What will be the issue God knows. they are now parading. if they have a head I believe that business will be of service, if they have not one, they will disperse as all tumultuous assemblys have done, that have not had a leader, . . .[45]

A committee was formed, and on May 26, 1779 they issued a price list, supposedly prices as they were on May 1, and demanded that prices be rolled back to those levels. This was to be just the beginning of a series

Table 2.3. *Prices in Philadelphia during 1779*

Month	Actual price index	Percentage change from preceding month[a]
January	100	12.7
February	133	28.9
March	152	13.1
April	188	21.4
May	217	14.2
June	220	1.1
July	210	−4.3
August	232	9.9
September	289	21.8
October	367	23.9
November	541	38.8
December	654	19.0

[a] Percentage changes are differences in the natural logarithms of the data underlying column 1.
Source: Bezanson (1951B, Appendix Table 3, Weighted Average, p. 344).

of rollbacks. The public was asked to support the list with a boycott. In the following weeks the committee did not hesitate to call merchants before it. It asked them, among other things, for an elementary form of rationing in which a family would be limited to one barrel of flour at the regulated price. Even Robert Morris, "the financier of the Revolution," was not immune from a visit from the committee. If the enmity of the committee was not enough, the artillery company of Philadelphia passed a resolution offering to support the work of the committee by force of arms.[46]

Table 2.3 shows the price index in Philadelphia during this tumultuous period. Clearly, the efforts of the "mob" had an impact on the prices merchants recorded in their books. The index rose only 1.1 percent in June and then actually fell 4.3 percent in July. But just as clearly, the effort soon collapsed and prices went up again at hyperinflation rates.

I used the roundabout phrase the "prices merchants recorded in their books" because there appears to have been some evasion of controls during this period. An upstate merchant complained in August 1779: "I cannot purchase any coffee without taking to one bill a tierce of claret and sour and at £6.8 per gallon."[47] This is an early example of a tie-in-sale, a method for evading controls frequently used in later episodes. There is also some evidence (a complaint from army suppliers) of shortages caused by the Philadelphia effort,[48] although the episode was too brief to have caused much privation. Recent claims that the army suffered greatly from various local attempts to fix prices are exaggerated.

The events in Philadelphia inspired a similar experiment in Massachusetts. On May 25, 1779 Boston adopted a report that called for fixing the prices of fifteen selected commodities on a month-to-month basis. But this apparently failed to satisfy the more radical citizens. On June 17, 1779 Bostonians awoke to find that the following handbill had been posted the previous night.

SONS OF BOSTON! SLEEP NO LONGER!

WEDNESDAY, *June* 16, 1779

You are requested to meet on the floor of the *Old South Meeting House* to morrow morning, at 9 o'clock, at which time the bells will ring.

Rouse and catch the Philadelphia spirit; rid the community of those *monopolizers* and *extortioners*, who, like *canker worms*, are knawing upon your vitals. They are reducing the currency to waste paper, by refusing to take it for many articles; the infection is dangerous. We have borne with such wretches, but will bear no longer. Public *examples*, at this time would be public *benefits;* You, then, that have articles to sell, lower your prices; you that have houses to let, refuse not the currency for rent; for inspired with the spirit of those heroes and patriots, who have struggled and bled for their country, and moved with the cries and distresses of the widow, the orphan and the necessitous, Boston shall no longer be *your* place of security! Ye inhabitants of Nantucket, who first introduced the accused crime of refusing paper money, quit the place, or destruction shall attend your property, and your persons be the object of VENGEANCE

N.B. – Lawyers, keep yourselves to yourselves.

† It is our determination to support the reputable merchant and fair trader.[49]

That very day the merchants of Boston met and resolved to eliminate the abuses complained of in the handbill. They agreed to neither buy nor sell specie, to expose violators, and to bring justice to monopolizers and forestallers. They also agreed not to advance prices further, and after July 15, to lower them. On this basis Boston's Committee of Correspondence called for a statewide convention to meet at Concord on July 14 to fix prices. Concord welcomed the convention with enthusiasm. One hundred and seventy-one representatives of 141 towns met on the appointed day and agreed on a set of maximum prices for a list of critical commodities. Wages, and the prices of other goods and services, were to be set by the towns in proportion to the list laid down at Concord. Violators were to be identified in the newspapers as enemies of the country, not a pleasant prospect with characters such as Vengeance about.

The agreement seems to have been a failure, however, because when sessions resumed (as scheduled) on October 6, distrust prevailed between representatives of urban and rural areas.[50] Distrust followed from economic specialization. The country blamed the city for violations on imported commodities. The city blamed the country for violations on, and shortages of, agricultural products. Attitudes of this sort put tremendous burdens on the controls because they rationalized violations.

Still, the second Concord Convention reached agreement on an even longer list of prices than the first one. This agreement appears, however, to have broken down rather quickly. Morris reports that a Boston committee appointed to fix certain prices concluded that it could not do so, and that the publishers of the Boston newspapers shortly raised their prices with the explanation that the regulations had not been effective.[51] Likewise, a Concord committee appointed to fix supplementary prices "postponed" the attempt because the regulations were being violated by Bostonians.[52]

There does not appear to be a price series for Massachusetts comparable to Bezanson's. Nevertheless, some inferences can be drawn on the basis of the prices Abigail Adams included in letters to her husband. These are shown in Table 2.4 along with the corresponding maxima set at the Concord Convention. It appears that it was the intention of the Convention to roll back prices (at least in these cases) from their previous levels. This is inevitably harder to accomplish than merely restraining increases, in part because once someone has been paid a price he begins to think of that price as a right. Unfortunately, Mrs. Adams did not report any prices in the immediate aftermath of the Convention. But the prices in October 1780 make it clear that by then the maxima set at the second Concord Convention were a dead letter.

The efforts to enforce these controls – here I am speaking generally of the Revolutionary controls – were what one might have expected from sporadic attempts, often local, based on waves of public indignation. Morris found that enforcement in the courts was rare, although some of the cases he uncovered have an intrinsic interest. For example, in "May 1780, Thomas Younghusband, a country justice, was indicted in the Edenton, N.C., district court for saying publicly: Damn the Congress! and Damn the Currency! and for refusing to take paper money for liquor purchased at his inn."[53]

Other methods of enforcement were also used but there was considerable variation from place to place. In Concord, the Committee of

Table 2.4. *Prices in Massachusetts, 1779–80 (dollars)*

Commodity	March 20, 1779 (A. Adams)	June 8, 1779 (A. Adams)	July 14, 1779 (Concord - I)	Oct. 6, 1779 (Concord - II)	Oct. 15, 1780 (A. Adams)
Wheat (bu.)	n.a.	n.a.	30.00	30.00	n.a.
Flour (cwt.)	166.67	n.a.	n.a.	100.00	450.00
Corn (bu.)	25.00	80.00	15.00	14.00	100.00
Rye (bu.)	30.00	n.a.	20.00	19.00	90.00
Beef (lb.)	1.17	1.17	1.00	0.83	8.00
Sugar (lb.)	2.00	4.00	2.33	n.a.	6.17[a]
Butter (lb.)	2.00	n.a.	2.00	2.00	12.00
Tea (lb.)	n.a.	n.a.	19.33	20.00	90.00

[a] This was derived from the price for a hundredweight. The price for one pound bought separately would have been somewhat more.
Source: Harlow (1918J, p. 168). I have converted all prices into dollars at the rate of 6s per dollar. The Boston prices are from letters written by Abigail Adams to John Adams. Where Harlow has used a range of prices I have substituted the mid-range. See Adams (1876B, p. 388).

Correspondence tried briefly to enforce the Massachusetts price-fixing law of January 1777, the one passed in the wake of the Providence convention. At least five cases were heard, but only a newcomer to Concord, a man named Walker, was found guilty. He was simply ordered to refund the amounts by which he had overcharged his customers.[54] In Albany, on the other hand, the committee forced violators to stand on a scaffold in the center of town and pledge allegiance to the committee. In other towns violators were fined, or forced to pay the overcharge, or publicly denounced. Their names were even cried throughout the town.[55] On occasion, violations of price-fixing laws were the justification for punishments meted out by vigilantes. In April 1777, Joyce Junior, the leader of a vigilante movement in Boston, succeeded in getting five "Tory Villains" carted across the Boston line for profiteering. In New York, a party descended upon the home of Peter Messier, seized some of his tea, refused his wife the price she asked, and left what they considered a fair price. Later he and his servants were beaten and his property vandalized. According to Morris, incidents of this sort were not unusual.[56]

But despite them, it is reasonably clear that the attempts to control prices during the Revolution, whether state or local, hardly made a dent on the upward curve of prices. The exact extent of the side effects of these efforts is not yet known, although there is evidence of rationing, shortages, and evasion. We can infer, however, from the failure of any program to survive for more than a short time, that these experiments, like those in the seventeenth century, were widely regarded as failures.[57]

The reasons for failure

Some observers have interpreted the failure of these early efforts as simply a particular case of the general proposition that the cost of controls (such as shortages) always outweighs the benefits. I will argue in subsequent chapters that this inequality does not always hold. Here, it will serve to bring together the reasons why controls, which have been useful on some occasions, failed in the particular circumstances of seventeenth- and eighteenth-century America.

First, the coverage of controls during these experiments was incomplete. Either certain commodities potentially under the control of the government were left exempt, or parts of the relevant market were under the control of governments that did not participate in the effort. In either case, there was a tendency for supplies to be diverted to the uncontrolled markets. The clearest examples of this problem are from the Revolution. Local experiments in the Northeast were doomed to failure, as long as merchants in this region could divert supplies to the South where prices were uncontrolled. As has been shown, the proponents of controls during the Revolution frequently used this argument to explain the failure of controls and to argue for broader experiments.

A second reason for the failure of these experiments went unnoticed at the time and since. The authorities in this era typically tried to stop inflation in its tracks, or even roll it back, by issuing a set of fixed maximum prices. Such a policy could work if the prices fixed were close to their long-run equilibrium values, and the fundamental causes of inflation had been dealt with in a similarly decisive fashion. In other words, these maxima could have worked if the only force behind further increases was the momentum of expectations of further increases. But as it was, controls were generally used to try to suppress powerful forces pushing prices upward. This problem was manifest in the early Puritan experiments that tried to fix wages below the market equilibrium and in the later Revolutionary experiments that tried to fix prices despite the rapid increase in money per unit of real output, the fundamental determinant of the inflation.

Both of these reasons are linked to the third, and the fundamental, reason for the failure of these experiments: The Colonial and Revolutionary governments lacked sufficient resources to plan, administer, and enforce the controls they imposed. It is a commonplace of economic theory that when the price system is prevented from operating by controls, something must be put in its place. Typically, this means rationing by the government, the physical allocation of supplies. The point here is that the price system does a great deal of work. The mechanism that replaces it inevitably requires a substantial commitment of men and money, and this the Colonial and Revolutionary governments could not afford to make.

These experiments, to put the point in a somewhat broader context, were doomed to failure because they occurred before what economist John Hicks has called the "Administrative Revolution" in government. He identifies this revolution as the tremendous increase in the ability of government to undertake the economic tasks formerly left to the market, a change that has taken place largely in the past century. This revolution was partly the result of technological changes (the typewriter is a homely example) and partly the result of changes in the resources available to government. It can be dated, or at least full recognition of it can be dated, as having occurred during the First World War.[58]

The American Civil War, the next era of significant inflation, might have produced further examples of controls worth exploration; the inflation both in the North, where prices doubled, and in the South, where it approached hyperinflation, was sufficiently severe. But, with the exception of a few isolated incidents, no resort was made to comprehensive controls. Partly this was the result of the triumph of a laissez-faire economic ideology in the intervening years. But partly, too, it may have been the consequence of the failure of controls during the Revolution. The experiments to which I now turn, beginning with World War I, occurred during and after the administrative revolution. These are the first experiments in which the technical ability of government to manage comprehensive controls was a plausible match for the size of the task.

3. World War I

> Prices mean the same thing everywhere now. They mean the efficiency or inefficiency of the nation, whether it is the government that pays them or not. They mean victory or defeat. They mean America will win her place once for all among the foremost free nations of the world, or that she will sink to defeat and become a second rate power alike in thought and action.
>
> Woodrow Wilson, July 11, 1917

To control prices in World War I the United States relied on a large set of agencies created ad hoc to deal with problems as they arose. Four of these organizations will concern us here: the War Industries Board, particularly its Price Fixing Committee; the Food and Fuel Administrations; and the Bureau of Industrial Housing and Transportation. In each case I will be concerned with the major questions raised in the debate over controls. Were controls evaded? Were shortages produced? Was rationing used? Did the system of regulations grow ever more complex and limiting? Did the introduction of controls cool the inflationary fever? Questions such as these, particularly the first four, must be answered on an agency-by-agency basis.

The Price Fixing Committee and the Food and Fuel Administrations were independent agencies responsible to the President, while the Bureau of Industrial Housing and Transportation was in the Labor Department. A measure of coordination was achieved through the "war cabinet," which consisted of the chairmen of the War Trade Board, the War Industries Board, and the Shipping Board; the Food and Fuel Administrators; and the Director General of the Railroads. They met weekly with Wilson from March 1918 until the armistice. But these were essentially independent agencies that must be considered separately.

The Price Fixing Committee

The appropriate starting point for this agency is August 1916, when an army appropriation bill provided for the establishment of the Council

43

of National Defense and an associated Advisory Commission. The Council was conceived as a peacetime organization that would survey the economy and advise on appropriate measures to prepare the nation for war. Appointments were made to the Commission in October, and after considerable debate over what the Commission was supposed to do each member took on a special problem related to his area of expert knowledge. Daniel Willard was in charge of transportation and communication; Howard Coffin (a disciple of Frederick W. Taylor, the proponent of scientific management), munitions and standardization, Julius Rosenwald, supplies, including clothing; Hollis Godfrey, engineering and education; Samuel Gompers, labor; Franklin Martin, medicine, surgery, and sanitation; and Bernard Baruch (who was later to head the War Industries Board) raw materials, minerals, and metals.

Baruch was already an adviser to Wilson.[1] He was by profession a successful Wall Street speculator. But, perhaps because of his upbringing in the South and his Jewish heritage, he was sympathetic to Wilson and the liberal wing of the Democratic party, and he supported them generously with time and money. An early advocate of preparedness, Baruch brought to government a clear intelligence and a commanding personal presence. He made more of his position on the Advisory Commission than did the others. His strategy, as he later described it, was simple: get in touch with the "leading man or men" in an industry and ask them to form a committee that could serve as a liaison between the industry and the government. Baruch soon had operating, at least on paper, an imposing list of committees. From the first it was clear that one of the main functions of the government's war agencies would be controlling prices. Baruch took this function on, attempting to negotiate lower prices for government purchases. His first success came in March 1917 when he reached an agreement with the Guggenheims for 45,000,000 pounds of copper reportedly at well under the market price. Historian Robert Cuff has concluded that the sacrifice on the part of the copper producers was more apparent than real.[2] But in any event, Baruch's prestige was enormously enhanced.

Thus, when it became clear in early 1918 that the government's economic controls should be consolidated – a frequent demand by the business community – it was natural that Wilson should turn to Baruch. Wilson's letter to Baruch, asking him to head the faltering War Industries Board, makes it clear that the administrative problems were to be solved by putting one strong man in charge:

The board should be constituted as at present and should retain as far as consistent with the character and purposes of the reorganization, its present advisory agencies, but the ultimate decision of all questions, except the determination of prices, should rest always with the chairman, the other members acting in a cooperative and advisory capacity.[3]

Prices per se were left in the hands of a specially designated committee, but the board's other decisions were to be made largely by the chairman.

The most flexible tool that the newly reorganized War Industries Board possessed for coordinating economic activity was the "priority." Orders placed by government agencies or by their suppliers were given one of five ratings – AA, A, B, C, and D (the first three were further divided into AA-1, AA-2, and so on). A firm was required to give precedence to an AA order over an A order, to an AA-1 order over an AA-2 order, and so on. Giving precedence did not mean stopping everything until the highest rated project was finished. It simply meant that if, say, only one of two orders could be filled by the originally agreed-upon date, then every effort would be made to get out the higher rated order on time.[4] Essentially, the same system was adopted in World War II, although it evolved into a more complex form.

After the war, Baruch was extremely enthusiastic about the effectiveness of the priorities system. During the war there were complaints, however, that when the power to issue priorities was delegated to war contractors (in an effort to save administrative resources) the power was abused. Since the system was in operation such a short time during World War I this problem did not reach major proportions. In World War II, however, "priorities inflation," the overissue of high priorities, nearly wrecked the system of controls.

The business community, it should be noted, generally encouraged the introduction of the "priorities" system. Manufacturers who directly supplied the government needed guidance on which orders to fill first. Manufacturers who had placed orders with suppliers favored priorities as a costless way of expediting their orders. Even those manufacturers who were on the receiving end of high-priority orders had, in some cases, a sound business reason for welcoming the system: They could delay filling low-priority orders with less fear of reprisal after the war. Priorities in other words provided a way out for the producer who wanted to drop old-line customers in favor of profitable war contracts, while looking forward to a renewal of the long-term relationship after the war.

The War Industries Board had at its disposal a more powerful tool than priorities: curtailment (forced reduction of output in an industry), a device that promised an immediate savings of resources. The most obvious target for curtailment was the automobile industry since it used large quantities of a wide range of crucial resources. The industry was understandably dead set against a sharp curtailment. As Baruch tells the story, an agreement was finally hammered out in 1918 when he threatened the auto-makers with drastic sanctions:

"Just a moment, gentlemen," I said as I picked up the phone and put in a call to McAdoo at the Railroad Administration. With the auto people listening to me, I said, "Mac, I want you to take down the names of the following factories, and I want you to stop every wheel going in and going out."

The automobile men looked at me, astonished and outraged, as I read off the names of Dodge, General Motors, Ford, and other plants. This effect was heightened as I put in a call to Secretary of War Baker. "Mr. Secretary, I would like you to issue an order to commandeer all the steel in the following yards," I said. Then I called Fuel Administrator Garfield and asked him to seize the manufacturers' coal supplies.

That did it. Billy Durant, head of General Motors, said "I quit." The others capitulated soon after, but not before some had tried to bring political pressures to bear.[5]

Historian Robert Cuff ignores Baruch's self-serving tale of confrontation. Cuff tells a more complex and convincing story involving pleading, as well as threatening, by the War Industries Board.[6] As both versions of the episode illustrate, however, the Board could not rely on voluntary cooperation to achieve what it considered the appropriate reallocation of resources.

Prices, as noted above, were left outside of Baruch's direct control and were made the responsibility of the so-called Price Fixing Committee. Baruch was merely an ex-officio member of this group. The purpose of separating the price-fixing function from other parts of the program was to cloak price fixing with a quasi-judicial appearance. In part this approach reflected Wilson's aversion to concentrating economic power. But in part, it responded to critics who charged that the "dollar-a-year" men, the War Industries Board volunteers from the private sector, were still loyal to the companies which they had served, and which paid their salaries, and to which they would return after the war. The Board could not do without them, but they were not to be allowed to use their power to win excessively high prices for their companies. The make-up of the Price Fixing Committee reflected this intent: The members were, besides Baruch, the chairman, Robert S. Brookings, a prominent businessman and philanthropist; General Pierce of the War Department; Paymaster Hancock of the Navy; Garfield, the Fuel Administrator; Taussig, one of America's leading economists, from the Tariff Commission; Harris from the Federal Trade Commission; and Hugh Frayne, labor's representative on the War Industries Board.

The Price Fixing Committee took an opportunistic approach toward setting prices and was influenced by a variety of tactical considerations, including the interests of the military services or the public in a particular price.[7] Nevertheless, the Committee developed a sophisticated system for determining the appropriate level at which to fix prices, even if at times "the appropriate level" became only the starting point of a bargaining process. This system, known as bulkline pricing, is worth considering in detail because it reveals some of the difficulties and possibilities inherent in suppressing the price system in favor of regulation.

Bulkline pricing

Bulkline pricing was applied to a large number of strategic goods, such as coal and lumber. The essence of the problem was that different producers had different costs.[8] A price that would assure one producer large profits might not be sufficient to induce another to stay in production, since many production costs had risen substantially. Given this situation, there were three alternatives. One was simply to set a single price sufficiently high to cover the costs of the high-cost producer. A second was to set a different price for each producer: a low price for the low-cost producers and a high price for high-cost producers. This alternative could be worked out in several ways. The government could form a corporation to buy all of the output, entering into separate agreements with each producer and then selling the output at some mean price.[9] Or a similar result (in terms of price and output) could be achieved by allowing the firms in the industry to form a pooling arrangement in which the profits of the low-cost firms were used to subsidize the high-cost firms. The third alternative was for the government to nationalize the industry, or at least the high-cost producers and, if need be, run them at a loss.[10]

The first two alternatives were given the most consideration, and the decision was in favor of a single price – the alternative closest to free-market pricing. The advantages of a single price lay primarily in the area of efficiency. In the first place, with a single price every firm had an incentive to reduce its costs as far as possible. With a differential price system the incentive was almost the opposite: increased costs would be rewarded by a more favorable price. The single-price system also economized on the necessary amount of administrative activity. While it was useful to have a notion of the costs of all firms in an industry under a single-price system, only the costs of producers who were on the margin between producing and not producing had to be known with a high degree of accuracy. In contrast, under a differential price system the costs of each firm had to be calculated accurately, something that would require a good deal of work – if it could be done at all.

The disadvantage of the single-price system was simply that low-cost firms would make "unreasonable" profits. The Price Fixing Committee felt that the excess profits tax then in prospect would at least ameliorate this problem. Later, when the problem of differential costs was faced again in World War II, more weight was given to the profiteering argument and differential pricing was adopted. The difference in approach between the two wars reflects many factors, not the least of which was the role given to New Deal liberals in the price-fixing process during the 1940s.

Given that a single price was to be set, how high should it be? This is where the bulkline concept came in.[11] The costs and potential output of each firm in an industry were collected and displayed in the manner shown in Figure 3.1. In the industry portrayed in the figure, the lowest-cost producer could supply 30 percent of the output at a price slightly under a dollar, the next most efficient producer could supply an additional 20 percent at a cost of slightly over a dollar, and so on. To get the entire output of the industry it would be necessary to set an extremely high price to bring in the fringe of small, high-cost producers on the extreme right of the chart. But if one were satisfied with, say, 80 percent of the total output – with the "bulk" of the output – then a much lower price could be set. So the government first decided how much of the output of the industry it needed and drew a vertical bulkline. From the intersection of this line and the cost curve it determined the costs of the bulkline producer, and then added a "reasonable" profit margin to induce this firm to produce. As the figure shows, while this firm was held to a relatively small profit margin, the other firms earned much larger profits, at least before taxes. Still, bulkline pricing had

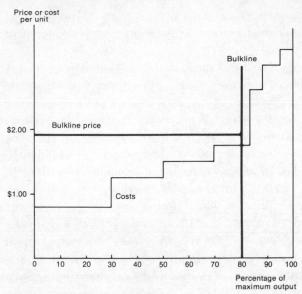

Figure 3.1. Bulkline pricing.

established a price that assured that the "bulk" of the potential output would be produced, while avoiding the extremely high price necessary to bring forth all of the potential output.

Nothing so far has been said about demand. It is likely, given wartime conditions, that demand at the bulkline price would be far greater than the 80 percent of the maximum output, the amount shown here. Some system was needed to ration this output among the firms demanding it. This is where priorities and curtailment came to the rescue. Curtailment reduced demand – the auto industry, for example, would demand fewer strategic resources after curtailment – and priorities, in principle, allocated the available output to where it was most needed. In a free market, in contrast, "need" would have been determined by the willingness of manufacturers to pay for available supplies.

The bulkline-priorities system did not run long enough to justify our reaching firm conclusions about its effectiveness as a temporary wartime measure. But we can say that it was at least a rational response to the problems created by suppressing the price system, one that was not grossly inadequate for a short-term application of controls. Perhaps the greatest practical weakness of the system was that it viewed costs statically. What was to be done in an industry in which costs were increasing rapidly and at varying rates, and what if some firms realized that the bulkline system would lead automatically to price increases to cover these costs?

The War Industries Board and the Price Fixing Committee took few actions to stabilize the cost of living directly, although they were repeatedly urged to do so. There was, however, some interest in this side of the problem. Robert Brookings wanted to see various industries produce low-cost standardized items. A beginning was made with the shoe industry. Negotiations were carried out for production of a "liberty" model, and after considerable persuasion and threatening by Baruch, a compromise was reached with the industry calling for a limited set of styles within certain price ranges. With the armistice, however, the plan was abandoned.[12] In World War II similar suggestions were made, but again (as will be shown in the next chapter) they were never carried very far. Nevertheless, it is clear that the standardization of models would be a powerful aid to price control at the consumer level. Such plans are likely to become an unpleasant part of any permanent system of controls adopted in the future. During World War I, however, stabilization of consumer prices was the more immediate responsibility of the Food and Fuel Administrations, which relied on other measures.

The Food Administration

The strong man of the Food Administration was Herbert Hoover, whose talents as an emergency organizer had first been revealed as early as 1900 when he was caught in Tientsin, China, during the Boxer Rebellion. But it was his organization of the American Relief Committee while in London at the outbreak of World War I (an organization that became the Commission for Relief in Belgium after the German invasion) that brought him to the attention of the Wilson administration. In May 1917, just a month after America declared war, Hoover set up an office in Washington at Wilson's request and became Food Administrator of the United States. A short time later the passage of the Lever Act, also known as the Food and Fuel Control Act, clarified Hoover's duties and gave him the power to enforce his actions.

The Lever Act, in its approach to food price control, was as much concerned with the limitation of profits as with the controls of prices. Only one price was mentioned explicitly, the price of wheat ($2.00 per bushel), and this was to be a minimum. All prices that were "excessive" (in the sense of producing excessive profits), however, were prohibited. Numerous provisions dealt with the prevention of speculation, and the medieval prohibitions against "enhancing and engrossing," holding food back from the market to increase price, were invoked. Although these provisions may have been somewhat vague, the penalties for violating the law were explicit enough; the Administrator was given the power to issue and revoke the licenses of dealers in necessary commodities, to requisition commodities for the armed services, and to seize firms when necessary. Violators were subject to fines and imprisonment.

The licensing power turned out to be the weapon relied upon to achieve compliance when voluntary cooperation failed. It placed the burden of proof on the merchant, a procedure that would not have been acceptable in peacetime but which considerably reduced the costs of administration. Reliance on criminal proceedings would have involved time-consuming delays. Under this procedure, businesses dealing in controlled commodities were automatically licensed, and the Administrators could revoke the license, prohibiting the firm from doing business, if there was evidence of a violation.

For the most part the Food Administration, in line with its Congressional mandate, did not attempt to fix the price of foodstuffs, but rather the markups of middlemen and retailers. One of the most perplexing issues was whether markups were to be figured on the original cost of a commodity or its replacement value. In other words, were merchants who had been smart enough to lay in a stock of a particular commodity before the market price had risen going to be allowed to realize a capital gain? The Food Administration's answer was no. Prices had to be based on what the merchant had actually paid for the commodity. This rule was, of course, designed to prevent profiteering. But as economist Charles Hardy has pointed out, it would not make much sense in a permanent system of controls.[13] There are several reasons. First, the historical cost rule delays the impact of higher prices and so postpones the time at which demand is reduced to a level consistent with current supplies. In addition, the benefits of the historical cost rule are likely to be rather arbitrarily distributed. Some consumers will find that the merchant they frequent has a low-price stock, and they will reap the benefit while depriving other consumers who happen first on merchants with high-priced stocks. Finally, if prices remain at a permanently higher level, those merchants who were forced to sell at their low historical costs will find their working capital impaired. This piece of analysis is a further illustration of an important general rule: Measures that lend themselves to short-term programs of price control, because they are fair and administratively simple, are usually inadequate for the long run.

A second issue that had to be settled was what constituted a "reasonable" markup. The answer was that "reasonable" referred to the prewar period (three years preceding the outbreak of the European war), on an even market, and under freely competitive conditions. This standard obviously gave the individual merchant a good deal of leeway and was of little value when a merchant did not have accurate records, had not been in business before the war, or had not sold a particular commodity. It soon became clear that the administration would have to issue specific numerical markups, and it began to do so in the spring and summer of 1918. Typically, the administration fixed two margins, one for low-cost dealers and a higher one for those who provided credit and delivery or other services.

Eventually the markups worked out by the Food Administration in Washington were utilized by local interpreting boards to compute so-called fair price lists that were published in local papers. A system of independent price reporters was also developed, so that prices paid by consumers could be checked against the fair price lists. Thus in foods, as in the industrial sector, price control led by stages to the control, and to some extent the hardening, of profit margins.

It is well to consider here, therefore, one of the important implications of the control of these margins: the control of investment. The rate of profit determines which industries are to expand and which to contract both because it determines which industries are most attractive to outside investors and also which will have the most surplus funds to reinvest themselves. Once prices were suppressed, a control mechanism for investment had to be developed. The attempt to maintain efficiency under controls leads in this way to the multiplication of bureaucracies and the further extension of the regulatory system. In this case, two agencies were created, although both had other, somewhat narrower surface objectives. The Capital Issues Committee was concerned in the first instance with stopping firms from issuing securities if their expansion was not important to the war effort. The War Finance Corporation was concerned with the opposite problem: supplying additional funds to war industries that needed them.[14] During the war this control raised few protests, since there was wide agreement that all investment should be concentrated in the war sector. In peacetime this would probably not be the case. It seems likely that under peacetime controls the nationalization of investment decisions would be viewed as one of the most significant departures from the decision-making process of the marketplace.

All of the wartime agencies gradually developed tighter and more complex controls. In several cases, for example, the Food Administration went beyond merely setting margins for middlemen and attempted to fix the price itself. Two commodities where this was the case, sugar and wheat, are of particular interest because they were important to the consumer and because the government formed corporations – the United States Sugar Equalization Board and the United States Grain Corporation – for buying and selling them. These corporations had the power to fix their prices at levels very different from what would have resulted from the free interplay of supply and demand.

Sugar was relatively easy to deal with at the producer level because of the willingness of the Cuban sugar producers, who supplied a substantial share of the market and who had the lowest costs in the hemisphere, to negotiate a common price for their output. In the second half of 1917 and the first half of 1918 the contracts between the sugar producers and refiners were still at least nominally voluntary, but considerable leverage was exercised by the Food Administration through its licensing of the refiners. Nevertheless, in 1918 the newly organized United States Sugar Equalization Board became the sole buyer of raw sugar and sole supplier of the refineries for the duration of the war. As the name of the Board implies, one of the functions of the Board was to equalize the supply prices of raw sugar, making a profit on its Cuban purchases while paying a higher price to American producers.

In the fall and winter of 1917 there was an acute shortage of sugar, particularly in New England. Although certain steps were taken toward rationing sugar (they will be discussed below), distribution in New England was not satisfactory and shoppers sometimes had to wait in long lines. Some observers blamed the Food Administration's pricing policies. One critic was Senator Lodge, who blamed the shortages explicitly on the fixing of the price below the market's equilibrium. In a Senate speech he proclaimed that "the gratitude which the vast majority of people of a large section of the country ought to have felt for the low prices of the Food Administration did not seem to comfort them when they sat at a table where sugar had become a memory."[15] Some support was given to Lodge's analysis by economist Roy Blakey, a knowledgeable observer, who was generally favorable to the Food Administration's efforts. According to Blakey, the Administration had expected that Louisiana sugars would tide New England over the period before the arrival of the Cuban crop. But the price for raw sugar set by the Food Administration was so low, it was more profitable for the Louisiana producers to prepare the sugar on their own plantations. Thus the raw sugars counted on by the Food Administration did not reach the Atlantic coast refiners. Western beet sugars might have filled the gap, but again the price set by the Food Administration prevented this from happening. In a free market the Atlantic coast refiners would have bid the raw sugars away from other areas, but controls prevented this adjustment. The Food Administration implicitly acknowledged that its pricing policies were partly at fault by revising the sugar price structure in a way that promoted the movement of raw sugars to the eastern refiners.[16]

Still, the Food Administration was determined to hold down the price of sugar and this meant considering what mechanism was to replace rationing by price. The long lines that had formed during the sugar famine were clearly undesirable, and there were suggestions that "good customers" and "unreasonable customers" (the latter category, in the paranoia of the times, seems to have included both foreigners and disloyalists) were getting around the restrictions. One alternative was formal rationing; giving each consumer a certificate entitling him or her to a fixed allotment of sugar. This was not considered administratively feasible at the consumer level. At the manufacturing and retailing level, however, a system was worked out so that buyers of sugar received certificates permitting the purchase of sugar in amounts related to prewar use. These certificates, then, accompanied payment for the sugar and were returned by the receiver to the State Food Administrator who issued them. This system could not eliminate shortages, but it did reduce the chance that the shortage would be concentrated in a particular area.

Rationing by certificates probably would have been extended to the consumer level if the war had lasted longer. As it was, a makeshift approach was adopted. First, retailers were asked to limit sales to one customer to a certain number of pounds of sugar per person per month, This system, however, even if adhered to, did not prevent a consumer from going from store to store, and did not prevent the unscrupulous

merchant from tying the sale of sugar to related hard-to-move merchandise. This technique, the "tie-in sale," or as it was then known,
the "combination sale," was recognized as a threat to the price stabilization
program and most forms were prohibited. But one form of combination
sale, because it seemed to favor low-income families, was specifically
exempted from the ban: The sale of sugar could be tied to the sale of
cornmeal in the ratio of two pounds of cornmeal to one of sugar. This
effectively raised the price of sugar by the difference between what the
consumer was forced to pay for the cornmeal and what he or she would
have paid voluntarily. Thus, in the end, the Food Administration relied
on a concealed price increase to ration sugar. It was, however, a price
increase that was smaller for the person who bought sugar for a large
low-income family, one that could really use the cornmeal.

Wheat was undoubtedly the most important commodity whose price
the Food Administration attempted to stabilize. The Food Administration
did not want to roll back the price of wheat and was limited, in any
case, by the guaranteed minimum provided by the Lever Act. It did
want, however, to protect consumers from prices that might be even
higher than the high prices prevailing in 1916–17. This it achieved
through its control of the millers and later through the United States
Grain Corporation.

Expert observers were divided on whether the fixed price of wheat
had caused inefficiency. George Warren, an agricultural economist who
was generally critical of controls, argued that the fixed price caused
the 1917–18 crop to move too fast. Normally, the price rose late in the
year as grain became scarce, which provided an incentive for storing
grain and leveling marketings between harvests. With the price fixed
throughout the year it made sense for farmers to market all of their
grain at once, thus producing late season shortages.[17] There can be little
argument that grain, in fact, moved extremely rapidly in 1918. Marketings
from July to October of 1918 equaled seventy percent of the total crop.
In comparable months of 1915, another large crop year, they had been
forty-seven percent. More sympathetic observers, however, such as
Frank Surface, an official with the Food Administration and its authorized
historian, did not interpret rapid movement off the farm as a failure.
They saw it as a favorable result. They might also have argued that
rapid marketing was a successful implementation of the Food Administration's general policy of making as much grain as possible available
for export.[18] At any rate, the crop did move to market at a significantly

faster pace as the result of the new system – a change of the sort that can always be expected when controls are introduced. This change could have been avoided only by announcing early in the year that the price of wheat would be raised from month to month by an amount sufficient to compensate some farmers for the cost of storage. But computing the exact amount of the necessary increase would have required more information and more resources than were available to the Food Administration.

In another case, however, Surface conceded that controls had created an undesirable situation. He pointed out that Western millers had traditionally made somewhat less on flour, which sold in a national market, and somewhat more on feed, a by-product, which sold locally. The Food Administration set what it considered reasonable markups separately on feed and flour, but failed to consider the overall profit position of the millers. As a result, some Western millers were forced to suspend operations.[19]

While the Food Administration could reduce price uncertainty in the wheat market it could do so only by increasing uncertainty in other markets, although this was generally not appreciated. The funds that the Grain Corporation used to support wheat prices were acquired either from the government or from foreign purchasers. Thus, either tax rates or interest rates or the rate of inflation (depending on how the government financed a deficit in the Corporation's budget) or prices in foreign markets had to reflect the fluctuations that in a market economy would have been absorbed by the domestic price of wheat. The real contribution of the Food Administration, aside from the benefits of shifting fluctuations in the price of food to shoulders more able to bear them if this in fact was the case, was its contribution to the general reduction of inflationary expectations. Food price controls alone could not have accomplished much along these lines. But controls on food prices were a necessary part of any program designed to convince the public that inflation was being brought under control.

In addition to shortages, there is also some evidence of evasion. Some millers padded their cost reports with improper items, including new construction, increased salaries, and so on, in order to qualify for higher margins. Some even created bogus jobbing departments because margins on jobbing were somewhat more favorable than on straight milling. There was also a bit of chiseling, to use the contemporary term, with inferior grain being sold at the price of the best grade.[20]

These problems undoubtedly would have been much worse if the Food Administration had not found a mechanism to substitute for the price system. Initially, it tried appeals for voluntary conservation, such as wheatless days. These appeals failed, however, so it turned to the same mechanism that was used in the sugar market: tie-in sales. The so-called 50–50 rule was introduced in January 1918, requiring millers, wholesalers, and retailers to tie the sale of one pound of wheat to the sale of one pound of the approved substitutes. This rule was modified in August to an "80–20" rule, one pound of an approved substitute (this list was also modified) for every four pounds of wheat. It was assumed that the substitute would then be used with the wheat flour in baking bread – "Victory Bread."

The lesson to be learned from both the sugar and wheat controls is that with prices fixed, the government must substitute some form of rationing or other means of reducing demand for the price system. Appeals to voluntary cooperation, even when backed by patriotism, are of limited value in solving this problem.

Evasion and shortages were probably less of a problem in other foods because less of an attempt was made to control the retail price. But even these products were not free of trouble. As one critic pointed out, the markup on cold storage eggs made storage unprofitable and, as a result, producers began marketing too many hens.[21] In fact, the Food Administration in February 1918 issued an order banning the sale or shipment of freshly killed hens and pullets until April 30, 1918. (The ban was actually lifted in mid-April.) Paul Garrett, one of the official historians of the controls, discusses this ban as an example of the foresight of the Food Administration. But it is probable that the government's restrictions on markups for eggs in storage contributed to the problem.[22] The Food Administration was also forced to issue detailed regulations covering egg crates, even specifying the number and size of nails to be used, showing that controls on the price of eggs were being evaded by reducing the quality of the crates in which they were shipped.[23]

It is difficult to form a firm judgment about the total extent of evasion of food price controls. But Albert Merritt, an economist who worked in the distribution division of the Food Administration, was probably right when he argued that the level of compliance was generally good. He based his judgment on comparisons of the fair price lists (what prices were supposed to be) with the actual prices being sent to the Food Administration by its independent price reporters.[24] The best

Table 3.1. *Sanctions imposed by the Food Administration*

Type of sanction	Aug. 10, 1917– Dec. 31, 1918	Jan. 1, 1919– Nov. 30, 1919	Total
Unlimited revocations	249	57	306
Limited revocations	187	5	192
Unlimited unfair orders	58	5	63
Limited unfair orders	43	0	43
Refunds and contributions	4,123	6	4,129
Temporary suspensions and minor penalties	3,658	7	3,665
Requisitions, etc.	65	0	65
Stop orders	210	84	294
Cancellations	10	2	12
Criminal cases	72	0	72
Total	8,603	166	8,769

Note: Revocations of licenses were either until further notice (unlimited) or for a specified period (limited). Unfair orders were issued to licensed dealers forbidding them to trade with another firm, typically an unlicensed retailer. This sanction was used because the Lever Act exempted firms doing less than $100,000 of business annually from the license requirement. The other sanctions are self-explanatory.
Source: Mullendore (1941B, p. 334).

additional evidence consists of enforcement activity, which should have been roughly correlated with the volume of illegal activity. Table 3.1 shows the sanctions imposed by the Food Administration in Washington; an additional but unknown number were imposed by the State Food Administrators. As can be seen from the table the Food Administration relied on the less severe forms of penalties. Unlimited revocation, cancellations (for the duration of the war), and criminal proceedings were resorted to in only a small percentage of the cases.

Little use was made of criminal proceedings, in part because of administrative delays. These were partly caused by the need to coordinate the work of two agencies: the price agency and the Justice Department. It is also true that the Food Administration may have sensed that criminal proceedings against people not identified as part of the "criminal element" would have aroused public opposition. It is not surprising that the government's first criminal case was the United States versus The Germania Catering Company and Rudolf Oelsner, a sugar-hoarding case. Oelsner, who ran a famous German restaurant in New York, was an importer of German beers.[25] It is difficult to avoid the striking parallel with the attacks on Tory merchants during the Revolution.

A perspective can be gained on the number of sanctions shown in Table 3.1 by comparing them with the number of firms the Food Administration had its eye on. These numbered about 140,000 judging by the Administration's peak mailing list.[26] Thus, about 6 percent of the firms being scrutinized closely had sanctions imposed. To be sure, there may be some double counting of firms for whom weak penalties were followed by stronger ones. But this bias is at least to some extent offset by the neglect of penalties imposed by State Food Administrators. In principle, of course, the Food Administration had more dealers under observation. If one uses Hoover's figure of 400,000 firms in the industry, the number of firms subject to sanction was about 2 percent (assuming no double counting). Hoover may have gone too far in claiming that 99 percent of the businesses in the industry were honest.[27] But it appears that for the short period of time controls were in effect the enforcement problem remained within manageable bounds.

The Fuel Administration

Coal prices rose spectacularly in the summer of 1917. Between August 1916 and August 1917 the War Industries Board's index of coal and coke prices went up 54 percent.[28] Since coal was then an important component of the cost of living, it is not surprising that the Lever Act reserved some of its strongest language for the control of coal prices. The President was empowered "to fix the price of coal and coke wherever and whenever sold" and to "requisition and take over the plant, business, and all appurtenances thereof" of any firm in the industry when he deemed it advisable. In addition, a violation was punishable by a "fine of not more than $5,000, or by imprisonment of not more than two years, or both."[29]

On August 23, 1917 Wilson appointed Harry Garfield – the president of Williams College and President Garfield's grandson – to head the Fuel Administration. But the crisis was so severe that Wilson could not wait for the Fuel Administration to set prices. On August 21 he announced a tentative price schedule for bituminous coal, and on the 23rd he followed with one for anthracite. Garfield took up his duties in September and in January appointed a committee of engineers to examine costs in the coal industry. The data assembled were converted into separate bulkline curves for each coal district. Hardy has called the use of bulkline pricing by the Fuel Administration the most systematic in any field.[30] For the most part, however, the bulklines confirmed the prices set earlier by the President along with adjustments made in the interim. In anthracite, for example, only a few changes were made in the President's schedule: a reduction in the price for one of the smaller size coals in October 1917, and two upward adjustments for wage increases in December 1917 and November 1918, just before the armistice. Bulkline pricing was acceptable to the industry because much of the coal came from the lowest cost mines. In other words, the cost curve turned up sharply toward the end, so that a price that brought a substantial part of the potential output to market was highly favorable to the firms producing most of the coal. Indeed, at the beginning of World War II the anthracite industry was one of the few that remembered bulkline pricing and urged its use.[31]

Finding an alternative to the market for allocating scarce supplies of coal was not easy. The crunch came in the winter of 1917–18, when the distribution of coal became chaotic during what was probably the nation's first "energy crisis." Clearly the main reasons for this state of affairs were the unusual severity of the winter and the unusual demands on the railroad system imposed by the war effort. Government policies, however, were also criticized. *The Commercial and Financial Chronicle* was quick to cite the Railroad Administration (then three weeks old), which was now running the railroads, and the Fuel Administration.[32] One might be tempted to discount the partisan position of the *Financial Chronicle*. But some observers closer to the scene, and more sympathetic to intervention, also placed the responsibility for the crisis on some aspect of government policy. Wayne Ellis, who wrote the final report on the zone system for allocating coal (discussed below) for the Fuel Administration, criticized the War Industry Board's priority system.[33] Shipments of coal got low priorities and other cargos that should not have been given high priorities got them. The result was that stocks were dangerously low when they were needed to meet the cold spell. Lesher, another official at the Fuel Administration, suggested that prices, despite the relatively small fringe of high-cost producers, were too low to bring out sufficient supplies.[34] The diversity of explanations suggests that this episode was not well understood, but there can be little doubt that the problem lay in part somewhere in the array of mechanisms assembled to replace the market.

The Fuel Administration's immediate response to the crisis was an order issued in January 1918 which closed all but a few coal-burning factories for five days running and several succeeding Mondays. This order gave the railroads a breathing spell in which to get coal and other cargo moving. Later, the Fuel Administration's Distribution Division relied on a variety of tactics to allocate coal. In some cases coal was simply diverted from a purchaser low on the Fuel Administration's "preference list" to a user more important to the war effort. In other cases forced exchanges were made so that crucial plants could get the kind of coals they needed.[35] In August and September 1918 the Fuel Administration issued temporary embargoes on shipments to plants which already had ample reserves. The Fuel Administration also issued a number of orders cutting back usage in "nonessential" industries. Breweries and factories making window glass for example, were cut back fifty percent, while country clubs and yachts received nothing. How much coal was saved is debatable, but the Fuel Administration estimated an overall saving from industrial restrictions of 6,000,000 tons, a bit over five percent of total coal consumption during the two-month period.[36]

The Fuel Administration also developed what came to be known as the zone system for allocating coal.[37] In the period before the war most coal was sold to users close to the mines where it was produced, but some particularly desirable coals were hauled long distances. During the War, long hauls appeared to be an unnecessary luxury; they worsened the already severe railroad congestion. So the Fuel Administration divided the country into a series of coal zones, based on prewar practice, and prohibited the shipment of coal outside the zone in which it was produced. This system was easily administered. The agents of the railroads, then under government control, simply refused to accept any coal for shipment beyond the boundaries of the zone. The main purpose of the system, it should be emphasized, was to reduce railroad congestion, although it had the incidental effect of altering the allocation of certain high-quality coals.

There was some evasion of the Fuel Administration's controls, although it was of minor proportions. The enforcement department prepared 244 cases for the Justice Department, a rate of roughly 12.8 cases per month, and a grand total of $763,547.89 in refunds was paid by coal dealers.[38] This was a tiny fraction of the nation's coal bill. There was also some enforcement, most of it informal, at the state and local level, but the picture of good compliance would probably not be altered if the details on enforcement at this level were known.

Scattered evidence suggests that quality deterioration was the main form of evasion. One of the few licenses the Fuel Administration revoked was that of a New York coal dealer who sold low-quality coal for use in a steamship in violation of an explicit order issued by the Fuel Administration.[39] The state Fuel Administrator for Alabama also reported that he had to intervene in order to prevent the shipment of improperly prepared coals.[40] In March 1918 the National Fuel Administrator issued an order providing for the inspection of coal. The shipper of unsatisfactory coals was given the choice of bringing them up to standard or of having fifty cents per ton deducted from the price. It was provided, initially, that the buyer could waive the deduction, but the latter provision was struck out in a June revision.[41] All of this suggests that there was some evasion, mainly through quality deterioration, in coal markets but that in general compliance was good.[42]

Compliance in the fuel markets was facilitated by several circumstances. One was patriotism, which was doubtless reinforced on a day-to-day basis by the presence of a number of coal men in the Fuel Administration. A second was the simple fact that controls did not really hurt in the coal industry, since the bulkline pricing system assured most producers a healthy profit. A third favorable circumstance was that most coal was sold under contract, and Fuel Administration prices applied only to so-called free coal. This meant that as old contracts ran out they could be renewed at higher prices, provided those prices were under the Fuel Administration's ceilings. Thus, coal prices continued to rise, even after the price of free coal was fixed. Lesher calculated "weighted realization" prices for free coal and coal under contract.[43] His series for bituminous peaked in August 1918, a year after controls were imposed in spot markets, and his series for anthracite peaked in November 1918.

While coal was the main concern of the Fuel Administration, it also took responsibility for oil. Oil, however, was not yet a crucial fuel for heating and oil prices had not increased to the same extent as coal. So oil was given correspondingly less attention. Evidently, the industry itself enforced controls after an agreement with the Fuel Administration was reached in August 1918. There was also an attempt to conserve oil through a program of "gasless Sundays." Some vigorous enforcement of the driving ban was apparently provided by "volunteers" because, in his final report on the Fuel Administration, Garfield wrote:

The people of this liberty-loving Nation . . . had become tyrannous, and the stories of punishment meted out to those who disregarded the request to save gasoline would have staggered the imagination of Americans 12 months earlier.[44]

Rent control

During the war average rents did not increase as fast as the cost of living, mostly because rents are contractual. But those seeking new quarters were not protected and they pressed for rent controls. Shortages were acute in the industrial communities that had been expanded by war contracts, particularly the steel-making towns in the East and the shipbuilding communities on the Pacific coast. Inevitably, too, the population of Washington, D.C. expanded, reportedly at the rate of 1,000 newcomers per week, and here also the problem was severe.

In Washington rents were controlled by the Saulsbury Resolution, which Congress passed on May 31, 1918. Subject to various reservations, it protected tenants holding leases of one month or more against increases. This control was not extended to other cities, although protection was given to soldiers renting quarters for less than fifty dollars per month. Permission was granted to the Navy to requisition housing for construction workers making torpedo boat destroyers, and to the Shipping Board for similar purposes. On the supply side of the housing market the Bureau of Industrial Housing and Transportation of the Department of Labor instituted building projects in several cities. In addition, it made some efforts to improve transportation (primarily in New Jersey), to encourage private investment in housing, and to encourage homeowners in critical areas to take in boarders.

The Bureau also organized seventy-six community committees (generally with members representing the real estate business, the legal profession, and the public) to settle rental disputes. In fifty other communities existing organizations were used to help achieve this end. Essentially, three formulas were used to determine "fair" rents: (1) the rent on some given base date, perhaps increased by a standard percentage; (2) a standard (gross) rate of return on investment; and (3) a standard (net) return plus costs. A variety of enforcement tactics were used, including appeals to reason and patriotism and threats of punitive action by other government agencies. Several states passed laws that aided rent control. In Massachusetts it was Calvin Coolidge, Acting Governor, who in August 1918 issued a proclamation under Massachusetts' rent control law conferring on a state official the power to seize rental properties for war workers.[45]

There is some quantitative evidence on the extent of evasion in this market. Schaub reported that forty-eight "active" committees reported only 8,029 complaints. Of these, 6,073 were classifiable: 1,102 decisions upheld the landlord, 3,436 favored the tenant, and 1,535 were compromises. Hardy viewed this as evidence of good compliance, and while the evidence is far from conclusive, I agree with him.[46] But this level of compliance depended on the short length of time controls were in effect. With most renters protected by actual or implicit contracts, and with "unfair" rents considered unpatriotic, controls could hold average rents down. In a permanent system of controls the problems involved in holding the rents down would be many times greater.

Thus, the agencies controlling prices during World War I were faced with the full array of difficulties that the critics of controls have posited. There is evidence of evasion, of quality deterioration, of shortages, and of a clumsy and growing network of rationing and similar controls. But how severe were these costs? Like contemporary observers, current readers will impose their own standards and reach various conclusions. My tentative assessment is that with the possible exceptions of the coal and sugar shortages – episodes that certainly call for further research – the difficulties created by controls were relatively manageable. In the pages that follow I will discuss some additional evidence that reinforces this judgment. But at this point it will be useful to examine the effect of controls on prices. What were the gains controllers had to show for the pains they took and the inconveniences they caused?

The effect on prices

Controls did not cover every good and every service at every stage of the production process. Instead, they were confined primarily to the raw-material processing stages of production and to prices that had risen dramatically. The main reason was administrative. It took relatively few government workers to control the small number of large firms that typically dominated the beginning of the production process: As one moved downstream toward the consumer, of course, the number of firms grew ever larger. There seemed to be no point, moreover, in controlling prices that were not yet a source of trouble. Because of this structure we must answer several questions if we are to understand

Table 3.2. *A comparison of changes in the prices of ten uncontrolled manufactured products with the changes in the prices of their controlled raw materials*

Product	Raw material price[a]	Manufactured product price[a]
Copper wire	102	97
Chains	77	100
Saws	77[b]	117
Lead pipe	129	122
Woolen yarn	98	100
Woolen cloth	98	103
Rubber tires	97	100
Men's shoes	93	130
Fuel oil	100	100
Kerosene	100[b]	111

[a] The prices given are those as of November 1918 as a percentage of the price when controls were inaugurated.
[b] The same raw material as for the preceding product.
Source: Garrett (1920G, pp. 536–9).

the effects of controls on the price level: Was control at the raw-material stage of production successful in the sense that prices downstream did not rise as much as they would have in the absence of controls? Were there "spillover" effects; that is, did prices in the uncontrolled sector rise faster because purchasing power was shifted from controlled to uncontrolled markets? Most important, did controls slow the rise in the general price level? Or, to put the matter another way, were spillover effects so strong that no reduction of inflation was achieved?

Controls on raw materials or incompletely processed materials might slow the rise of final product prices for either of two reasons. In the extreme short-run manufacturers and distributors might tend to add a conventional markup to their costs because of inertia or perhaps for patriotic reasons. It is hard to imagine, however, that in the long run they would not take advantage of their ability to raise their traditional margins and earn greater profits. A more plausible reason for expecting upstream controls to be successful turns on the role of expectations. If the increase in demand that is producing large price increases is based on hoarding in anticipation of still higher prices and shortages, then the imposition of controls may moderate this component of demand, even in downstream markets.

Table 3.3. *Controlled and uncontrolled wholesale prices (annual percentage rates of change)*

Index	May 1916– Aug. 1917	Aug. 1917– Mar. 1918	Mar. 1918– Nov. 1918
Controlled			
Constant composition	41.8	−6.0	5.2
Chain	—	−46.7	.4
Uncontrolled			
Constant composition	22.0	20.0	14.1
Chain	—	21.7	14.1
Percentage controlled[a]	0	17.9	38.2

[a] This is an average for the months in the period shown. It consists of the percentage of prices in the War Industries Board's index of wholesale prices which were under control. Each price is given an equal weight in calculating the final percentage.
Sources: Constant Composition Indexes: Garrett (1920G, p. 427). Chain Indexes: Ibid., p. 500. Percentage Controlled: Ibid., p. 417.

Table 3.2, which compares controlled raw materials with uncontrolled manufactured products in ten cases where this comparison could be made, provides a tentative answer: The attempt to control downstream markets was partially successful. In six of ten cases control of the raw material price is associated with stabilization in the product price. But in four cases – chains, saws, men's shoes, and kerosene – prices seem to have advanced despite the stabilization of raw materials costs. Whether this was due to increases in other production costs or to demand pressure cannot be determined from price data alone. But if we assume that demand would have been strong in all of these markets in the absence of controls, then Table 3.2 can be read as providing some evidence that upstream controls worked.

Given this degree of success in controlling downstream markets, was there a tendency for buyers to shift their hoarding to other markets that were not influenced by controls? Carefully compiled indexes of controlled and uncontrolled prices exist for the war years, so a tentative answer is possible. Table 3.3 gives percentage rates of change for the two sectors during three periods: the fifteen months prior to controls, the first seven months of controls, and the eight months following Baruch's appointment to head the War Industries Board.[47] Two kinds of indexes were used in computing the percentage changes shown in Table 3.3: Constant Composition Indexes and Chain Indexes. The two are useful in different contexts. The Constant Composition index of controlled (uncontrolled) prices shows changes in a market basket consisting of goods that became (were never) subject to price controls at some point in the period. Constant composition indexes are most useful for examining the period leading up to controls, for seeing whether there was anything distinctive in the behavior of markets that were later controlled. After controls were in place constant composition indexes are less useful. In particular, the constant composition index of controlled prices is contaminated by prices still to be brought under control. The chain indexes compare the price of commodities which were controlled (uncontrolled) in a particular month with the same market basket in the preceding month. Chain indexes are more useful for comparing price behavior in the two sectors while controls were in place.

Two striking features characterize the precontrol period. One is the extremely rapid rate of inflation. It is clear why controls were imposed. Even the business community welcomed them in "runaway" markets – to use the contemporary term. The other feature is that increases were greatest for those commodities whose prices were eventually subject to control. The authorities sought to bring under control those prices that were rising at unusually rapid rates. These were the commodities critical to the war effort and which therefore faced the strongest and most persistent demand. When a new commodity was placed under control, the price was frequently rolled back. This explains the large decrease in the chain index of controlled commodities for the first seven months of controls. But once the commodities were under control, prices were usually adjusted upward to compensate for increased wages or other costs.

Table 3.3 suggests that spillover effects were limited. After controls were imposed, uncontrolled prices continued to rise at about the same rate as before, reflecting perhaps a lag in the effect of changes in the size of the controlled sector on the free prices, a lag analogous to the one observed in the effect of monetary policy. Then, with the consolidation of power at the War Industries Board, and the passage of the Lever Act, the rate of increase of uncontrolled prices actually decreased, reflecting perhaps a more rapid response to events that directly influence expectations of inflation. This analysis suggests that we must use a more sensitive test to detect spillover effects. They were not of sufficient magnitude to show up clearly in the raw data. One test that suggests itself is a regression that relates percentage changes in uncontrolled prices to lagged values of percentage changes in the money stock (to represent the fundamental source of the inflation), lagged values of the size of the controlled sector (to capture the effect of changes in the size of this sector on uncontrolled prices), dummy variables for events that radically changed expectations about future inflation, and a constant term (to represent trends in velocity, and output in the two sectors). If there were spillover effects the sum of the coefficients on money would exceed one and the sum of the coefficients on the controlled sector would be positive. In other words, spillover effects imply that the effect of monetary increases on the uncontrolled sector would be magnified, and this magnification would be greater as the size of the uncontrolled sector increases. This is the result I obtained from a regression using the data underlying Table 3.3 (although the coefficient on the size of the controlled sector, while positive, was not statistically significant).[48]

This evidence also disposes of an alternative hypothesis concerning the effects of selective controls. It is sometimes argued that controlling part of the price structure will tend to reduce inflation in the uncontrolled sector. Since controlled prices are sometimes costs of production in the uncontrolled sector, controlling these costs might reduce the rate of increase in the related uncontrolled prices. And, since uncontrolled prices are sometimes costs of production in the controlled sector, controls that limit the income of producers in the controlled sector might limit the amount these producers could spend to bid up the price of uncontrolled inputs. It is clear, however, that in World War I these effects were negligible.

The existence of spillover effects, however, does not necessarily undermine the case for controls. That depends on whether the imposition of controls tended to reduce the overall rate of inflation, even if there was some increase in the uncontrolled sector relative to what might have occurred if prices in the controlled sector had been held down with a tight money policy, rather than with controls. In World War I, in fact, it is clear that controls had a stabilizing impact on the overall rate of inflation. This shows up rather dramatically in Figure 3.2, which depicts the difference, each month, between the rate of inflation from a year earlier and the rate of change of money per unit of real output (approximated by industrial production), also from a year earlier. It is

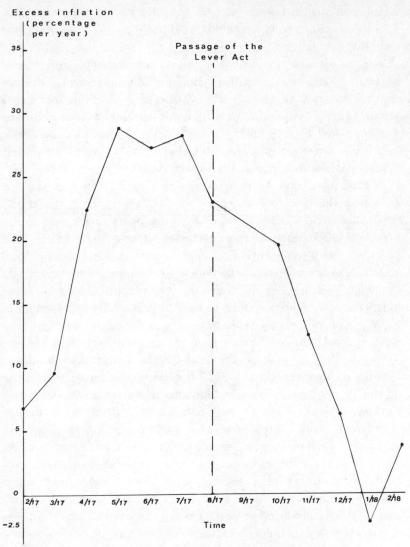

Figure 3.2. Inflation in excess of the growth of money per unit of real output.

a kind of "fever chart" of the inflation. For example, in June 1917 the rate of inflation since June 1916 was 40.5 percent, while the ratio of money to real output had increased only 13.3 percent. The difference in these rates, 27.2 percent, is recorded in Figure 3.2 above June 1917. The significance of this number is that it shows the "excess" inflation, the inflation produced by wartime fears of further inflation and shortages. This component of inflation could be suppressed without crippling the economy.

It is not possible to identify a precise moment when the fear of runaway inflation was calmed. Events in the spring and early summer of 1917, however, must have suggested to most observers that strong actions to suppress inflation were under way or soon would be. Hoover was appointed Food Administrator in May, for example, and during July it was obvious that a Food Bill (the Lever Act) would be passed, although it was not signed until early August. But it is clear from Figure 3.2 that controls, or more exactly, the formation of the War Industries Board in July and the passage of the Lever Act, started a downward trend – controls cooled the inflationary fever.

It does not appear that there were any other changes in economic policy or other determinants of economic events that could have produced such a dramatic change in the course of inflation. The second best candidate is changes in the course of the war. But the break in the inflationary psychology appears to have come too early to be accounted for by events of a purely military nature. America entered the war in April 1917. Ahead lay the formation of a unified allied command, the Treaty of Brest-Litovsk between the Central Powers and the Soviet Union which permitted the Central Powers to concentrate their forces on the Western front, and the German counteroffensive, the second battle of the Marne, which was stopped in August 1918. Yet the momentum of inflation in the United States seems to have been broken between July and August of 1917. If anything, a close look at the course of the war over these crucial months makes the achievement of controls appear all the more outstanding. Despite the uncertainty about the potential length and intensity of American participation in the war, uncertainty that must have produced at least some fears of inflation and shortages, controls were able to quiet these fears and reduce inflationary pressures.

Imposing controls protected the real incomes of those who could not readily adjust to the inflation and this substantial benefit outweighed, in my opinion, the inconvenience of controls. The real earnings of workers in manufacturing rose from 1916 to 1917, and the average real earnings of all workers remained about constant. But for those for whom adjustments came slowly, such as ministers or public school teachers, there were substantial declines in real incomes. For those for whom no adjustments were possible, those on fixed incomes, the situation was still worse. Without the moderating effect of controls, the decline in real income for these groups would have been more severe from 1917 to 1918 than it was. It is hard, moreover, to conceive of a feasible alternative mechanism for protecting these groups. In any case, no alternative was seriously discussed at the time.

It was clear to contemporaries that controls had worked, had slowed inflation. They did not have access to the measures shown in Figure 3.2. Indeed the estimates of the money supply which are crucial to the figure were not then available. Contemporaries could, however, compare what was happening to prices under controls with what had been happening before. In the fifteen months prior to the introduction of controls, wholesale prices increased at an annual rate of 32.4 percent, while during the fifteen months controls were in effect the index rose at an annual rate of only 7.1 percent per year. To be sure, the index under controls understates prices because of increased chiseling and because of shortages. Prices that included adequate monetary allowances for decreased quality and for the inconvenience of shortages would have been higher. But the overall impression of a substantial slowing of inflation is correct. Consider the following – a kind of thought experiment of the sort that might have been in the mind of a contemporary observer of controls. Suppose prices had continued to rise after the imposition of controls, for six months, at the rate they had been rising before controls were imposed. But then, due to other policies, the rate of increase had fallen for the remainder of the period of controls to a rate equal to only half of what it actually was under controls. Assume in other words, that the price spiral continued for only a short period of time longer than it did. How high would prices have been when controls terminated under this hypothetical scenario? They would have been about 10 percent higher than they actually were. Even a short continuation of "runaway" inflation, combined with extremely favorable conditions afterward, would have been worse than the actual course of events.

The opportunity created by controls to reduce the fundamental pressure on prices was grasped. As can be seen in Table 3.4, the rate of increase of money per unit of real output, the long-run determinant of the price level, was slowed whether one uses the national security version of national product or the civilian version. Using the national security version produces the most dramatic change. While money per unit of real output was rising at an annual rate of 14.6 percent before controls were imposed, the ratio was almost stable afterward, rising at an annual

Table 3.4. *Prices, money, and related data, before, during, and after controls*

Index	May 1916 (15 months before)	Aug. 1917 (beginning of controls)	Nov. 1918 (end of controls)	Feb. 1920 (15 months after)
Wholesale prices	100	150	164	189
Money	100	122	136	168
Monetary base	100	122	157	172
Money per unit of real national product (national security version)[a]	100	120	122	150
Money per unit of real national product (civilian version)	100	127	141	157

[a] This variable includes national security outlays in the denominator.
Sources: Wholesale prices: Warren and Pearson (1933B, p. 13). Money: Friedman and Schwartz (1970B, Table 1, column 9, pp. 15–17). Monetary base: Friedman and Schwartz (1963B, Table B-3, column (1), pp. 801–2). National product: Kendrick (1961B, Table A-1, columns (5) and (6), pp. 290–1).

rate of only 1.3 percent. This result, however, was fortuitous. While growth of the money supply stock slowed during the period under controls, from an annual growth rate of 15.9 percent in the fifteen months prior to controls to an annual rate of 8.7 percent after, this was not due to the actions of the monetary authority. Indeed, the growth rate of currency and bank reserves, the monetary base, actually increased. Yet, this is the instrument that the Federal Reserve used to influence the money supply. The reason for the slowdown in the monetary expansion was the tendency of the public, after the imposition of controls, to convert bank deposits into currency, a tendency which had a contractionary effect on the banking system because it drained the system of cash. The reasons for this tendency are not clear. A similar development occurred during World War II and Philip Cagan, studying that episode, suggested that it might be explained by the superiority of cash for travelers at home and abroad and for individuals trying to evade income taxes or price controls.[49] Friedman and Schwartz have suggested that similar forces may have been at work in World War I.[50] If so, and if the last-named factor was important, then there may have been an indirect connection between the imposition of controls and the slowing of the growth rate of the money supply. Whether this was the case or not, however, we can conclude that controls were successfully combined with a restrictive monetary policy. Separately, neither policy would have worked so well.

The size of the bureaucracy

Controls, it was shown above, did produce many of the ills that critics of controls would expect. But it was also argued that those ills appear to have been of manageable proportions. Given the evidence that controls cooled the inflationary fever that had gripped the nation, it begins to appear that the use of controls in World War I was justified. This tentative assessment is reinforced when we turn to those costs of controls that can, to some extent, be quantified. To start with a simple question, but one that plays a large role in the case against controls, how large was the bureaucracy created to manage controls? How did it compare with existing bureaucracies?

The bureaucracy created to control prices and allocate resources and output during World War I was, by design, temporary and small. The functions taken on by the War Industries Board and the Food and Fuel Administrations could have been performed by existing agencies such as the Federal Trade Commission (which in fact did considerable accounting work for these agencies) and the Department of Agriculture. But new agencies were free from the image of partisanship which sometimes adhered to established agencies, and new organizations could be expected to disappear, as in fact they did, when the war was over. Had they been mere additions to existing agencies it is far more likely that the resources they employed would have been permanently captured by the bureaucracy. The war agencies, moreover, tried to rely as much as possible on voluntary cooperation rather than bureaucratic commands. For example, the Food Administration, as we have seen, relied first purely on appeals for restraint, and later on the sanctioning of tie-in sales, another way of saving administrative resources, compared to the issue of ration cards.

Table 3.5 shows the expenditures of four of the civilian war agencies crucial to the system of control, including the three discussed above; these agencies performed a substantial share of the price fixing and related tasks. The expenditures of the Post Office, a large but familiar and unfrightening bureaucracy, are given by way of comparison. Table 3.5 shows that controlling prices in World War I did not involve a costly

Table 3.5. *Expenditures by agencies controlling prices, 1918–19 (thousands of dollars, years ending June 30)*

Agency	1918	1919
War Industries Board	n.a.	1,939
Food and Fuel Administrations	5,331	17,645
War Labor Board	n.a.	1,022
Total	n.a.	20,606
Post Office	324,833	362,497
Total as a percentage of Post Office	n.a.	5.7

Sources: War agencies: U.S. Treasury Department, *Annual Report*, 1919, pp. 191, 194, 195. Postal Service: U.S. Bureau of the Census (1960G, series R141, p. 496).

expansion of the bureaucracy. In fiscal year 1919 the agencies listed in the table spent only about 5.7 percent as much as the Post Office. Of course, other agencies were involved with controlling prices. It has already been mentioned that the Federal Trade Commission did numerous studies for the war agencies, and the Commission expanded its staff of accountants for this purpose. There were also agencies that might be included in Table 3.5 that were not. The War Trade Board, the Bureau of Industrial Housing and Transportation, the Farm Labor Project, the Capital Issues Committee and War Finance Corporation, the Shipping Board, and even the War and Navy Departments all took on functions that the market would have performed in peacetime. The addition of these agencies would raise the total shown in Table 3.5 somewhat, but would not change the general picture.

The expenditure data are also somewhat misleading because the civilian war agencies relied to some extent on volunteers. They did so at two levels. The top echelons were filled with volunteer executives from the private sector, the dollar-a-year men. Then, at the local level, the Food and Fuel Administrations were staffed by part-time volunteers. On the other hand, paid employees filled the middle level of clerical staff. Typical was the experience of the Food Administration. In July 1918 the Washington staff of the Food Administration consisted of 1,805 paid employees and 120 volunteers. In December 1918, just after the Armistice, there were 1,338 paid employees and 90 volunteers. In that same month the staff outside Washington numbered 1,538 paid employees and 7,984 volunteers.[51]

I have not found comparable data for other agencies, but my impression from scattered evidence is that the War Industries Board had a Washington staff roughly equivalent to the Food Administration's, but no comparable staff outside Washington. There were industry committees, but frequently their work was limited. The War Labor Board was even smaller. The Fuel Administration's operation was roughly of the same size as the Food Administration's. Thus, even if one were to compare the total employment of the civilian war agencies with the total for the Post Office (188,000 in 1919),[52] the appearance would be that of a rather small bureaucracy. The December 1918 staff of the Food Administration, to carry out the comparison, was about 5.8 percent as large as that of the Post Office. Overall, the bureaucracy might have reached a number equal to fifteen percent of the Post Office.

There was a private-sector bureaucracy opposite the government's bureaucracy. Firms had to assign personnel to deal with the rules and regulations promulgated by the government agencies. For World War I there is no evidence, that I have been able to find, on the potential extent of this bureaucracy. The evidence from later wars is that taking the private-sector bureaucracy into account would not overturn our ideas about the size of the total bureaucracy. It should also be noted that while price controls increased the need for personnel for certain purposes, controls decreased the need to allocate personnel to watching prices and other market trends. To a considerable extent the private-sector bureaucracy that stood opposite the government's bureaucracy could have been staffed with personnel drawn from these superfluous jobs.

It is true, of course, that great oaks grow from little acorns. The civilian war agencies were hastily assembled in an environment of genuine labor scarcity, and their temporary character discouraged people who were seeking long-term careers in government from joining them. It seems inevitable that had their functions become a permanent part of the economy, these agencies would have grown significantly relative to the existing bureaucracies. As it was, however, these trees were still just bureaucratic seedlings at the war's end.

Seizure

Behind much of the "voluntary" compliance that permitted the use of a relatively small bureaucracy lay a simple threat: seizure of the output of a firm or even the firm itself. There have been scattered references to seizure in the discussion above, but the issue is of sufficient importance to justify explicit discussion. Why rely on such a drastic threat rather than on some traditional penalty? The answer lies in the delays and uncertainties of the legal system. A price controller faced with a recalcitrant industry wants a threat that can be applied right away, not one that may take months to wend its way through the courts and may in the end be denied. When wages were part of the problem, enforcement through the courts appeared even less attractive. A Democratic administration did not want to appear antiunion, so attacking striking unions through court-enforced injunctions was out of the question. But permitting a firm that had a strike on its hands to buy its way out with a wage increase (to be passed on as a price increase) would endanger the stabilization program. In this case seizure emerged as an attractive alternative.

During the war three outright seizures were made by the President: the railroads, beginning with the major long-haul lines in December 1917; the wire services, in July 1918; and the Smith and Wesson company, in September 1918.[53] All three were seized because of labor troubles. The railroads were taken over because of a threatened strike and the other two because of failures to comply with decisions of the National War Labor Board. Seizure did not necessarily mean losses for the shareholders. Indeed, the terms under which the long-haul lines were operated were so favorable that the short-line operators petitioned to be seized as well, a wish that was eventually, but reluctantly granted. The seized firms were protected, moreover, by the Constitutional provision which calls for just compensation when private property is taken by the government. But despite the favorable terms in these cases most businessmen were probably worried about the threat of seizure. There was always the possibility that the terms in their cases might turn out unfavorable.

While the profits of shareholders might be protected, at least from outright losses, management faced the destruction of its traditional privileges, and even dismissal. In the particular cases cited above, the fear of seizure was enhanced by the government officials in charge of the industries who campaigned to make seizures permanent. There were arguments in all three seizures that the industry was a special case, that seizure was not a general weapon. Nevertheless it is easy to imagine that these examples served as a warning to businessmen of the ultimate costs of noncompliance with the government's program.

In other cases seizure was only threatened. This happened several times in the coal fields. The Fuel Administrator threatened to take over some Midwestern coal mines in labor disputes, an action sanctioned by the Lever Act, as did President Wilson with respect to some Alabama coal mines in similar circumstances. The U.S. Shipping Board threatened to seize ships and shipyards in several labor disputes. The War Department actually ran Blue Spruce logging operations in the Northwest as a result of a long loggers' strike.[54]

Paradoxically, the small firm was less vulnerable to a government takeover than the large one. While the small firm feared the government's ability to harass it through judicial proceedings, it had little to fear in the way of outright seizure. Public opinion, except in extreme cases, would have strongly opposed attempts to nationalize a small, independent business. With the giant corporation, on the other hand, the potency of the alternatives was reversed. The corporation was prepared to fight long legal battles in the courts. In the Progressive Era, however, it could not rely on public opinion to oppose seizure. Quite the contrary, many people would have welcomed the nationalization of certain giant corporations.

The Price Fixing Committee of the War Industries Board also eschewed legal actions to enforce its decisions, relying instead on the "more or less veiled threat of commandeering."[55] The War Department and the Navy were both represented on the Price Fixing Committee. Both resorted to commandeering and compulsory orders on a fairly extensive scale. The total value of requisitions and compulsory orders of the War Department alone (presumably at the "just" price) were $141,687,000, about one percent of total wartime expenditures by the War Department, but about 77 percent of departmental expenditures in 1916, the last full year of peace.[56]

The most dramatic examples of the threat of seizure are those that Bernard Baruch later recounted. I have already referred to his threat to commandeer the coal and steel of the automakers. He also claims to have pressured the steel industry in a similar way. According to Baruch, no agreement could be reached on the price of steel until he showed Judge Elbert Gary, chairman of the board of U.S. Steel, a letter from Wilson expressing the President's willingness to nationalize United States Steel. As Baruch remembered the encounter:

> Gary read the letter with an expressionless face and handed it back.
> "You haven't got anybody to run the Steel Company," he said.

"Oh yes I have, Judge," I told him.

"Who?"

"Oh we'll get a second lieutenant or somebody to run it."

That must have stung Gary to the quick.

"But that won't trouble you very much," I added. "If those mill towns find out why we've taken over, they'll present you with your mills brick by brick."

Gary rose from his seat and walked away. I could see the fingers of each hand rubbing one against the other. You could almost hear his mind turning over.

Suddenly he turned around, came back, and said, "Can't we fix this up?"

"Sure we can," I said.[57]

Even the copper industry, the site of Baruch's triumphant initial negotiations for price restraint, apparently had to be threatened with seizure at a later point.[58] In short, while there were often good working relationships between the government and industry during the war, there was, below the surface, a crude but effective threat to enforce compliance. No other aspect of the wartime experience reveals so clearly why controls must be viewed as an emergency measure. Seizure was tolerated because of the overwhelming case for controlling inflation as part of the process of winning the war. It is conceivable that peacetime inflationary emergencies might justify similar, but more limited, grants of power to those controlling prices. But permanent controls would require a broad array of legal safeguards to prevent the misuse of power that would considerably complicate the process of controlling prices.

Aggregate productivity

While the creation of more bureaucracies, and their resort to extreme threats, is clearly alien to the American spirit, the heart of the case against controls, as it is usually developed, is that controls are an extremely imperfect substitute for the market. The distortions created by controls, it is charged, outweigh the benefits. But the evidence that controls produced difficulties in certain markets, for example, sugar or coal (even if evidence were unambiguous, and it is not) would not prove that controls had severely damaged the allocative efficiency of the economy. Even without controls one could always construct a list of mistakes made by private entrepreneurs, actions which in principle might have been avoided. To take a recent example, several automobile manufacturers appear to have delayed overlong in changing over to smaller models. In principle, far-seeing regulators could have prevented this mistake

Table 3.6. *Year-to-year percentage changes in productivity,*
1913–23

Years	Labor productivity (BLS)	Total factor productivity (Denison)	Total factor productivity (Kendrick)
1913–14	−3.02	−4.12	−7.36
14–15	−.38	1.24	2.43
15–16	1.15	−1.02	7.19
16–17	−3.09	−3.23	−5.76
17–18	5.72	6.13	6.65
18–19	3.64	2.29	5.18
19–20	−3.27	−6.91	−1.27
20–21	0.37	−3.40	4.79
21–22	9.13	8.79	0
22–23	4.59	4.38	5.73

Sources: U.S. Bureau of Economic Analysis, *Long Term Economic Growth,*
1860–1970 (1970G). Column 1: series A168, p. 211. Column 2: series A162,
p. 209. Column 3: series A161, p. 209.

by altering the relative prices of large and small cars. The real question
is whether or not the volume of difficulties created by controls was
greater than the volume of similar difficulties that would have been
encountered had the economy been left uncontrolled. In part the answer
would depend on how skillful the authorities were in controlling prices.
Could they do as well or better than the market in adjusting relative
prices – the price of one product compared with close substitutes, the
price of one product compared with its inputs, and so forth? In part
also, the answer would depend on whether controls were being used
to keep the general level of prices below its long-run equilibrium, or
merely to bring the level of prices down to the long-run equilibrium.
In the former case, even skillful tuning of relative prices would not
prevent shortages in some markets. In World War I, however, the latter
case applies.

Economists have computed several estimates of aggregate productivity
that can provide a tentative measure of the overall damage to the allocative
mechanism caused by controls. In essence, these are estimates of the
ratio of output to input. Percentage changes in the three most commonly
used estimates are shown in Table 3.6. The labor productivity index
is the ratio of real output to total labor hours, while the Denison and
Kendrick indexes are ratios of total real output to the theoretically

superior alternative, a measure of total inputs. The Denison and Kendrick measures, in turn, differ in the weighting of inputs (the Denison measure uses the arithmetic sum of the value of inputs while the Kendrick measure uses a geometrically weighted sum) and other details. The three measures are correlated, but the differences in the way they were computed sometimes produce moderate differences when percentage changes in the two measures are compared.

The measures presented in Table 3.6 provide no support to those critics who have contended that controls must severely damage the allocative mechanism of the economy, even in the short run. All three indexes show strong gains in productivity from 1917 to 1918 and again from 1918 to 1919. These gains appear substantial, moreover, whether compared with the precontrol or postcontrol average gain.

There are some reasons to suspect that the true picture may not be quite as rosy as these data suggest. These were years of high aggregate demand, which fosters productivity growth, so the gains might have been there even in the absence of controls. Wartime output, too, is of a form different from that of peacetime output – more uniform, and therefore easier to produce – so that the comparison with peacetime production may not be entirely fair. Finally, the indexes used to deflate the value of real output may not reflect the full effect of chiseling, and thus real output may be overstated. But it seems unlikely that these effects could reverse the finding of strong productivity gains during the control period. This finding implies that the positive effect of controls on price expectations must be given considerable weight in the overall assessment of controls. The burden of proof on the issue of allocative efficiency in the First World War falls to the critics of controls.

Why not make controls permanent?

On reading the firsthand accounts of World War I controls, one is struck by the frequency with which the assertion that controls worked much better in wartime than free markets was combined with the assertion that we should return to free markets, or some slightly modified form of them, after the war. Seldom was the crucial question addressed. If controls were a more efficient way of allocating resources in the stress of war, would they not have been more efficient (even if by a smaller margin) in peacetime? Why go back to free markets? One of the clearest examples of the failure to face this question can be found in Baruch's final report on the War Industries Board. After telling the "inspiring" story of the Board, its absolute superiority over reliance on the market, he then weakened when it came to recommending that a system of price controls and priorities be continued in the postwar period. Instead, he made a milder recommendation. The government should validate trade organizations, agreements reached between them and the government, and cooperative agreements among firms when the government agreed they were in the national interest.[59] But clearly this vague prescription bore little resemblance to the wartime experiment.

Fortunately we can now reconcile these conflicting positions. Controls, as we have seen, were useful during the war because they quieted the fears that caused the rapid increase in prices that preceded the imposition of controls. Controls were not used to push prices below the level dictated by the long-run determinants. In peacetime, when, normally, the price level is closer to its long-run equilibrium, controls might well be disequilibrating. In that case the costs of controls would no doubt outweigh the benefits. This argument – that controls were useful precisely because of the disequilibrium in the price system – was not appealed to by people such as Baruch (as far as I am aware), despite the seriousness of the intellectual dilemma they faced. They did, however, produce several arguments worth considering for the light they shed on the experience of controls.

One argument, implicit in many of the firsthand accounts, could be put this way: Central planning is more efficient in peace as well as war, but free markets and the economic freedom entailed are good in themselves. In wartime, reliance on free markets would have meant catastrophic inflation and fewer arms with which to fight the war; in peacetime, no such disastrous consequences flow from reliance on the market. Economic freedom is a luxury we can afford only in peace. The notion that freeing the public, but particularly businessmen, from having to worry about an endless series of government edicts was worthwhile in itself appealed to a man like Baruch, who had considerable personal experience in business.[60] Someone who identified with a different constituency would have felt differently.

A second argument was based on the role of patriotism. During the war controls had worked, it was argued, because business and labor had cooperated voluntarily. In peacetime there would be more resistance to government authority and more evasion; controls would never work as well in peace as they had in war. As Hoover put it in his final report:

During war a high degree of altruism maintains initiative, but in peace there can be but one basis of economic control, that is, freedom for normal processes of business with prevention of domination by the few.[61]

There is undoubtedly some truth in this. But it should be remembered that behind much of the "voluntary" compliance lay the threat of seizure. It was not so much the willingness of Americans to comply that made controls work, but their willingness to tolerate extraordinary interference with traditional rights. One variant of this argument, moreover, seems to me to be patently thin. It was sometimes argued that controls worked so well during the war because they were administered by extremely able businessmen from the private sector drawn to Washington by a desire to serve, men like Baruch and Hoover, of course, but also men like J. Leonard Replogle, Baruch's steel expert, who had been president of the American Vanadium Company. Once the war was over most of them returned to private business. How could mere government bureaucrats run things as well? While in fact most of these men did return to the private sector, surely this outcome was not inevitable. There must have been some combination of monetary and other rewards that would have kept them in Washington, or permitted the government over the long term to find suitable replacements. Neither the private nor the public sector in our society has a monopoly on administrative talent.

A third argument is in some way both the most interesting and the most convincing. It can be put this way. The most important functions of the market are to reveal information about people's tastes and preferences. What kind of automobiles should we make, what kind of clothing should be manufactured, even what kind of sports should be played? These are all questions that in peacetime most people are willing to leave to the market because it responds to "dollar votes." Consumers get what they really want. But in wartime this information becomes superfluous. The needs of the military are relatively obvious, and in any case, cannot be clarified by market activity. Thus, in wartime the balance of virtues swings in favor of central planning; while in peacetime, because of the information it generates, the balance favors the market.[62]

This view was articulated with some degree of thoughtfulness by Lesher of the Fuel Administration, who asked himself why the zone system for allocating coal should not be continued after the war.[63] The zone system, you will recall, limited the shipment of coal to users close to the field in which it was produced. There was an obvious saving in rail miles from the system. Why return to the wasteful prewar system in which Eastern coals were sometimes carried halfway across the nation? The answer that Lesher gave was that in the absence of a clear standard – does it contribute to the war effort? – there was no basis for denying high-quality coals to users located far away if they were willing to pay. Lesher pointed out that when the Fuel Administration expanded the zone in which Iowa coal had to be used, outraged consumers, who wanted to pay the additional costs involved in buying the higher-quality Illinois coals, bombarded the Fuel Administration with complaints. That episode, Lesher thought, could be taken as a model of the dissatisfactions that would plague a permanent zone system. One can imagine alternative ways of generating the information ordinarily produced by the market. But without some such alternative, and it is hard to imagine a fully satisfactory alternative generator of information, one can anticipate that dissatisfactions of the sort that the zone system produced would be endemic.

Benefits and costs

During World War I, controls, to sum up, accomplished their major purpose of arresting the inflationary spiral. From May 1916 to August 1917 (when controls were imposed) wholesale prices rose at an annual rate of 32.4 percent. Under controls, wholesale prices rose at a rate of only 7.1 percent per year. This slowdown was facilitated by a reduction in the rate of monetary expansion relative to output. But monetary factors cannot fully account for the slowing of inflation. It is hard to imagine that a more restrictive monetary policy alone could have produced such dramatic results, or indeed, that such a monetary policy could have been long pursued in the face of price increases fed by fears of further inflation. Slowing inflation reduced the incidence of arbitrary and in some cases painful redistributions of income. This result was achieved without the imposition of a large bureaucracy and without substantial damage to the productive efficiency of the economy.

Balanced against this success were the headaches that in a more severe form would plague any permanent system of controls. There was some cheating, which required detailed bureaucratic intervention, and the appropriate allocation of supplies required the substitution of clumsy, authoritarian devices – priorities, tied sales, driving bans, threats of nationalization, and so forth – for the price system. The historical record of these controls thus suggests to me that the United States made the right choices both when it imposed controls in World War I and when it removed them.

During the 1920s the combination of conservative national leadership and a relatively stable price level meant there was little interest in controls as a way of improving economic performance. But in the early thirties economic conditions seemed to be almost the reverse of a wartime inflation; prices and wages spiraled downward, creating expectations of further decreases, and leaving severe unemployment in their wake. The Roosevelt administration responded by providing for the reverse of wartime controls, government action to set a floor on prices and wages. This policy was embodied in the National Industrial Recovery Act (NIRA) which sponsored cartels that sought to maintain minimum prices and minimum wage scales. The NIRA period ended abruptly when the law was declared unconstitutional. But, during its short existence, it represented an attempt to control the general price level through direct government intervention. The experience might reasonably have been included in this history. My concern, however, is with inflation, and it was not until the outbreak of World War II renewed the threat of inflation that Americans began again to think seriously about controls as a supplement to monetary and fiscal restraint.

4. World War II: Attacking inflation directly

> The executive order I have signed today is a hold-the-line order.
>
> To hold the line we cannot tolerate further increases in prices affecting the cost of living or further increases in general wage or salary rates except where clearly necessary to correct substandard living conditions. The only way to hold the line is to stop trying to find justifications for not holding it here or not holding it there.
>
> Franklin Delano Roosevelt, April 8, 1943

The experiment with controls during World War II was the longest and most comprehensive trial in America's history. The program evolved through a series of phases from early exhortations to an elaborate series of formal controls. An examination of the effects of these policies requires, at the minimum, a working knowledge of these phases since each one left a distinct imprint on prices, the black market, and so forth. But in laying out the "life cycle" of the controls it is worth asking what political forces produced this changing pattern. The answer to this question will tell us something about how the changing balance of costs and benefits was perceived by the public, by business, and by the government, something that the statistical record alone cannot reveal.

Thus, a political history of controls is presented in the first section. The second section, "The Effect on Prices," launches the examination of the statistical record with a look at the positive side of the ledger, the reduction of inflation. The questions asked are whether controls reduced inflation, by how much, for how long, and in what relationship to the structure of controls. The next section, "The bureaucracy," takes up the first of the side effects identified by the critics of controls: the extent of the bureaucracy. In the first section of the next chapter, which is also on World War II, I will look at a related issue, the extent of rationing during the government's most systematic attempt to replace the allocative function of the market. The next section in that chapter examines the efficiency of the war economy, and asks whether controls damaged that efficiency. The third section takes up what for many will be the most fascinating part of the story, the black market. Here the questions are how extensive was the black market, and how confining were the methods used to suppress it. Finally, the last section suggests some tentative conclusions.

It may be of some use, at this point, to anticipate these conclusions in order to provide a guide through what is at times a somewhat round-about argument. The general impression of controls during the war is that they "worked," in the sense that they produced a significant reduction in inflation with only moderately costly side effects. This picture contains a strong element of truth, but it needs to be modified, and in these two chapters I will try to provide the information and ideas needed to develop those modifications. Thus, the reader will be able to understand why controls worked during part of the period, but not all of it. It will be seen that, by the end of the war, controls had worn out their usefulness. Their removal, although perhaps not done in the most efficient manner, was the correct decision. At first controls were used to equilibrate the system. Prices were being pushed toward a level consistent with monetary and production trends. By the end of the war, however, controls were being employed to maintain the system in a disequilibrium. Then, the costs outweighed the benefits.[1]

Evolving the rules of the game

As World War II approached, country after country established price controls. The totalitarian states moved first. The Fascist party in Italy had tried to fix the prices of certain key commodities as early as 1924. In October 1935, shortly before the invasion of Ethiopia, a Permanent Committee for Price Watching was appointed. On October 5, 1936, a royal decree-law fixed commodity prices, utility rates, and rents. The Germans began experimenting with controls in 1931. In October 1936, Germany issued the famous *Preisstop*, which froze virtually all prices.[2] The democracies, and particularly the United States (as might be expected), were slower in adopting controls. A tentative move was made in the summer of 1939 in the United States when the assistant secretaries of War and Navy appointed the War Resources Board to draw up a plan for mobilizing the economy in the event of war. The plan included a provision for price controls, but the Board was disbanded in November, and its report was not made public.[3] The country was not yet ready for full mobilization.

The first phase of price controls in the U.S., a period of growing but selective control, lasted for almost three years, from the formation of the Price Stabilization Division of the National Defense Advisory Commission in May 1940, to the issuance of the General Maximum Price Regulation in April of 1942. This period is of particular interest because it reveals clearly the limits of a policy that seeks to avoid a thorough repression of the market and a major commitment of resources to the administration and enforcement of controls.

The organization that eventually grew into the Office of Price Administration (OPA) was born on May 29, 1940 when President Roosevelt revived the Council of National Defense, a World War I device, and its National Defense Advisory Commission. The latter consisted of seven "prominent" persons brought together to advise the President on defense matters. Roosevelt chose Leon Henderson to head the Price Stabilization Division. It was a fateful choice. Henderson became an effective advocate of broad and strongly enforced price controls. Although he had an academic background, there were probably few if any men in government who had more experience with fixing prices. He had been the chief economist at the National Recovery Administration (a depression-era device concerned with setting minimum prices), a chief economic coordinator for the Temporary National Economic Commission (which investigated antisocial business practices), and an economist at the Securities and Exchange Commission. He was also given credit for predicting the downturn of 1938 using the theory that prices were rising too fast relative to wages and that therefore too much of the increase in revenues was being impounded in profits.[4] Economists have generally cited other causes for the downturn, but this prediction added substantially to his credentials.[5]

In the summer and fall of 1940 Henderson and his staff prepared themselves for the coming ordeal by studying examples of controls adopted in other countries and in the United States in World War I. They also tried to limit certain price increases by securing the voluntary cooperation of business. There were examples both of success and failure with this policy. The first attempt was made in July of 1940. Paper pulp prices had shown signs (in the Price Division's opinion) of spiraling toward unwarranted heights. A meeting with the important producers of the industry was held in New York on July 23, and a promise to hold prices down was obtained. Whether this was the cause or not, pulp prices retreated.[6] A similar situation developed in lumber. But in this case Henderson was rebuffed. To secure compliance he was forced to threaten seizure of lumber inventories. Again the advance was halted. But already it was clear that without some means of enforcement the government's notions of reasonable price behavior could not be made to stick.[7]

We cannot know for certain whether businessmen today would be more amenable to voluntary agreements than they were in the summer of 1940. On the one hand, business had been profoundly alienated by the New Deal; today, it is more reconciled to government intervention. But on the other hand, the world in 1940 was engulfed in war. Henderson and his lieutenants could make an appeal to patriotism that would be meaningless today.

The movement toward formal controls accelerated in February 1941. Demand for machine tools in particular was high and substantial price increases had occurred. This was the logical outcome of the mobilization process: Demand for munitions created a demand for the machines to make them. Apparently, some control was achieved over the prices being charged for new tools through voluntary agreements with major producers. But there were so many dealers in used machines that this technique was not feasible. Therefore, on February 17, 1941, the Price Division issued Price Schedule No. 1, the first formal control, a list of maximum prices for used machine tools expressed as a percentage of the price when new, the percentage varying with the age and condition of the machine.[8] Issuing the price schedule apparently involved a certain amount of bravado; it was not clear that the ceilings were legally enforceable. The schedule itself promised only that violations would be publicized and that the Price Division would attempt to get other government agencies to use their influence against the violators.

The official historians of the early days of OPA report that this first price schedule "met with almost universal approval from industry."[9] The word almost is probably used to exclude the owners of second-hand machine tools. The point to be noted here is that while businessmen generally oppose ceilings on their own prices they may well support certain controls and even rationing. Businessmen are buyers as well as sellers. They have long-term as well as short-term interests. Not infrequently, powerful blocs of businessmen favored the imposition of a given set of controls. In this case it is not hard to imagine that the industrialists who found themselves being squeezed by increases in second-hand machine tool prices were as influential, if not more influential, than the dealers in used machine tools. This theme will recur in more complex circumstances; it has an important bearing on the ability of the controllers to maintain an equitable system.

Some quantitative evidence on the attitudes in the business community at this time is available. A survey of executives was conducted by *Fortune* in October 1940. The executives were given a choice among three alternatives for regulating prices: direct government intervention; trade association activity; and free markets. Thirty-five percent favored direct intervention; 25 percent, trade association activity; only 27 percent favored the free market (14 percent expressed no opinion).[10] An even more dramatic result was reported somewhat later in *Modern Industry*, a magazine intended for business executives. In August 1941 *Modern Industry* published one of its regular debates. The question was, Should a ceiling be set on prices and wages? The "No" side of the debate, incidentally, was argued by Irving Fisher, generally considered one of the greatest American economists of the twentieth century. Readers were invited to vote their preference after reading the debate. Of those responding, 82.5 percent agreed that ceilings should be placed on prices, and 17.5 percent disagreed.[11] While one cannot put great weight on this evidence since it may not be representative, it is nevertheless intriguing. It suggests that well before Pearl Harbor there was in the business community considerable support for a freeze.

In all, only five price schedules were issued during the National Defense Advisory Council period, in part, perhaps, because of the weakness in their legal foundation. To strengthen Henderson's hand, President Roosevelt created the Office of Price Administration and Civilian Supply on April 11, 1941. Henderson was immediately dubbed the "price czar" by the press. The agency derived its authority from the President's war powers, but it still did not have a foundation in the sort of Congressional action that would have allowed it to enforce compliance in the courts. The Civilian Supply part of the name expressed the agency's responsibility for rationing and similar measures, if they became necessary. Later the power to order rationing was shifted to the War Production Board as a result of a power struggle between the agencies that was to surface in other contexts. From this time on the agency controlling civilian prices was known simply as OPA.

Perhaps as significant as the creation of OPA itself was the creation of the Price Division of OPA, headed by John Kenneth Galbraith, an enthusiastic and skilled administrator, and a leading theoretician of controls. During the remainder of the prestatutory period Galbraith continued the policy of issuing price schedules and arranging voluntary agreements. But the emphasis shifted, particularly after August 1941, to formal schedules. In that month, Galbraith's division issued more formal orders than in all the previous months combined. Overall, by the end of the prestatutory period, about 50 percent of the nation's wholesale prices had been placed under control by issuing fifty-three price schedules, arranging 120 voluntary agreements, and sending several hundred warning letters and suggestions.[12]

The Emergency Price Control Act

Perhaps from the beginning OPA had felt that it needed a legal mandate to succeed in controlling prices. In any case, it was now clear that such a mandate was essential. Early in 1941 drafts of a proposed law were circulated in the agency, and the appropriate strategy for obtaining approval was considered. The proposed bill was finally introduced in the House on August 1, 1941. Competition in the House came from a bill introduced by Gore of Tennessee. His bill, closely in tune with ideas long advocated by Bernard Baruch, called for an across-the-board freeze, embracing wages, interest rates, and prices. While there was some sympathy for this approach at OPA it was felt that administrative and political considerations ruled it out in the summer of 1941.[13] The price control bill passed the House a few days before Pearl Harbor.

The bill was similar to, but weaker than, the one originally planned by OPA. A key provision created a single administrator, who was given considerable discretion in choosing the type of controls to be applied. Prices, where it was practical, were to be set at the level prevailing between October 1 and October 15, 1941. But the Administrator could set any prices he deemed "generally fair and equitable." He could make adjustments for individual firms. He could use overall ceilings, allowance of certain margins over costs, and various devices for securing the output of high-cost producers without raising the average price in the industry. There were, however, certain goods and services specifically exempt from control: wages, fees for professional services, insurance rates, public utility rates, prices charged by the "media," and agricultural prices until they reached certain predetermined levels. The bill provided for several penalties to enforce compliance. Either buyers in the private sector or the Administrator could sue for treble damages. The Administrator could also seek court injunctions and criminal penalties for willful violators. He was empowered to issue and revoke licenses for firms dealing in controlled commodities. The measure provided a special Emergency Court of Appeals to hear challenges to the constitutionality of the regulations; its decisions could be appealed only to the Supreme Court.

The bill was far from satisfactory from OPA's point of view. For one thing the bill no longer included wide powers to ration civilian goods, powers that, as noted above, were given to the War Production Board.[14] The latter agency soon delegated control over the administration of consumer rationing back to OPA, but not the power to initiate rationing. At the wholesale level OPA never had authority over the production of goods or their distribution.

Of more immediate concern, however, were the limitations which the law placed on the agency's ability to fix agricultural prices. No price could be set below the highest of (1) 110 percent of parity, (2) the market price as of October 1, 1941, (3) the market price as of December 15, 1941, and (4) the average market price during the period July 1, 1919 to June 30, 1929. This complicated provision was used to assure high ceilings to a number of specific commodities.[15] Galbraith strongly opposed this part of the Act because he thought it would prevent effective price control. He recommended a veto of the bill.[16] His advice was not followed, but an amending act, the Stabilization Act of October 2, 1942, modified this provision, limiting agricultural prices to 100 percent of parity or the maximum reached between January 1 and September 15, 1942. This latter Act also brought wages under control, an area which OPA had omitted from the original bill for political reasons.

Galbraith's position in this matter is of some interest. In later discussions of price controls he has argued that controls over industries dominated by a few large firms and unions would be sufficient in peacetime, and that controls over competitive industries including, presumably, agriculture would not be necessary.[17] Evidently, however, his discussion of peacetime controls assumes a stable level of aggregate demand. In the mobilization period when aggregate demand was surging ahead of supply, he felt that controls over agriculture were essential. Yet the implicit assumption that aggregate demand can be reined in more easily in peacetime can be called into question. While it is true that the "needs" of the government expand less rapidly in peacetime, the ability of Congress to raise the taxes necessary to finance additional government expenditures without inflationary pressures is also less; the patriotic justification for higher taxes is absent.

More important, the imposition of controls may itself have an effect on the level of aggregate demand. In a free market system the President, the Congress, and the Federal Reserve are responsible for controlling inflation. This responsibility creates the willingness to forego expansion of the money supply that might be attractive on other grounds. When a separate agency is created specifically to control inflation it is possible that the other agencies, mentioned above, will no longer take seriously their responsibility for controlling inflation. If prices advance the blame will fall on the agency charged directly with controlling prices. The result could be an expansion of the money supply and the creation of excess demand. A situation might well emerge in peacetime similar to what developed in 1940 and 1941, when across-the-board controls were needed to stabilize the cost of living. The implication of all this is that even with selective controls it is necessary to impose simultaneously a set of institutional constraints sufficient to slow the growth of aggregate demand. Without such constraints peacetime selective controls are likely to prove a bad bargain in the long run.

Across-the-board controls

Public opinion polls at this time showed strong support for more vigorous action to stabilize prices. The Gallup Poll in late 1941 and early 1942 asked the public whether the United States should adopt a policy similar to Canada's, which froze both prices and wages.[18] In three separate polls, from 63 to 67 percent answered in the affirmative.[19] Surprisingly, farmers seemed to be as enthusiastic about a freeze as other groups, with 64 percent favoring the Canadian system.[20] Polls taken by the National Opinion Research Center also showed strong support for across-the-board controls. The Center asked a somewhat vaguer question – Should the government regulate prices? – and got an affirmative response from 88 percent.[21]

Partly in reaction to these pressures, Roosevelt, on April 27, 1942, sent a comprehensive seven-point, anti-inflation program to Congress. The proposal called for increased taxes, across-the-board ceilings, in-cluding ceilings on agricultural prices, wage controls, rationing, war bond sales, and credit controls. Part of the plan required additional Congressional and Presidential action, but the price ceilings were already within the power of OPA.

The next day, OPA issued the General Maximum Price Regulation (GMPR), affectionately known as General Max, freezing prices at the highest level reached in March, 1942. This regulation, which became effective on May 15, inaugurated a period of over four years in which across-the-board controls would be maintained. Professor Galbraith has written that "with much refinement and modification" the GMPR remained the basic method of control.[22] This description, however, is somewhat misleading. The GMPR was essentially a stop-gap measure. As quickly as possible, OPA took prices from under the GMPR and placed them under specific regulations "tailored" to particular markets.

There were two problems with the GMPR. First, freezing prices inevitably created inequities and inefficiencies. If one seller had a temporarily favorable cost–price relationship in March 1942, he got to keep it. But if his profits were unusually low, his profits remained depressed. An agency whose relationships with business and with Congress were crucial could not long afford to overlook inequities of this sort. Moreover, if costs or demands changed, some adjustments had to be made in order to avoid shortages.

Even more important were the enforcement problems. It was difficult to enforce the GMPR in part because each seller set his own prices. Consumers could not be sure that a seller was overcharging just because the price was higher in one store than it was across town. From this standpoint "dollars-and-cents" ceilings were the most effective, so OPA tried to set as many ceilings in terms of specific amounts as possible. The OPA reported some outstanding successes in bringing prices down when dollar-and-cents ceilings were enforced by local volunteers.[23]

Enforcement of the GMPR was particularly difficult when a seller had to set a price for a commodity which he had not carried in March 1942. In that case the GMPR instructed him to use the price of the most "similar " item or, failing that, the price charged by the "most closely competitive seller of the same class." When both of these methods failed, the seller was instructed to use the current replacement cost of the item and a markup based on the highest March ceiling prices in that line. Obviously, reasonable people could disagree about what constituted a "similar" item or the "most closely competitive seller of the same class." And where reasonable people could disagree, the temptation to take the highest defensible price was at times irresistible. In fact, by deliberately changing product lines or brands the alert seller could virtually escape from the GMPR.

The changing of the guard

During 1943, while OPA was struggling to replace the GMPR with tailored controls and to introduce various rationing programs, the Henderson–Galbraith team was replaced by one headed by Chester Bowles. The inside story of this crisis and its resolution has not been told. But the public facts suggest that opposition from the business community to the "professors" at the OPA eventually soured relationships between OPA on the one hand, and business, the Congress, and perhaps the public on the other, to such an extent that a change of administration seemed the only practical course. Henderson resigned in January of 1943 and was shortly replaced by ex-Senator Prentiss Brown of Michigan. Brown's defeat for reelection to the Senate had been widely attributed to his support of Roosevelt's plan to bring farm prices under control at parity. So his support for controls was taken for granted. Moreover, it was felt that as a former Senator he would have the best chance of helping to win Congressional approval for the renewal of controls without weakening congressional amendments to the law.

Galbraith remained at the agency for some months after Henderson, but opposition from the business community and particularly from businessmen inside OPA remained strong. In May a number of key aides at OPA drawn from the business community resigned.[24] One of the most outspoken of the internal critics of the "professors" was OPA's information director Lou Maxon.

Maxon resigned in July of 1943 with a strong parting blast at OPA. In his resignation letter he said that he had had his fill of "slide rule boys, professors, theorists, and lawyers."[25] He listed a series of complaints that are worth recounting for the light they shed on business opposition to the leadership of OPA. One complaint concerned OPA's regulation concerning women's hosiery prices. This regulation, which had been strongly attacked by industry groups, did not provide for a price premium for branded hosiery. Maxon saw this omission as an attempt to "reform" long-standing business practices, an action that had nothing to do with emergency price control. Similarly, Maxon objected to the plan to introduce grade (quality) labeling as an adjunct to price control. "Grade

Table 4.1. *A poll on OPA and other wartime agencies,*
November 1943

Roper: "How do you feel about the State Department, Office of Price
Administration, War Labor Board, and War Production Board – do
you rate the job they have done as good, medium, or poor?"

	State	OPA	WLB	WPB
Good	42.7	29.4	38.6	62.6
Medium	18.8	24.0	18.2	11.3
Poor	9.9	30.8	16.5	5.0
Don't know	28.6	15.8	26.7	21.1

Source: Fortune, "Fortune Survey," Vol. XXVIII, No. 5, November
1943J, p. 20.

labeling," Maxon wrote, "in my sincerest estimation, presents the greatest
threat to American industry and our way of life that ever existed,
because it is without question the spearhead in a drive to eliminate
brands, trademarks, and eventually free enterprise."[26] Maxon also complained that certain regulations were reflections on the efficiency of the
merchant; in other words, propaganda disguised as regulation. On an
even more general level, Maxon lashed out at the alarming way the
government's regulations had grown in length and complexity. His
example, a six-page order concerning fruit cakes, was memorable.

There is evidence that public support for OPA reached a low ebb
during this period. In November of 1943, *Fortune* published a survey
of public opinion, presumably taken a month or so earlier, concerned
with the kind of job various government agencies were doing. The
results are reported in Table 4.1. The OPA got low marks. More people
thought that it had done a poor job than a good job, and fewer people
thought that it had done a good job than thought the same about three
other civilian war agencies.

Opposition to the kind of job that OPA was doing, however, did not
imply opposition to controls. Most people wanted controls continued,
but with more vigorous enforcement. Even in the business community,
which was beginning to feel the effects of controls, a reservoir of support
remained. Between 1942 and 1944 George Katona did a series of interviews
with Chicago businessmen. He found 19 percent of his interviewees
fully cooperative with controls (aware of the need for control and for

keeping their own prices down), only 24 percent hostile, and 57 percent falling somewhere between.[27]

Galbraith resigned in May of 1943, but even if he had not, he soon would have been forced out by a remarkable provision of the 1942 extension of the Emergency Price Control Act. The law required people in policymaking positions at OPA to have five years of business experience! As a result, a number of administrators drawn from academic backgrounds were forced out of their jobs. The "slide rule boys" had created too many enemies in the business world to hang on at OPA.

Meanwhile, Administrator Brown had been rapidly promoting a rationing official from the Connecticut office, Chester Bowles. Brown eventually resigned and Bowles's accession was confirmed by the Senate in November 1943. The agency could not have hoped for anyone better. For one thing, Bowles had made a fortune in advertising during the depression; critics could not charge that he was a professor without experience in the real world. Moreover, Bowles believed passionately in price control and adopted a policy of aggressively defending the agency. He put his advertising experience to good use in constructing the case for controls which he laid before the public in speeches, radio broadcasts, agency publications, and in Congressional testimony backed up with dramatic charts. The popularity of his regime was also helped by events partially beyond his control. By the time he came to power the agency had embarked on a policy of "holding the line," preventing increases across the board, a policy that is easier to enforce and to defend before the court of public opinion than selective controls. By the time Bowles left office, OPA had significantly improved its position in the "ratings."

Hold the line

The GMPR, like the selective controls that preceded it, failed to bring price stability in the elementary sense of a low rate of inflation. Between April 1942 and April 1943, the consumer price index rose at an annual rate of 7.6 percent. Given the evasions that took place under the GMPR, the true increase was probably somewhat more. The GMPR may have been more successful than selective controls in the sense of keeping price increases below what they would have been in a free market. But this is obviously a difficult basis on which to defend a policy.

It is therefore not surprising that in April of 1943 President Roosevelt issued his famous Hold-the-Line Order prohibiting most increases. The opening paragraphs of the order are quoted at the beginning of the chapter. Under Bowles, OPA followed both the letter and the spirit of this directive. The line was held. From December 1943 until June 1946, when controls expired (roughly Bowles's tenure at OPA), the annual rate of increase in the official consumer price index was only 2.8 percent per year. True, the official figures understated the true increase to some extent. But based on an attempt to incorporate estimates of the errors, discussed below, the rate of increase could be put at 3.2 to 3.4 percent per year – still an impressive performance.

Holding the line on prices meant developing a tough standard by which to judge an industry's request for a price increase. The basic standards that emerged set two profit criteria. First, an industry was allowed to earn the same dollar amount of profits before taxes that it had earned on average in the period 1936–9. Second, the industry was entitled to recover out-of-pocket expenses on all major product lines. In practice, of course, numerous exceptions and special considerations were taken into account, but this is the basic idea. If the industry was above these minima, then it was supposed to absorb cost increases out of profits. A similar standard was developed for the distributive trade.[28]

Naturally, the standard was strongly criticized by industry. The debate was as inevitable as it was unresolvable. The OPA pointed out that the base years were the ones used for computing excess profit taxes; that it included two good years, one mediocre year, and one bad year by prewar standards; and that in order to have good records it was useful to have a fairly recent period.

The standard was, however, a tough one for businessmen to accept. The late thirties were depression years in which profits were lower than they typically had been before 1929. More important, prices had run up considerably since 1939. Profits equal in nominal terms to what they were in 1939 would be worth much less in real terms. A stockholder, in principle, could find the real value of his dividends much reduced by a strict application of OPA's standard. In practice, however, profits were generally high. Operating at full capacity produced economies of scale which increased profits in many industries, and the OPA standards had no impact on prices in war contracts where profits were generous.

In addition to adopting this standard, the OPA attempted to extend price control into the remote nooks and crannies of the economy. Its philosophy was well illustrated in a letter by deputy administrator Elliot Brownlee to the *New York Times* concerning the pricing of "luxury" goods. The *Times* had argued that luxury goods should be exempt from price control, partly because it would not hurt and partly because it would prepare the way for the removal of controls after the war.[29] Brownlee replied, and his arguments, although directed to the luxury issue, summarized the case for across-the-board controls. First, and most important, if luxuries were freed from price controls, resources would be reallocated from the production of necessities to luxuries. Second, the definition of a luxury, in many cases, would be arbitrary. Endless debates would revolve around particular commodities. Third, the exemption of certain commodities from control would create an impression of unfairness and so reduce business support for controls.[30]

One sensitive aspect of the transition to across-the-board controls involved the prices of newspapers, books, movies, and so forth. These prices were exempt under the Emergency Price Control Act, although newsprint was subject to allocation by the War Production Board. There was a legitimate concern that the freedom of the press would be endangered by placing this set of prices under regulation. The power to refuse a price increase might be the power of life or death over a newspaper or other publication. Even the authority simply to delay making a decision might be a source of considerable control over the media, and particularly over new and struggling enterprises that had not built up enough capital to outwait the agency. Price controls as a whole might not be a danger to political liberty, but in this area the probablility seemed too high to take the risk.

Reconversion

The period from VJ day to the termination of controls is of special interest because it was the only phase in which the "civilizing influence of common adversity," to borrow a useful phrase, was absent.[31] To be sure, these months were far from normal. The process of reconversion, a job of no small magnitude, was unique. Nevertheless, if we are to search the World War II episode for clues as to what would happen if controls were adopted in peacetime, then the period following VJ day must claim special attention.

Victory over Japan brought a significant change in wage policies. Roosevelt had received no-strike and no-lockout pledges, but these were for the duration of the war only. The first official recognition of the need for a new policy came on August 18, 1945, when President Truman issued an executive order significantly altering the hold-the-line policy. Direct wage controls were removed. But for a wage increase to be considered as the basis for a price increase it had to be approved first by the National War Labor Board or some other designated agency.[32] On October 30 a second order modified this standard. This order catalogued the variety of wage increases that the National War Labor Board could approve. It also liberalized the conditions under which wage increases could be used as a basis for raising prices. Approval of higher wages could be sought after they were agreed upon, and if the wage increases produced a violation of OPA profit standards, price relief was to be granted.

Labor troubles, however, soon doomed even this moderate policy: A wave of strikes spread through the economy. Among the more important were the walkouts by the United Auto Workers in November and the Steelworkers in January. Truman attempted to deal with them by appointing "fact finding" commissions. But the agreements proposed by the commissions were not acceptable to the industries involved. Negotiations continued. When word leaked out that a deal was about to be struck with government concurrence that involved a steel price increase which violated OPA's standards, Bowles wrote to the President urging him to take a stronger stand. Bowles wanted Truman to seize the steel industry, along with the meat industry which was also experiencing difficulties.[33] Seizure, although it seems a drastic measure now, was (as we will see below) frequently resorted to during this war as well as in World War I. Truman had used it a number of times after the surrender of the Japanese. Indeed, widespread seizures were made in the meat-packing industry on January 26.[34] But to solve the problems in steel Truman preferred to oppose OPA and establish a new price policy.

The new policy was announced in mid-February. Worked out in a conference attended by Bowles and John W. Snyder of the Office of War Management and Reconversion (among others), it provided for a liberalization both of the wage and price restraints. On the wage side, the National War Labor Board was to grant increases if (1) they were consistent with the pattern already established in the industry or area or (2) they were necessary to correct inequities or to raise substandard living conditions or to offset the change in the cost of living from January

1, 1941 to September 1945. On the price side, the policy defined several new criteria, most important of which was the right of an industry to earn a rate of return to net worth as high as in the base period. As part of this agreement Bowles replaced Snyder as head of the Office of War Mobilization and Reconversion, and Bowles was replaced at OPA by Paul Porter (who had been at OPA earlier and was currently at the FCC).[35] The new policy permitted the announcement of a new higher price for steel, which in turn permitted the settlement of the steel strike. With the announcement of this policy the hold-the-line phase came to an end.

The new policy also ended the remarkable stability that had characterized the official consumer price index. From VJ day until February of 1946, the consumer price index had increased at an annual rate of only 0.5 percent. But from February of 1946 until June of 1946, when the price control law expired, prices rose at an annual rate of 8.4 percent. As in the pre-hold-the-line period, controls failed to work in the simple sense of maintaining a low rate of inflation. Only a pervasive and rigid set of controls could hold inflation in check by this time.

During the reconversion period OPA faced two new problems. First, it had to decide what prices were to be set on goods produced by industries converting to civilian production. Here OPA provided a choice of two alternatives. A producer could use the ceiling that existed for the product when production stopped. Or, if this price was not relevant because of increased costs or because the product was substantially different (the normal case), the producer was entitled to use his 1941 costs, increased by certain standard ratios and a margin reflecting normal industry profit rates.[36] This policy was strongly assailed on the grounds that it inhibited reconversion. It was argued that these prices did not fully reflect current costs of production; this point was, for example, part of Senator Taft's criticism of OPA's pricing policy.[37] The OPA's response was that high costs were typically a transitory result of low volumes that industry could easily absorb.

The much larger issue facing OPA was how and when to terminate controls. The OPA's general philosophy was that controls should be continued as long as they were "necessary" to prevent inflation. Individual items should be decontrolled only when supply and demand were roughly in balance.[38] At a minimum, according to OPA, this would require extension of the Emergency Price Control Act for a year beyond its June 30 termination date.

Table 4.2. *Two Gallup Polls on price controls in 1946*

Commodity group	Percentage who want to		
	Keep price ceilings	Remove price ceilings	No opinion
	April 26–May 1, 1946		
Food	75	21	4
Clothing	70	26	4
Rent	78	17	5
Automobiles, radios, and other manufactured goods	66	27	7
	September 12–18, 1946		
Meats	42	53	5
Other foods	42	51	7
Clothing	49	44	7
Rents	67	27	6
Automobiles, radios, and other manufactured goods	45	46	9

Source: Gallup (1972B, pp. 579, 602).

The notion that OPA should be continued for a time beyond June 30, 1946 was widely shared by the general public. The testimony of the public opinion polls is unanimous on this point. A Gallup Poll taken in August 1945, just after the dropping of the atomic bombs, showed that 77 percent of the public favored keeping price and wage controls.[39] In October 67 percent favored keeping the regulations.[40] In January the proportion was 73 percent.[41] Other pollsters came up with similar results.[42] In April support for controls, as shown in Table 4.2, which is discussed below, ranged from 66 percent in the case of manufactured goods to 75 percent in the case of food in late April. From VJ day through June 1946 public support for controls was thus very strong.

Perhaps even more remarkable than the support among the general public for the extension of controls was the unanimity among professional economists. In April 1946, fifty-four economists addressed a letter to the *New York Times* urging the extension of control.[43] The economists' basic recommendation was the same as OPA's: Individual prices should be decontrolled only as supply and demand came into balance. The signers ranged the political spectrum among American economists. There were distinguished conservatives such as Henry Simons and

Frank Knight of the University of Chicago; liberals such as Paul Samuelson, later the first American Nobel Laureate in economics, and Alvin Hansen, the leading American interpreter of Keynes; and the Marxist, Paul Sweezy. The signers also included Arthur Burns, later an advisor to President Eisenhower and chairman of the Federal Reserve Board; and Simon Kuznets, the developer of national income accounting, and the second American Nobel Laureate.

On the surface the case for selective decontrol was so persuasive that almost no one noticed that in the circumstances it had little chance of success. The problem was the enormous gap that existed between aggregate demand and full employment supply at the OPA price level. The excess demand was due primarily to the increase in liquid assets, money and government bonds, that had accumulated in the hands of the public during the war. Any prices that were freed separately, before others, would simply face that much more demand on their own and would be bound to rise dramatically. Waiting for demand and supply to be in equilibrium before releasing controls meant, in effect, waiting forever. In principle, of course, various devices could have been used to dry up, or at least immobilize, the excess demand. The economists recommended various measures along this line: a moratorium on tax reductions; reduction of the government deficit; maintenance of consumer credit controls. But given the unwillingness of the Congress to pass adequate tax measures during the darkest days of the war, it would have been unreasonable to expect more vigorous action in peace. As drastic as it may seem, the real choices were the continuation of controls indefinitely or their removal en masse (although the latter policy might have been phased over a period of time to permit a more gradual adjustment to the higher price level).

Where the economists went wrong, and the public as well, was in their analysis of inflationary pressures. Those economists who looked at inflation from the cost side saw the inflationary problems as separate problems in separate markets: low volume during a start-up period; excess demand for consumer durables because civilian stocks had run down during the war; "bottlenecks"; and so forth. Solve these problems and the danger of inflation would disappear. Even those economists who viewed inflation primarily from the demand side tended to focus on the current flows of expenditure rather than the purchasing power stored in liquid assets. Bring savings and investment into line through appropriate tax policies, these economists reasoned, and the inflationary problem would be solved.

In the event, the actual process that was followed – the sudden removal of controls on June 30, 1946, an abortive attempt to reinstate them, and their final removal – was probably as realistic as the policy of item by item decontrol that almost everyone thought made the most sense.

The death throes of controls

Despite strong public support for controls, the legislation renewing the Emergency Price Control Act was passed with amendments that made it unsatisfactory to OPA. The legislation was introduced in the House early in 1946. When Bowles reviewed the amendments that had been tacked on, he termed the result a "joy ride to disaster."[44] Two of the most undesirable features from his point of view were the limitation of the extension to nine months, and the requirement that OPA set prices that covered costs plus a "reasonable" profit for producers, wholesalers, and retailers.

The latter feature was objectionable because it hit at the cost absorption principle. Now that wage control was gone, OPA felt it crucial that it be able to force firms to absorb wage increases. Without absorption, OPA would be forced to pass increases along to consumers. To be sure, the OPA profit standards in principle limited the ability of OPA to force firms to absorb wage increases. But, as noted above, OPA's standards were relatively strict, guaranteeing only the nominal profits earned in the latter years of the depression. Since profits in 1946 were, in general, much higher than those of the depression, OPA's standards permitted considerable absorption before they would call for price increases.

Part of the explanation, perhaps the most important part, for the barrage of weakening amendments was the change in the attitude of business toward controls. A poll of 17 leading industrialists (reported in August 1944) showed that although they found controls personally exasperating, they favored continuation, even strengthening, of controls, and continuation of controls after the war until inflationary dangers had passed.[45] But after VJ day the opinion of the foremost industrialists seems to have shifted against controls. Perhaps they at last preceived how rich postwar markets would be. The most vociferous group was

the National Manufacturers' Association, which ran a vigorous advertising campaign against OPA.[46]

In the Senate, Taft, the Republican leader, had regarded price controls
as a necessary evil during the war.[47] But now he was determined that
controls should be eliminated as soon as possible, and that in the meantime
business should not be made to bear an "unfair" share of the cost of
stabilizing prices. His thinking was included in Senate amendments
providing for an independent, three-person decontrol board which would
have the power to overrule OPA decisions that continued controls on
particular items, and in the pricing formula which would guarantee
producers their 1941 price plus subsequent cost increases. Other Senate
amendments decontrolled meat, poultry, and milk (although the decontrol board could recontrol these prices if necessary).

These and still other amendments which OPA considered weakening,
survived the House–Senate conference and were included in the bill
presented to President Truman. His Congressional leaders advised him
to sign it. But Bowles strongly recommended a veto, and on June 28
he resigned to counteract the argument (he said) that he was fighting
for OPA to maintain his personal power. It could have been worse for
Bowles. In the words of detective fiction, "Events took a more sensational
course."[48] This, in fact, was the course Truman chose to follow. The
legislation reached his desk at the "eleventh hour" and he vetoed it,
sending a strongly worded message critical of the legislation to the
House.

Truman prefaced his veto message by arguing that the bill represented
a choice between "inflation with a statute and inflation without one."[49]
He singled out the Taft amendment assuring producers their 1941 price
plus cost increases, and a similar amendment covering distributors
added by Senator Wherry. He went on to urge the Congress to pass
a more satisfactory measure, and to pass an extension of the old act in
the interim.

The veto was sustained, but efforts to pass an extension were thwarted.
After more than six years the United States suddenly returned to free
markets. The pent-up demand had a predictable effect on prices. From
June 15 to July 15 the consumer price index rose 5.4 percent. By December
15 it had risen 14 percent. As in earlier periods, however, the price index
probably misrepresents matters, this time overstating the inflation, because
the lifting of controls reduced black marketeering. The food price index
is the most important case in point. From mid-June to mid-July the

food index rose 12.9 percent fueled by meat prices which rose 29.6 percent.[50] But the meat price in June was largely a fictitious price. Most people found that meat was only available on the black market at prices above the ceiling. The prices that the Bureau of Labor Statistics was recording were simply the prices of meat when last available. The rise in the official meat price index was probably accompanied by a decline in the real price of meat.[51] Overall, however, my impression is that the prices did increase substantially, if not by the amount shown by the official index.

The Administration's hope that a strong dose of inflation would frighten the Congress into passing a tough bill was not realized. In the final law the Taft profit amendment was replaced by the so-called Barkley amendment, which was weaker but based on a similar formula. The base period was moved back one year to 1940, when prices and profits were somewhat lower; and the increase in costs was to be an industry average, making the law easier to administer. But numerous additional commodities were exempted from control.

Politically, the month was not a profitable one for the Administration. True, many people saw the issues from the Administration's point of view. In Boston an OPA tea party was held, and Taft apples sold for a dollar each.[52] Nevertheless, Senator Taft could argue correctly that the country was without controls because the President had vetoed the legislation, not because he had voted against it. In any case, when the new legislation was finally passed toward the end of July, President Truman decided to follow the advice of his Congressional leaders and sign the bill. He did so "reluctantly" on July 25, 1946.[53]

The Price Control Extension Act with its welter of exceptions for particular commodities is not easy to summarize.[54] The most unusual feature of the bill was the three-person price decontrol board appointed by the President, a feature that clearly reflected the suspicion that OPA intended to drag its feet on decontrol. The board was given three principal tasks. First, if an industry advisory committee petitioned the Price Administrator for decontrol of a particular commodity and that appeal was denied, the Board could reverse the decision. Second, before OPA could recontrol a free price that had risen substantially, it had to get the Board's permission. Third, livestock, milk, cottonseed, soybeans, and certain products made from these commodities were decontrolled automatically by the Act and could be recontrolled after August 20 only on the decision of the Board.

The Price Administrator was ordered to decontrol all nonagricultural prices that were not important to the cost of living by December 31, 1946. Other nonagricultural prices were to be decontrolled when supply and demand were in balance. But they could be recontrolled after a test period if prices increased "excessively." Agricultural prices were left to the Secretary of Agriculture, reflecting the farm bloc's opinion that the Secretary would decontrol prices more readily than would OPA. The profit standards for prices still under control were weakened, as noted above. The ceiling price on manufactured products had to cover the average price in 1940, plus the average increase in costs since 1940. The basic standard for wholesalers and retailers was the average current cost of acquisition, plus the average percentage markup in effect on March 31, 1946. These were the central provisions. But numerous commodities were treated separately in the legislation. The OPA was ordered to wind up its business by June 30, 1947. As it turned out, it finished sooner.

In retrospect, it was inevitable that the blank check OPA had been given during the war would be taken back and that the legislation would be riddled with amendments reflecting the influence of special interests. Even during the War, pressure-group politics had not come to a complete stop. The farm bloc had still been potent – the Bankhead–Brown amendment to the stabilization Extension Act of 1944 had forced OPA to set ceilings on textiles that assumed a parity price for raw cotton even when the market price was lower. This amendment, and an interpretation issued by the Senate Banking and Currency Committee in 1945, forced OPA to grant large price increases to which it was opposed.[55] But despite this example, prior to VJ Day a courageous congressman had an answer for a constituent seeking special favors: "We must all make sacrifices to help win the War; compare your sacrifices with those of our men in uniform." After the War it was politics as usual.

On July 27 Truman appointed three men to the price decontrol board: Roy L. Thomas, President of the Federal Land Bank; George H. Mead, head of Mead Corporation; and Daniel W. Bell, a Washington Banker.[56] Ironically, given the name of the Board, their most important decision was to recontrol meat prices. With this authority restored, OPA decided to roll back meat prices on September 9 to their June 30 level, a portentous move.

The result was another severe meat shortage. Bowles saw the shortage as a conspiracy. In a speech given on September 24 he argued that "every time it's to the benefit of the meat producers to have a meat shortage, somebody pulls a switch and presto, we have a meat shortage."[57] But clearly controls laid the groundwork for a successful withholding action. Farmers have often tried to organize strikes, but they have seldom been successful. The reason is that typically while it is in the interest of all farmers to withhold part of their product from the market, it is in the interest of each separately to sell as much as he can. Cheating undercuts the strike. In the fall of 1946, however, the situation was very different. Prices were controlled, but the betting had to be that in the not-too-distant future controls would be lifted and prices would be higher. Thus, it made sense not only from a collective point of view for producers to withhold meat, but also from the point of view of each producer separately.

The meat shortage, and the general dissolution of the hold-the-line philosophy, led to a rapid decline in public support for controls. The change could be observed by the end of the hiatus in controls. A Gallup Poll taken about the 24th of July asked people how they felt about price controls, giving them a set of representative statements to choose from. Forty-three percent said the former OPA was all right. Nine percent thought the new OPA law was an improvement. Twenty percent wanted to do away with all price control except rent control. Twenty-three percent wanted to do away with controls completely.[58] Clearly a majority still favored controls, but it was a much slimmer majority.

By mid-September support for controls had declined further. The extent of the change is illustrated in Table 4.2. In every category a sharp decline had taken place, and a majority clearly favored removing controls on food. This poll was released on October 5, 1946. Without assigning undue weight to the poll itself, we can assume that President Truman was cognizant of the change in public attitudes when on October 14 he announced that he was lifting controls on meat in order to end the shortage.[59] Other controls, he added, would have to be removed at an accelerated pace. Truman blamed the meat shortage on Congress, which had allowed control to lapse, encouraging excessive slaughter in July, and thus producing the subsequent shortage. He also blamed the producers. He had considered seizing the cattle, he said, but the prospect of sending Federal authorities onto thousands of widely scattered farms and ranches a year after VJ day was not acceptable.

Price controls from this point on were lifted rapidly. On November 9 Truman ordered the removal of all remaining controls except those over rents, sugar, and rice.[60] The reasons for doing so, in addition to the lack of public support, were the familiar problems of selective and temporary controls. Selective controls diverted resources from controlled to uncontrolled sectors, and temporary controls promoted speculative hoarding. The official end of the World War II price controls came at 12:01 A.M. Sunday, November 10, 1946.[61] Received enthusiastically, and for a time highly popular, controls had finally worn out their welcome.

The effect on prices

In a sense the democratic process wrote its own evaluation of controls: Selective controls were a failure; the hold-the-line policy was initially a success; but failed when, at the end of the war, the constraints on collective bargaining and rationing became too confining. The statistical record, on the whole, tends to confirm this judgment. Perhaps the simplest question is, Did controls "work" in the elementary sense that the rate of inflation was kept below some arbitrarily small figure, say 5 percent per year? The answer that emerges (Table 4.3) depends on the particular subperiod one examines. From April 1943, when President Roosevelt issued the Hold-the-Line Order, until June 1946, when controls temporarily expired, inflation was held to a measured rate of only 2.3 percent per year. The true rate was probably somewhat higher, but even with an allowance for errors in the published index – an estimate of inflation partially corrected for these errors is in parentheses – controls were a success in this elementary sense. On the other hand, under less than total control the rate of inflation was not effectively restrained. Of particular interest are the periods April 1942 to April 1943 and February 1946 to June 1946 which give the rate of inflation under the General Maximum Price Regulation and under President Truman's reconversion policy, respectively. In both cases the economy was under extensive price controls, but in neither case was the rate of inflation held down. The difference seems to be that during the high tide of price controls, they were backed up by a vigorous enforcement effort and three important supplementary measures – wage controls, the seizure of noncomplying industries, and rationing both of resources and of final products.

Strong conclusions cannot be defended on the basis of World War II alone. But, the relationship between the degree of control and the rate of inflation during the War suggests that if the goal is to reduce

Table 4.3. *The degree of control and the rate of inflation*
May 1940–March 1947

Period	Method of control	Rate of inflation[a]
May 1940–April 1943 (Starting-up)	Selective	7.3 (8.3–9.3)[b]
May 1940–April 1941	Exhortation	2.1
April 1941–April 1942	Selective	11.9
April 1942–April 1943	GMPR	7.5
April 1943–June 1946 (High tide of controls)	Across the board	2.3 (3.2–3.4)[c]
April 1943–February 1946	Hold the line	1.6
February 1946–June 1946	Adjustable	8.4
June 1946–March 1947 (Reconversion)	Selective	21.4 (11.2–15.6)
June 1946–July 1946	No controls	67.4[d]
July 1946–October 1946	Selective	21.0
October 1946–March 1947	No controls	12.3

[a] The annual percentage rate of change was calculated by subtracting the natural logarithm of the consumer price index at the first date from the natural logarithm at the second date and dividing by the number of intervening years.
[b] This is an estimated range which takes certain weaknesses in the published index into account. See Evasion and the Black Market, Findings of the Mitchell Committee, in Chapter 5, for the details of these adjustments. For this period, the adjustments actually apply to January 1941–December 1943; the Bureau's measured increase was 7.2 percent per year in this period.
[c] December 1943–June 1946; the Bureau's measured increase was 2.8 percent per year.
[d] The percentage increase during this one month was 5.4.
Source: Various issues of the *Monthly Labor Review*.

the rate of inflation to low levels by direct controls, while allowing aggregate demand to grow rapidly, then half measures will not work. Only a thorough regimentation of economic life will be successful.

The record during the first period in which regulations were limited to a broad array of strategic prices, April 1941 to April 1942, was also discouraging.[62] Consumer prices rose at an annual rate of 11.9 percent. As a purely arithmetic matter, this record was the product of rapid increases in uncontrolled prices with slower increases in prices subject to some form of controls. This is demonstrated in Table 4.4, which shows the rate of change of wholesale prices classified by the type of controls imposed. Formally controlled prices were those for which an official price had been issued by the OPA, while informally controlled prices were those over which some sort of agreement had been reached between the authorities and the industry. Formally controlled prices

Table 4.4. *Annual percentage rates of change of wholesale commodity prices by degree of control, August 1939 to April 1942*

Commodity group	August 1939– April 1942 (WWII-GMPR)	August 1939– April 1941 (WWII-OPACS)	April 1941– April 1942 (OPACS-GMPR)
All commodities	10.4	6.3	17.2
Formally controlled	9.2	6.4	13.8
Informally controlled	5.5	3.4	9.0
Uncontrolled	12.4	6.9	21.7

Notes: These calculations are based on constant composition indexes with control status defined as of April 28, 1942 (just before the General Maximum Price Regulation). The rate of change was calculated by subtracting the natural logarithm of the index at the initial date from the natural logarithm at the final date and dividing by the number of intervening years.
Source: U.S. Office of Price Administration, "Indexes of Wholesale and Retail Prices," Price Control Report No. 11, June 1, 1942, p. III – B1.

show greater increases than informally controlled prices because formal controls were imposed when informal controls, in the judgment of the authorities, had failed. Taking the whole period of selective controls, from one month before full-scale war in Europe (August 1939) to the month when across-the-board controls were first attempted (April 1942), formally controlled prices rose at an annual rate of 9.2 percent per year while uncontrollable prices rose at an annual rate of 12.4 percent. Thus, there is some evidence that selective controls had an impact. But the difference in the two rates of increase does not measure the impact of selective controls. Even at this early date, some black markets developed; the black markets in scrap metals at this time were "notorious," to use the adjective employed by the official historians of the period.[63] During the first half of 1942, the iron and scrap regulation (with the exception of waste paper) generated more complaints of overcharges than any other.[64] Since wholesale prices were collected from sellers, it is likely that the official index of controlled prices understates the true increase. I will return to this problem below. The judgment of the official historians, however, is that the errors were small at this time, a judgment I share.

A more important reason for thinking that the gap between the increase in uncontrolled prices and the increase in controlled prices overstates the effect of controls is the existence of spillover effects. If prices are being pulled up by demand, perhaps generated by anticipations of future shortages, then controlling prices in one sector simply means that there is more purchasing power to spend in the uncontrolled sector. Uncontrolled prices, according to this argument, rose *faster* than they would have if there had been no controls at all. A regression, similar to the one described for World War I, was run that related the percentage change in uncontrolled prices to the percentage change in money and the size of the controlled sector. It revealed substantial evidence of spillover effects.[65] This does not mean, of course, that selective controls produced no slowing in the rate of inflation; rather, it indicates that the gap between uncontrolled and controlled prices misstates the benefits of controls.

While the experience under selective controls was ambiguous, it is clear that once across-the-board controls were in place the rate of inflation was held to low levels, even if some allowance is made for evasion, black markets, and so on. But were the benefits of this policy temporary or permanent? Was the reduction of inflation achieved during the war bought at the cost of more rapid inflation after the War?

Milton Friedman has attempted to supply an answer within the traditional monetary framework that also underlies my analysis.[66] His argument is that the rate of inflation is determined by three principal variables: the amount of dollars added to the economy; the amount of new goods and services produced; and changes in the rate at which people spend money (the velocity of money). The old cliché that inflation is caused by "too much money chasing too few goods" captures the spirit of this view. If money is added to the economy faster than new goods and services can be produced (and if the rate at which people spend money does not slow down), inflation will result. In the long run, controls will have their principal effect on inflation, Friedman argues, through the velocity variable, since the stock of money is determined largely by the Federal Reserve and the banking system, and the volume of real goods and services by the fundamental productive forces of the economy.

Thus, in the postcontrol period the money created during the war will have its full impact on prices – in other words, there will be "catch-up" inflation – unless controls during the war could somehow reduce velocity after the war. But how could that happen? While in fact velocity was somewhat lower in 1945–7 than it had been before the war, Friedman argues that there are other explanations of this phenomenon (most prominently, the fear of renewed depression which led people to hoard money) that are more plausible than a residual effect of wartime price controls. His conclusion is that since there is no reason to expect temporary controls to permanently lower velocity, there is no reason to expect temporary controls to permanently lower the price level. All controls accomplished, according to Friedman, was to convert a steady rise in prices into a slower rise followed by a more rapid rise.

Friedman arrives at this position by concentrating his attention on a comparison of velocity before controls with velocity after controls. In doing so he misses two essential points. First, there was a temporary surge in velocity – or what comes to the same thing, a rise in prices relative to money per unit of real output – during the early years of the war. Suppressing the price level during this phase would not cause inflation after the war. Instead, controls would prevent a temporary rise in prices that would be followed after the war by a deflation. This is the equilibrating sequence described in Chapter 1.

That controls served this purpose, initially, is shown in Figure 4.1, which traces the price level (without an adjustment for black markets) and money per unit of real GNP from 1940 to 1948. Monetary velocity is the ratio of these two magnitudes. During the first part of the period, controls were pushing prices toward their long-run equilibrium path. Only later did controls have a disequilibrating effect. The break in the inflationary psychology seems to have come with the announcement of the General Maximum Price Regulation in April of 1942. Had a restrictive monetary policy been imposed simultaneously, some of the later difficulties could have been avoided. The "crossover," the point at which prices fell below their long-run determinants corresponds to the point in time at which evasion began to take on major proportions. Since controls had a disequilibrating effect only later in the war, the postwar catch-up inflation, while severe (measured prices rose at an annual rate of 21.4 percent from June 1946 to March 1947), appears small when allocated across the large number of years controls were in effect. There was, to make the point differently, only 2.6 percent of suppressed inflation per year from May 1940 to June 1946.[67]

A second reason why ignoring the behavior of velocity within the war leads Friedman to underestimate the impact of controls turns on an analysis of the determinants of the supply of money. Controls made it possible for the government to acquire the same volume of resources while creating a smaller volume of money. A specific example will make the process clear. Suppose a munitions manufacturer had trouble acquiring

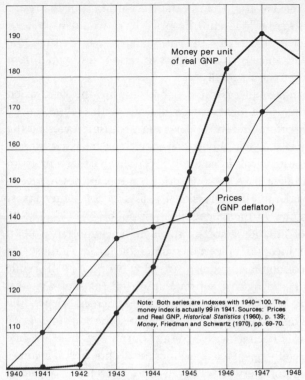

Figure 4.1. Prices and money per unit of real output, 1940–48.

all of the steel he needed. Under the system that evolved in World War II, the munitions maker could get an order forcing a manufacturer to sell him steel at the ceiling price. In the absence of such an order, the manufacturer would have had to bid the steel he needed away from competitors. This would have meant higher armament prices, and in raising the funds to pay for those arms the government, since it was unwilling to rely on higher taxes, would have been forced to expand the money supply.

The process, of course, was not so simple as in the Revolution when the government created the money to buy arms simply by printing it. During World War II the Treasury raised the funds it needed (in excess of tax revenues) by issuing bonds. But because the Federal Reserve was pledged to keep interest rates, and hence bond prices, constant, the Federal Reserve had to enter the market as a buyer of these bonds, pumping new money into the system. The institutional framework was more complex in World War II than in the Revolution, but the result was similar. Thus, in the long run the price level would have been higher in the absence of controls than it actually was, because the government (in the absence of a willingness to raise taxes) would have created more money than it actually did.

To sum up, controls reduced inflation both during the war, when they calmed the initial inflationary surge, and hence the self-defeating fears of runaway inflation, and in the long run because they eased the government's financial burden. These considerations are what explain the mildness of the postcontrols inflation. It is conceivable that a program of rigorous taxation might have substituted for controls in these respects, but there was considerable Congressional resistance to higher taxes, even when the outcome of the war was still in doubt.

This reduction of inflation, moreover, played an important role in protecting the real incomes of certain vulnerable groups, those for whom adjustments of nominal incomes came slowly or not at all. While real wages in manufacturing rose substantially from 1939 to 1943, real wages of workers in public education fell from 8 to 15 percent, depending on the assumptions one makes about the accuracy of the consumer price index.[68] Much of this decline was made up during the hold-the-line period. For the retired living on fixed incomes the decline in real incomes during the first years of the war was even more substantial. While to some extent these developments may have reflected changes in relative demands or supplies, it is hard to escape the conclusion that the most vulnerable groups needed some form of protection, and that controls were the only widely considered method for providing it. It is undoubtedly this measure of protection that explains public support for controls during the war.

The bureaucracy

The OPA was only one part of a large mosaic of agencies erected to control the wartime economy. This is important to keep in mind because it is sometimes assumed that OPA was the only agency controlling prices. By extension, some writers argue that prices could be controlled today by creating an agency similar in size and authority to OPA. It is more reasonable to suppose that to achieve a similar level of price control, under a similar regime of strong aggregate demand, it would be necessary to create a set of agencies that could re-create the theme of the entire mosaic. I will show below that the total bureaucracy was smaller than is usually imagined. But to confine one's attention solely to OPA is to carry a good argument too far.

Some of the complementary agencies were organized to deal with specific sectors of the economy; for example, the War Food Administration, and the Petroleum Administration for War. But the three I will discuss in detail, the War Production Board, the War Labor Board, and the War Manpower Commission, were created to deal with economy-wide problems which were consequences of price control.

The War Production Board (WPB), created in January 1942, was the last and most powerful in a line of agencies established to expedite the production of war goods.[69] Since the economy was rapidly approaching full employment by the time the WPB was formed, this meant transferring resources from the civilian sector to the war sector. A dramatic example of this process was the Board's order shutting down the production of private passenger cars so that the assembly lines in Detroit could be used for the production of tanks, planes, and other weapons of war. But the Board's job went beyond actions of this sort. It was also concerned with the everyday problems faced by producers in a controlled economy. By 1944 the WPB had worked out a fairly detailed system for rationing scarce materials among different types of war goods and between the war and civilian sectors.

The key to the system was the so-called Controlled Materials Plan, which provided for the allocation of the three critical war metals (carbon and alloy steel, copper and brass, and aluminum) among various "claimant agencies" (Navy, War Food Administration, and so on).[70] The primary purpose of the Controlled Materials Plan, of course, was to make sure that the production of munitions was not distorted by critical shortages.[71] Nevertheless, the rationing of strategic materials was an important supplement to consumer price controls because these materials also entered the production function for civilian goods.

Beyond its primary responsibility for assuring production of the required volume of war goods, the WPB was also responsible for assuring an efficient distribution of the civilian residual. This responsibility directly touches our main concern. Since the price system could not be used to allocate civilian goods, some form of rationing had to be substituted. The administration of rationing, as noted above, was delegated to OPA, but the WPB retained the authority to decide which goods should be rationed and when, and to delegate rationing to some other organization. This division of authority often brought the two agencies into conflict, typically because OPA thought a particular good should be rationed while the WPB was reluctant, and in some cases, because OPA thought that the WPB was telling OPA how to ration as well as what to ration.

Beyond formal consumer rationing the WPB, through its Office of Civilian Requirements (OCR), tried to channel resources into areas in which shortages were severe.[72] In the early days of the OCR, typically, it identified a shortage by the volume of complaints coming from users of a particular commodity. But later the OCR undertook formal surveys to learn civilian needs and to pinpoint areas in which shortages were severe. There were several things that the OCR could do to alleviate shortages, the simplest being to issue "priorities" to manufacturers of scarce items similar to the priorities relied on in World War I. These were an important help to manufacturers of essential civilian goods.

The first assignment of the OCR was to increase the volume of nonmachinery farm supplies, such as fencing, sprayers, hardware, and twine. Late in 1942 and early in 1943 numerous complaints were reaching the OCR about the shortage of these supplies. In a free market their price would have run up and drawn resources from other sectors of the economy. But with prices fixed, this automatic process was aborted. Instead, the government had to close the gap through direct allocation.[73] The action finally taken was simple. The Army, Navy, and Office of Lend Lease were forced to cut back their demands, and manufacturers of the critical supplies were required to ship a fixed percentage of their output to wholesalers serving the farm trade.[74] This example was not an isolated one. The OCR attempted to deal with dozens of similar shortages as they surfaced.[75]

Two programs which were tried only on an experimental basis are of some interest because they point to the sort of thing that would have to be tried on a larger scale if price controls were instituted on a permanent basis. These were the concentration and standardization programs. The basic idea of concentration was simple. If a large proportion of the total output in an industry consisted of war goods, then the consumer residual should be concentrated in a few plants. The alternative was to have each plant produce both war and consumer goods. One motivation, of course, was the potential for economies of scale in production. But there was another major advantage of concentration that was not overlooked; it would facilitate price control by reducing the number of plants that OPA had to police. The plan ran into considerable opposition from industry, however, because it tended to weaken the value of trademarks and long-established customer relationships. The firms in which production of civilian goods was concentrated would be at a distinct advantage in the competition for postwar markets. The problem of compensation for plants closed by concentration orders also proved difficult to resolve. By late fall of 1942 only five industries – stoves, bicycles, typewriters, farm machinery, and pulp and paper – were affected by concentration orders, and in early 1943 the entire plan was abandoned.[76]

Closely related to concentration was the principle of standardization and simplification. Here the idea was to limit the range of products that could be produced in a particular industry to a few simple and standard models for the duration of the war. Simplification and standardization could aid concentration by solving the trademark problem. No manufacturer would be able to gain on his competitors by imprinting his trademark on the public's mind during the war while his competitiors were producing war goods. But standardization and simplification had several additional justifications. First this program could be used to conserve resources by eliminating the use of materials that contributed only to the appearance of the finished product. More important, the program could contribute to price control. One of the most effective means of evading price controls, as we will see below, was to reduce the quality of finished goods. By forcing producers to make a smaller number of standard models the WPB could greatly ease the OPA's enforcement burden.

In fact the WPB did issue a number of standardization and simplification orders, although it did not go as far as OPA would have liked.[77] To take one example, Stanley Marcus of the Neiman-Marcus department store in Dallas was asked to develop the standardization order for women's dresses. He decided to preserve the styles prevailing in the late 1930s and early 1940s and make only minor simplifications, even though these styles used considerable material. He reasoned that if dramatic changes were made, the dresses already in hand would go out of fashion and even more material would be used in meeting the demand for new styles.[78] This reasoning, however, was not followed consistently. For instance, a briefer two-piece bathing suit was introduced to "save material."[79]

In short, although the main concern of the WPB was the maximization of war production, it had important obligations to the civilian sector which the Board made some efforts to fulfill. These were obligations inherent in the suppression of the price system, whether it was done during a war or not; if a similar suppression were undertaken in peacetime a similar agency would have to be created to undertake these tasks.

On the labor front there were two agencies crucial to the effort to control the price level: the War Labor Board (WLB), which controlled wages; and the War Manpower Commission, which controlled the allocation of labor. In general, the powers of both agencies were increased as the economy moved toward maximum central control in 1944 and 1945. Initially, the WLB only became involved in disputes that threatened the war effort. If management and labor came to terms the WLB could not intervene even if the agreement involved a large wage increase. Perhaps the most important decision of the WLB during its period of limited authority was in the "Little Steel Case." This dispute, which involved wages in the steel industry, was settled by a decision of the Board announced in July 1942. The Board granted a small increase to the workers on equity grounds, but more important, it gave them an additional increment of 15 percent to make up for the deterioration in the value of the dollar as measured by the consumer price index between January 1941 and May 1942. This decision turned out to be extremely important because it served as the model for wage adjustments when the powers of the WLB were expanded. It also focused attention on the Bureau of Labor Statistics' consumer price index – it was then called a cost-of-living index – an issue I will return to below.

Greater power was given to the WLB in an executive order associated with the Price Control Act of October 1942. But under the system prevailing in early 1943, wage increases could be allowed for a variety of reasons, in particular if they contributed to "the effective prosecution of the war." This was a substantial loophole. It meant that the rapidly expanding war industries could get their increases approved. Roosevelt's Hold-the-Line Order, issued partially in response to the wage situation, considerably reduced the degrees of freedom available to the WLB.

This order was modified, and the basic policy for the duration was outlined, in a directive issued by the Office of Economic Stabilization, the agency that supervised the whole stabilization program in May 1943. Four criteria were established for wage increases. First, any wage could be increased by 15 percent over its level in January 1941, the "Little Steel" formula. Second, wages could be increased to 40 cents per hour without formal approval, and to 50 cents with the approval of the Regional War Labor Board. This was consistent with Roosevelt's desire to see increases in substandard wages. Third, ranges of wages (brackets) were established for each job. Wage increases to the lower end of the bracket (the lowest "sound and tested" rate) were permitted. Finally, increases to eliminate intraplant differences were allowed. Salaries of persons earning over 5,000 dollars, and of non-unionized persons earning less, were placed under the control of the Internal Revenue Service and were subject to a similar set of criteria.

The most vexing problem encountered in administering wage and salary limits arose from promotions. A genuine promotion, one which carried with it greater responsibility or more onerous duties, naturally warranted a higher wage. But an employer who wished to circumvent the wage controls could give an employee a phony promotion, one in which the title was different and the wage was higher, while the real duties remained unchanged. Detection was particularly difficult if the employee moved from one firm to another. This phenomenon may account, in some measure, for the high rate of labor turnover that prevailed after the economy was fully mobilized.

The ultimate threat used to enforce wage controls was the seizure of the firm or industry in which noncompliance was taking place. Two cases of seizure gained widespread notoriety. In one the government seized Montgomery Ward & Co., and met with dramatic resistance from its President, Sewell Avery, who had to be carried bodily from his office. The most important case, however, was the seizure of the coal mines, an encounter which featured Roosevelt's running battle with John L. Lewis, the leader of the miners. But these were not the only cases. In all, sixty-three Presidential seizures took place between 1941 and 1946.[80] The rate of seizure was not uniform. It rose, as Figure 4.2 shows, from 0.33 seizures per month in 1941 and 1942 to a peak of 2.0 seizures per month in 1945. In part the increase in the rate of seizure was the result of the growth in the amount of suppressed inflation. In

Seizures per month

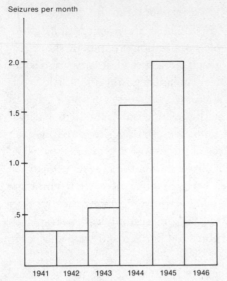

Figure 4.2. Presidential seizures during World War II. (Source: Blackman, 1967B, Appendix A, pp. 259–78.)

part, it could also be attributed to the passage of the War Labor Disputes Act (Smith–Connally) in 1943, which strengthened the legal basis for seizure; it was no longer necessary to carry out seizures under the President's war powers.[81]

Seizures were an important part of the stabilization program and not simply efforts to keep production going. To be sure, the war added special urgency to the need to settle disputes promptly. But in many cases the disputes could have been settled if the government had been willing to grant sufficient wage and price increases. Seizure, in these cases, was an alternative to inflation. This can be seen by contrasting the wartime policy of holding the line combined with seizure with two cases from the reconversion period when Truman decided against seizure: the steel strike and the meat shortages. In the steel strike the government granted a price increase that could be rationalized only by giving up the hold-the-line policy. In the latter case, Truman abandoned price controls altogether. The frequent resort to seizure in World War II is, perhaps, the clearest illustration that stable prices can be maintained in the face of excess demand only by adopting measures that would be unacceptable in peacetime.

Control over the allocation of labor was vested in the War Manpower Commission (WMC) and the Selective Service System.[82] Thus, the separation of powers in the labor area resembled the separation in commodities between OPA, on the one hand, and WPB and the other supply agencies on the other. In both cases the separation was somewhat artificial. It is impossible to set a price without at the same time setting the quantity, yet the wartime separation of powers between "price" agencies and "quantity" agencies assumed that this could be done. Conflicts between the agencies and failures to coordinate policies were inevitable. Some overall coordination was provided by the Office of Economic Stabilization, but clearly a permanent price control agency would have to be given authority over both price and quantity at a fundamental level.

In the labor field, attempts at rationing remained rudimentary because of strong opposition to compulsion from both labor and management. In the circumstance no great damage was done because a considerable amount of unemployed labor existed at the start of mobilization, and because munitions makers had considerably leeway inside and outside the stabilization rules for raising wages. In general, labor shortages did not hamper mobilization.

There are two exceptions, however, worth notice. The Selective Service System was obviously of considerable importance in the allocation of labor between the military services and the private sector. The demands of the military, of course, had top priority. But the decisions on how to allocate occupational deferments and whether to draft fathers before or after men with claims to occupational deferments had considerable impact on the economy.

It also appears that labor shortages became acute on the West Coast at the height of the mobilization. The WMC, in response to the West Coast situation, developed a system of labor allocation analogous to the WPB's Controlled Materials Plan. This attempt at labor allocation was also used, in a limited way, in other areas. It consisted of two major parts. Manpower priorities were developed for the industries in a particular area. The U.S. Employment Service, or other designated agencies, then referred workers to firms in the order of these priorities. In addition, manpower ceilings were applied to nonessential industries in order to make more labor available. Very little of this program was actually carried out, because of opposition from a variety of sources. But, according to one account, the first part of the program may have served a useful purpose by acquainting workers with openings in high priority plants.[83]

The WMC also attempted to deal on an ad hoc basis with particular shortages. For example, it appeared at one point that a serious shortage was developing in nonferrous mining. A free market would have solved this problem through increases in the price of nonferrous minerals and in the wages paid to workers in nonferrous mines. With this process suppressed, some alternative was required. In the event, the WMC used a relatively mild method for attacking the problem, paying the transportation costs for workers and their families who moved into these areas.[84]

But granted that agencies such as the OPA, the WPB, and the WMC were the product of the suppression of the price system, how large was the total bureaucracy? Table 4.5 provides a surprising answer. The total bureaucracy appears to have been rather small, smaller for example than that large, but hardly threatening, agency, the Post Office. It is true that the figures understate, to a small extent, the total size of the bureaucracy. For one thing, old-line government agencies devoted some of their personnel to the administration of price controls, and this is not shown in the table. The Justice Department handled much of the work involved in the criminal prosecution of price law violators; the Internal Revenue Service handled the administration of salary controls. Numerous other examples at the federal, state, and local levels could be given. But it seems unlikely that counting these workers would swell the total dramatically.

A more important reason for thinking that the table understates the labor power devoted to administering controls is that it ignores the corresponding bureaucracy that grew up in the business sector. For each bureaucrat writing orders in Washington there were, ideally, at least a few in the business sector reading them. The National Industrial Conference Board claimed, on the basis of a survey, that most large concerns were devoting (early in 1943) more than 1,000 labor-days, and that many were devoting more than 5,000 labor-days, to filling out forms required by OPA and other civilian war agencies.[85] These estimates, however, need to be taken with a grain of salt because of the tendency to overstate the burdens one is subjected to, and because the survey was taken early in the period of stringent control and so involved doing things for the first time. Nevertheless, it is of some interest to see what these estimates imply for the resources devoted to administering controls

Table 4.5. *Employees of the OPA and related agencies, 1942–6*

	1942	1943	1944	1945	1946
OPA	16,539	57,101	59,783	64,517	34,368
Volunteers in OPA[a] (full-time equivalents)	1,676	5,783	6,058	6,538	3,483
Related agencies[b]	31,406	94,702	85,604	81,496	46,698
Total war agencies	49,621	157,589	151,445	151,551	84,549
Post Office	319,762	316,357	352,773	378,849	488,623
Total war agencies as a percentage of Postal Service employment	15.5%	49.8%	42.9%	40.3%	17.3%

[a] In the month preceding July 23, 1945, 107,806 OPA volunteers worked an estimated 1,067,812 hours. See Putnam (1946), p. 166. Allowing 163.33 hours per full-time worker per month, yields 6,538 full-time equivalents. This was assumed to be the average for 1945, and the ratio of full-time equivalent volunteers in 1945 to full-time workers was then applied to full-time workers in other years to obtain estimates of full-time equivalent volunteers. See the text for more details.

[b] Includes the War Production Board, War Labor Board, Petroleum Administrator for War and several smaller agencies. Excludes the War Food Administration. It is not clear whether the dollar-a-year and without-compensation employees are included. The War Production Board, the major user of this group, had 63-dollar-a-year and without-compensation employees in 1940, 728 in 1941, 998 in 1942, 870 in 1943, 680 in 1944, and 454 in 1945.

Sources: U.S. Bureau of the Census, *Statistical Abstract of the United States, 1944–1945,* p. 179; 1947, p. 207 and U.S. Civilian Production Administration, *Dollar-A-Year and Without Compensation Policies, of the War Production Board and Predecessor Agencies, August 1939 to November 1945,* April 1947, pp. 104–5.

by the private sector. If we split the difference between the two estimates, and figure 245 labor-days per employee per year, we get a figure of about twelve employees per large firm. If this state of affairs existed in the 3,000 largest firms, it would imply only about 36,000 employees being used to fill out forms. Multiplying this number by an estimate of the ratio of the total civilian labor force to the labor force of these large firms yields a rough estimate of the total business bureaucracy of 161,000, a number roughly comparable to employment on the government side.[86] Perhaps other employees in these firms were doing control-generated work. But it is also true that while controls created the need for additional personnel to read and fill out forms, they also reduced the duties of other employees. For example, the need to devote personnel to keeping track of prices being charged by competitors was reduced by the imposition of controls. So the argument that controls created an enormous, new private sector bureaucracy is not compelling.

To return to the figures in Table 4.5 it is also conceivable that there are some upward biases in the figures, but these would have been rather small. The OPA, for example, started a program late in the war for finding postwar exmployment for its workers. The resources devoted to this activity were clearly not part of the price control effort. It could also be argued that the WPB was concerned primarily with allocating resources among munitions makers and therefore that only a part of its resources were devoted to price control. But as I tried to show above, this argument loses force on closer examination. The effective channeling of resources among these producers was crucial to the stabilization of costs to civilian firms. Had the munitions makers been producing civilian goods, the relevant situation from our perspective, moreover, even more labor would have to have been devoted to this phase of rationing because the relatively clear priorities established by the military would be absent.

The second row of the table presents an estimate of the number of volunteers in full-time equivalents. This estimate is based on data for only one month in the summer of 1945. But, from our perspective, this particular month is of special relevance. To use the actual number from the early months of the war, when, for example, thousands of school teachers were used to help issue ration books, or from the end of the war when the system was disintegrating, would not really tell us that much more about the efficiency of the system during its mature phase. The data, in effect, capture the system at its peak.[87] Contrary to what many believe, these figures indicate that the volunteers supplied only a marginal amount of labor power to the control effort.

One naturally wonders whether in peacetime the government could again recruit a core of volunteers much as does, say, the Red Cross. I think not. The wartime experience is itself not very encouraging. Once the war was over large numbers of volunteers began to resign. The problem was that much of the work involved unpleasant confrontations. This was sometimes true of the ration board, the more popular activity among volunteers, and nearly always true for the price panel volunteers, the "snoopers," as they were labeled by critics. It is not the kind of work that many people would volunteer for in peacetime.

The bottom two lines in the table provide the comparison between the civilian war agencies and the postal service. This is a good way of getting a feel for the size of the agencies because the postal service is one of the government agencies with which most people have contact on a week-in and week-out basis. As the table shows, when the civilian war agencies settled down in 1944 and 1945, they were employing a labor force about 40 percent as large as that of the postal service. While this was a large bureaucracy, compared with most federal agencies, few people would be prepared to argue that the equivalent of a 40-percent expansion of the Post Office over a period of several years was an inordinate price to pay for a substantial measure of price stability. The total labor force of the bureaucracy controlling prices in 1943, the peak year, amounted to only 0.3 percent of the total civilian labor force. Even if one allowed for the 161,000 business counterparts mentioned above, the total bureaucracy, government and business, would have been only about 0.6 percent of the total civilian labor force.[88]

When this analysis is carried out in terms of the expenditures of the controlling agencies rather than their personnel, the price control bureaucracy appears even smaller. It amounted at the peak to, perhaps, .4 percent of GNP, including an allowance for business expenses. The reason is that the OPA and related agencies were labor intensive; they used a larger share of labor resources than of total resources.[89] One can thus condemn price control for a variety of reasons but not for the great size of the organization needed to implement the policy.

To summarize the entire argument so far, controls succeeded, for at least part of the war, in their main task of holding the rate of inflation to a low level. Controls did not simply postpone inflation, although there was a sharp surge in prices when they were removed. Prices would have been still higher in the long run had controls never been imposed. This result was achieved, moreover, without the necessity of building up a huge bureaucracy that used a substantial share of the nation's resources. But before jumping to a favorable conclusion about World War II price control, we must examine the indirect costs of controls. How burdensome was consumer rationing? Did controls damage the productive efficiency of the economy? Finally, and perhaps most important given the usual discussions of the issue, how extensive was evasion? We must delay a final assessment of World War II controls until these issues have been dealt with in the following chapter.

5. World War II: The market under controls

Consumer rationing

Rationing of consumer goods was more extensive in World War II than in any previous or subsequent experiment with wage and price controls. At its peak rationing covered slightly more than 20 percent of the consumer price index at prewar prices. Table 5.1, which gives a complete list of the rationed items and the duration of the programs, conveys something of the significance and ubiquity of rationing in World War II. The OPA clearly had a major job on its hands with items as diverse as sugar and shoes to ration.

Two major questions concern us here. First, was rationing required by the stabilization of prices in the face of excess demand or was it a by-product of other war-related changes in the economy? If it was required by the stabilization program, then we are likely to need rationing in a similar peacetime program. Second, what were the nature and origins of the difficulties encountered? If there were a substantial number of tough problems to be solved in the course of producing an equitable program, and if these difficulties were inherent in consumer rationing, then the need to ration must be counted as one of the major drawbacks of controls when used to suppress an inflation generated by an expansionary monetary policy.

The simplest motive for rationing was what might have been called the siege motive. This motive is easy to understand if you will imagine a besieged city cut off from all supplies. Only a limited supply of bread is available; once it is used up, people will starve. The authorities would not want to rely on the price system to allocate the available bread. In part the market would be rejected because doing so would be grossly unfair: The rich would get all the bread and the poor would starve. In part the market would be rejected because people might be shortsighted and consume too much in the short run rather than reduce their consumption and stretch their supplies over a long period. The most likely

Table 5.1. *Effective dates of rationing programs administered by the Office of Price Administration*

Program	Effective dates
Food	
Sugar	May 1942 to June 1947
Coffee	November 1942 to July 1943
Processed foods	March 1943 to August 1945
Meats, fats, canned fish, cheese, and canned milk	March 1943 to November 1945
Footwear	
Rubber footwear[a]	October 1942 to September 1945
Shoes	February 1943 to October 1945
Fuels and stoves	
Fuel oil and kerosene	October 1942 to August 1945
Stoves	December 1942 to August 1945
Solid fuels[b]	September 1943 to August 1945
Transportation	
Tires	January 1942 to December 1945
Automobiles	February 1942 to October 1945
Gasoline[c]	May 1942 to August 1945
Bicycles	July 1942 to September 1944
Typewriters	March 1942 to April 1944

[a] Six heavy-duty types.   [b] Pacific Northwest only.
[c] Initially confined to the Eastern Seaboard.
Source: Redford (1947G, p. 2).

outcome would be that the authorities would requisition the existing stock of bread and dole it out in small equal shares.

The siege motive explains the initial rationing programs. Tires were first. Japanese expansion in the Pacific cut off our supplies of natural rubber. Until synthetic rubber plants could come on line, the supply of new tires was limited. If prices were allowed to allocate the tires available on dealers' shelves or produced from crude rubber stock on hand, the resulting distribution of tires would be unfair and the dealers and manufacturers would make "unconscionable" short-term profits. Rationing tires was the obvious solution, and a nationwide network of tire rationing boards was set up just after Pearl Harbor.

Before the full network was set up, a ban on the sale of tires was issued. According to a story told by Donald Nelson, John Kenneth

Galbraith and others at OPA perceived the danger to the tire stock as greater than did the corresponding officials at the Office of Production Management (OPM). The latter office was planning to issue an order limiting the sale of tires to four per customer. Galbraith managed to have the order spirited from OPM's office. The phrase permitting sale of four tires was crossed out, so that the order, when issued, had the effect of banning all tire sales.[1]

The main part of the stock of tires consisted of those on automobiles and the problem was how to get people to conserve them. Each driver obviously had an incentive to conserve, but the government did not want to gamble on the farsightedness of the public. Several schemes were considered, but the one which seemed feasible administratively involved rationing gasoline. By limiting consumption of gasoline, the government could curtail driving and conserve the stock of automobile tires. Thus, both gasoline rationing and tire rationing were introduced because of siege conditions. In the Northeast, where Nazi submarine activity limited the amount of oil that tankers could bring in, the use of gasoline had to be curtailed more sharply than in the rest of the country.[2]

The siege motive also explains the rationing of consumer durables. Producers of durables switched to munitions during the war. Consequently, many durables – stoves, automobiles, bicycles, and typewriters – had to be rationed. In 1943 the automobile industry sold a grand total of 139 cars, all out of inventories.[3] In a sense the disappearance of a commodity from the market was the fairest form of rationing. Each consumer got an exactly equal share: nothing.

Frequently there was a second motive for rationing (although this objective was usually minimized in communications with the public) – to aid the enforcement of price controls. By assuring each consumer a small share of the commodity, rationing inhibited the scramble for supplies that produces black markets or other forms of evasion. As with the siege motive, the fundamental problem was that a gap existed between the market clearing price and the price that people considered "fair." The difference between the two types of rationing was in the history and potential cure for the gap. In the siege model the gap exists because outside supplies have been cut off; the problem will be cured when the siege is broken and supplies return to normal. When rationing is an aid to price control, however, the gap may exist simply because

Table 5.2. *Relative supplies of foods during rationing*

| Foods | Civilian consumption during rationing relative to 1936–9 (percentage) | |
	Average to average[a]	Minimum to minimum[b]
Total nutrients (selected)		
Calories	101.5	101.5
Protein	110.7	111.1
Calcium	112.3	110.6
Vitamin A	112.3	112.5
Thiamine (B1)	141.3	143.4
Ascorbic acid (C)	108.3	104.3
Rationed foods		
Sugar	83.7	77.6
Coffee	91.5	97.0
Canned fruit	76.1	68.9
Canned vegetables	125.4	124.2
Meat	115.2	115.1
Edible fats	88.8	86.3
Canned fish	73.4	79.1
Cheese	96.8	90.7
Canned milk	103.3	98.7

[a] Average civilian consumption per capita during the years when rationing was in effect divided by the average for 1936 through 1939. If consumption was rationed for only part of a year, then consumption for that year was weighted by the proportion of the year rationing was in effect.

[b] The smallest annual consumption during any year rationing was in effect was divided by the smallest annual consumption of the years 1936 through 1939.

Sources: All items except canned fish: *Historical Statistics* (1960G, pp. 185–7). Canned fish: *Historical Statistics* (1960G, pp. 7, 327).

aggregate demand has increased while prices are held down. In this case there is no plausible hope that an increase in supply will close the gap.

During World War II the rationing of food was undertaken primarily to aid the enforcement of price controls. Table 5.2 shows that food supplies were generally well above the levels reached in the years 1936 to 1939. In every category of basic nutrients listed in Table 5.2, more was available to the civilian sector during the rationing period than in the base period, including the basic categories of calories and protein. The figures, moreover, understate the true amounts of nutrients available because certain foods were undercounted, particularly black-market beef. Even among the specific foods where rationing programs were introduced, supplies were frequently close to or above prewar levels. This was true in coffee, canned vegetables, meat, cheese, and canned milk. In these cases it is clear that rationing was the result of rapid growth in aggregate demand combined with price controls. It was not produced by a cutoff of supplies.[4]

For a few foods, notably sugar, supplies were reduced because of war-related activities. And since supplies of tin were limited (because of a shortage of shipping space to carry ore from Bolivia), the rationing of canned goods served to conserve this material. But the important conclusion to reiterate is that in many cases the rationing of food was a by-product of combining price controls with monetary expansion rather than being the by-product of a cutoff of supplies.

It is sometimes argued that rationing was introduced for efficiency reasons. One version of the argument holds that had workers not been able to get a fair share of meat or other critical supplies they would have refused to cooperate in the war effort. Since this assertion rests on assumptions about political behavior, it is difficult to test its validity. A more tractable argument runs as follows: Had the government tried to hold prices down by taxing away excess purchasing power, production would have been discouraged.[5] This argument, however, is incorrect, at least as an unqualified statement. It has been shown that there is no general presumption that taxation will reduce incentives in comparison with rationing.[6] The usual reason for introducing rationing, moreover, – to assure each consumer a fair share – conflicts with incentives for productivity. Think of it this way: no one can consume more of the rationed commodities by working harder. Even under a very heavy system of taxation, harder work will yield some benefits in terms of consumption of any particular commodity.

There were two basic techniques used to ration commodities at the consumer level during World War II. The simplest was the unit system. Under this program, which was used for most products other than processed foods and meats and fats, the consumer was given a ticket permitting him to buy a specified physical quantity of the rationed good. In addition, the consumer had to pay the fixed monetary price.

The share of each consumer might be equal, or as in the case of gasoline, a relatively complex system might be used to tailor the consumer's ration to his "needs."

A more sophisticated method, the so-called point system, was used to ration processed foods (the blue point system), and meats and fats (the red point system). Under point rationing the consumer was given a certain number of points that could be used to purchase a specified range of rationed commodities which sold at varying point prices. Again, the consumer had to pay money for the goods, as usual. The advantage of the point system was that it could assure the consumer a fair share of some basic commodity, say, animal fat, while allowing some freedom of choice in the form in which he took it. The system also gave the rationing authorities some flexibility: They could alter point prices to correct imbalances between supply and demand of particular commodities.

The rationing programs were in many ways analogous to monetary systems. Indeed, the various kinds of ration tickets were frequently referred to as ration currency. Many of the problems that afflict monetary systems thus arose in the rationing programs. Perhaps the most ancient problem in monetary history was counterfeiting, and the ration programs were hard hit by it. This was especially true in gasoline where counterfeiting reached epidemic proportions soon after the program was set up. In part, counterfeiting of ration currency was so severe because the OPA was not prepared for it. But the agency could not have been expected to issue currency as difficult to counterfeit, and to hunt down counterfeiters with the same ability, as more experienced agencies. Even when well policed, the rationing programs, by multiplying the number of currencies used in everyday life, made it more difficult for merchants to spot counterfeits. In this respect the situation was reminiscent of the period before the Civil War during which counterfeiting was aggravated because numerous banks were issuing different forms of currency.

A more fundamental problem also afflicted the rationing programs: the tendency of the government to overissue its currency. If the monetary authority engages in this activity in the absence of price controls, it produces commodity price inflation. If the rationing authority overissues its currency, it leads to point inflation, or bare shelves. Overissue became critical in late 1944. In order to make the ration currency operate more efficiently the OPA had issued tokens that could be used as change, and that could be stored and used to make purchases at a later date.

As it turned out, by late 1944 surveys showed that consumers had built up a large stock of ration tokens, and the OPA feared that a change in consumer expectations might lead to a run on the stores and empty shelves; to bankruptcy, if you will, of the rationing programs. How had this problem been allowed to develop? One cause may have been excessively rosy estimates of future supplies made by other agencies, an explanation favored by the OPA. Another factor may have been the ration currency issued by the military services, over which OPA had little control. But unpredicted changes in the demand for the currency may have played their role as well. In this respect, the price controllers were on a similar footing with a monetary authority. Changes in "velocity" had undermined policy.

In any event, the OPA was faced with a dilemma. If consumers were allowed to use their stored ration currency, they might completely buy out existing supplies. The basic purpose of rationing, a fair sharing of existing supplies, would not have been realized. On the other hand, if the OPA cancelled the ration tokens, it would explicitly break a promise to consumers. It was, according to Chester Bowles, the toughest decision he had to make as head of the OPA.[7] The decision was to invalidate the ration currency overhanging the market, an action similar to the monetary reforms that many countries suffering from severe inflation have undertaken.[8] On December 24, 1944 processed food and meat stamps issued before December 1, 1944 along with certain sugar stamps were invalidated. We cannot know for sure that this overissue of ration currency was the symptom of a chronic problem. This case, however, was not unique. Other programs, such as the one for gasoline, suffered from over issue at times during the war.

In short, whether undertaken because of a sharp decrease in supply (as in tires) or because of the sharp increase in demand (as in foods), rationing facilitated price control. It is noteworthy that the period of effective control over prices corresponds closely to the period in which the rationing programs were in effect. The siege programs were generally introduced soon after Pearl Harbor. But the major food programs were introduced in March 1943, a month before the Hold-the-Line Order. These programs, along with most of the others, were phased out in the summer and fall of 1945, just before the big cracks in the price line began to form. It cannot be proved with this one example that prices cannot be held in the face of excess demand without the aid of a comprehensive rationing program. But there is no counterexample in

American history. If rationing is required by controls of this sort, and if ration currencies are inherently hard to manage, as the World War II experience suggests, then the case for confining controls to periods in which the growth of aggregate demand is being decelerated is that much stronger.

Efficiency

Rationing, as we have seen, mitigated the worst effects of controls by preventing a scramble for supplies and the inequities that this would produce. In markets where formal rationing was not used, or where the program was limited by political considerations, the deleterious effect of holding prices below equilibrium levels can be seen more clearly. One example was in the market for fluid milk. Nationwide, per capita civilian consumption of fluid milk and ice cream was about 6.9 percent higher during 1942 and 11.6 percent higher in 1943 than during the period 1936 to 1939.[9] But demand had increased even more rapidly, and those milksheds that contained war centers experienced a greater increase in demand than was true nationwide. Normally, the price of milk in areas experiencing a rapid increase in demand would tend to rise and draw milk from adjoining sheds. In the long run a rising price would stimulate additional production. But with prices fixed, this process was aborted. Numerous shortages of milk developed. In 1942, "critical shortages" were reported in Mobile, Pascagoula, New Orleans, Jacksonville, Miami, Altanta, and Norfolk News in the South; and in Los Angeles, San Francisco, San Diego, Portland, Seattle, and Spokane in the West. In 1943 shortages spread to most of the major cities.[10]

In the absence of the market governments were called upon to solve the problem, but no effective means of rationing was instituted. Local governments, in some cases, relaxed health standards to permit the sale of milk that would not ordinarily have been sold in a particular area. The War Food Administration issued an order prohibiting the sale of heavy cream to increase the supply of whole milk. And the OPA granted what were in effect price increases for milk by permitting reductions in butterfat content without requiring price reductions. The OPA also made extensive plans for rationing fluid milk in areas experiencing shortages, the only measure likely to be effective in the long run. But these plans were prevented from reaching fruition by opposition from producers in the affected regions.

Misallocation also plagued the market for gasoline. In much of the country supplies were adequate for normal driving needs and gasoline rationing was a device for conserving automobile tires. But in the Northeast, as already noted, German submarine warfare prevented tankers from maintaining normal supplies and military requirements were heavy. In the absence of controls gasoline prices would have risen relatively higher in this part of the country and refineries would have had the means by which to draw supplies (by railroad tank car in the period before the pipelines were completed) from other parts of the country. With prices fixed this automatic process was prevented from working. The appropriate response was obvious: mimic the market by using government orders to move oil by tank car from the Midwest to Eastern refineries, and officials at the OPA favored this policy. But opposition from the ocean tanker firms, which were afraid of losing their postwar markets, apparently prevented this course of action from being taken. Instead, the OPA was forced to reduce civilian allocations in the Northeast and at one point to introduce bans on pleasure driving, although the latter proved to be short-lived.[11]

A third example of the mischief produced by fixing prices, and then failing to ration, is from the clothing sector. There were shortages of all forms of clothing in the sense that consumers could not purchase all they wanted at OPA ceilings. But there were also misallocations among regions (the West fared worse than other regions), between urban and rural areas (rural areas fared worse), and among different sorts of garments. Wide sheeting, for example, appeared to be in greatest demand; it was out of stock an average of 28 days in March 1945. On the other hand, men's pajamas, while still considered one of the items in which a serious shortage existed, was out of stock only 13 days on average.[12] The market solution was suppressed. The OPA, as we will see below, proposed many and implemented several measures to alleviate the worst of these shortages, but strict rationing was successfully resisted by the industry.[13]

In each of these examples price increases were suppressed, but no effective alternative allocative mechanism was substituted. The reason, uniformly, was political. The industry affected, or some part of it, was successfully able to resist controls by pressuring legislators or administrators. This sort of resistance is likely to be a part of any program of controls. A short-term program, supported by a broad consensus, is most likely to avoid extensive damage from this quarter.

While other examples of inefficiency induced by controls could be given – many will be touched on from a different viewpoint in the next section – there are two reasons for thinking that they may not have been important in the aggregate during the period when strict controls were in effect. First, prices become inefficient only with the passage of time. For some months after prices are frozen, resources continue to flow in channels where they can be effectively used. As Professor Galbraith has argued, "If the pre-control allocation was satisfactory, it will remain satisfactory at least for some period."[14] Second, evasion and black markets tend to limit the inefficiency produced by controls. If producers can conceal a price increase, say, by reducing the quality of their product, then the hidden price increase will tend to limit shortages just as would an increase that showed on the price tag. The only difference is that the hidden increase raises the cost to sellers of changing their price and the cost to buyers of searching the market for the best price. With either type of increase demand will be reduced and profits will be increased, drawing additional resources into the production of the commodity in short supply.

There is also important quantitative evidence that shows that controls did not severely damage the allocative mechanism. Economists measure the aggregate efficiency of the economy, as we saw in a previous chapter, by taking the ratio of an index of total output to an index of resources; the more output per unit input, the greater the efficiency of the whole economy. The concept is analogous to measuring, say, the efficiency of an automobile in terms of miles per gallon. In principle, these measures can show whether controls had a substantial impact on the economy as a whole, whatever their effect on particular markets might have been.

Table 5.3 shows the year-to-year percentage changes in the three most commonly used measures. While there are considerable differences in particular years, the overall impression conveyed by each series is similar. Productivity growth was rapid during the mobilization; it slowed in 1942 and 1943 as full employment was reached; and it surged again in 1944 and 1945 as the new industries created during the war began to overcome the inevitable wastes of rapid development. Labor productivity, the most familiar measure, is essentially the ratio of total real output to hours worked. It shows this pattern clearly. In fact the increases from 1943 to 1945, years of full employment and strict controls, were years of growth in labor productivity that compare favorably with the best postwar years (let alone the recent period of slow growth). This

Table 5.3. *Year-to-year percentage changes in productivity, 1938–48*

Years	Labor productivity (BLS)	Total factor productivity (Denison)	Total factor productivity (Kendrick)
1938–9	3.92	3.13	4.57
1939–40	4.01	3.82	3.23
1940–1	6.27	5.10	3.82
1941–2	0.86	1.58	0.42
1942–3	2.34	−0.37	1.10
1943–4	6.51	3.91	6.23
1944–5	4.05	2.38	4.40
1945–6	−3.46	−2.47	−3.63
1946–7	0.39	−1.44	−1.54
1947–8	4.39	1.26	2.94

Sources: U.S. Bureau of Economic Analysis, *Long Term Economic Growth, 1860–1970* (1973G). Column 1: series A168, p. 211. Column 2: series A162, p. 209. Column 3: series A161, p. 209.

measure, however, is not entirely satisfactory from a theoretical point of view since it confounds true changes in productivity with those produced by alterations in the amount of capital and other resources per unit of labor. The two measures of total factor productivity are designed to avoid this pitfall since they are ratios of real output to total factor inputs. The latter two differ in the way factor inputs are added together and in a host of smaller ways. Nevertheless, in terms of the broad question – did productivity decrease under controls? – the two measures are in agreement. Both show substantial gains in most years and very large gains in 1943 to 1945, the crucial years.

To be sure, the aggregate measures of productivity probably overstate the gains to some extent because the price indexes used to deflate output do not fully reflect indirect price increases (such as those due to deterioration in quality). But as we will see below, the price indexes were not as wildly inaccurate as sometimes supposed. It should also be noted that the output measures are not completely accurate either. They ignore output produced and sold on black markets, and ignoring this may lead to an understatement of total productivity. Price deflators were also used at points to estimate real resources. Here errors in the price indexes lead to an understatement of total productivity. In short, taking black markets and indirect price increases fully into account would lead to both upward and downward revisions of the productivity indexes that seem likely to leave the overall picture largely unchanged.[15]

The notion that there were substantial productivity increases during the war is shared by those observers who have surveyed developments industry by industry. Celia Gody and Allan Searle examined trends in labor productivity in industries producing for civilian consumption and concluded that while there was stagnation of productivity in some manufacturing industries (the sector hardest hit by cutbacks in output), there were substantial increases in other civilian sectors including electric light and power, and agriculture.[16] Likewise, Simon Kuznets, a contemporary observer whose opinion deserves our attention, examined (in the course of other work) the data on productivity change then available, with the purpose of forming an idea about general changes in productivity. His conclusion was that productivity of all resources in the civilian sector rose about 5 percent from the first quarter of 1939 to the first quarter of 1943 and then leveled off in 1942 and 1943, the last years he examined. Kuznets's estimates are merely a way of expressing his qualitative judgments, but they confirm in a general way the aggregate statistics if we assume that there were large gains in the industries producing war goods.[17] Thus, despite the damage to the allocative mechanism allegedly produced by controls, the economy managed to transfer a large volume of resources to essentially new industries, and to the armed forces, while maintaining and in some cases even increasing productivity in the older sector.

Controls and the misallocations they produced, moreover, were not the only forces working against productivity.[18] The most important additional factor was the dilution of the labor force. Experienced workers were drawn into the armed forces and replaced by less experienced workers on the home front. This process left considerable scope for productivity increases as the new workers gained experience, but initially it must have lowered productivity. In some industries the reduction in output – whether because of a cutoff of raw materials, or because of an explicit government order, or because of unfavorable price changes engineered by the controllers – reduced the scale of production and lowered productivity.

Indeed, the real question raised by the data is why, despite the allegedly damaging effect of controls, and despite the dilution of the labor force, productivity increases were so substantial during the war. Part of the answer, of course, was patriotism. Some people undoubtedly worked harder because they felt they were aiding the war effort. An extra dose of scorn fell on the slacker. But it should be noted that some of the largest productivity increases occurred after the military tide had turned and this motive had begun to flag. There were, in addition, several technical reasons for increased productivity. A return to full employment generally brings a rise in productivity, as the rate of utilization of fixed capital approaches an optimum. This process was at work in the early years of the war. In industries producing new products or making use of new raw materials there was a period of "learning by doing" while the new production processes were perfected. The rubber industry, for example, experienced productivity gains as increasing supplies of synthetic rubber permitted increases in the scale of operation and as engineers and chemists in the industry learned how to handle the peculiarities of the new materials.

Finally, the structure of economic incentives favored high productivity. Minority workers responded to a chance to prove themselves for the first time. It was also widely believed that after the war something like the depressed conditions of the late thirties would return. It therefore made sense to accumulate as much money as possible during the war, to spend on lower priced goods afterward and to provide a hedge against unemployment. It made sense, in short, to make hay while the sun shone.

With all of these conflicting forces affecting productivity, we cannot say that controls had no negative effects. What does appear clear, however, is that these effects from controls were so small that even working in tandem with other disruptive effects they could not offset the forces producing substantial gains. The burden of proof clearly falls to those who claim that even a short-term application of controls would severely damage the productive power of the economy.

Evasion

The evidence examined so far has been rather favorable to controls. While the difficulties encountered in the rationing programs raise disquieting questions, nothing has emerged that by itself strongly argues against the permanent adoption of the World War II model – tight controls combined with an expansionary monetary policy. When we turn to the issue of evasion, however, the picture changes. Evasion was so widespread, particularly toward the end of the period, that it raised serious doubts about the validity of the program. This is a controversial point, so below I will examine a wide range of evidence on the extent of evasion. In the course of that examination I will try to draw attention to an important, but neglected consequence of controls when combined with monetary expansion. For in order to suppress evasion the OPA was forced to seek more and more control over the market place. Suppression of the black market, to put the matter more simply, led gradually toward a significant regimentation of the economy. Ultimately, it is the inevitability of this process which makes permanent controls on the World War II model an unacceptable alternative.

Regimentation did not evolve along a straight line path. OPA was frequently frustrated in its pursuit of effective control. The black marketeers kept finding new schemes, the industries that OPA wanted to control sometimes opposed OPA successfully in the courts or in the legislature, and other agencies sometimes successfully opposed OPA in order to maintain their own sphere of influence or to win friends in the affected industries. Nevertheless, there is a clear chain leading from the suppression of inflation, to evasion, to the regimentation of the market place.

In order to define and illustrate this process I will examine evasion and the administrative response in five crucial sectors: food, clothing, shelter, fuel, and consumer durables. These sectors cover a sufficient range of market structures to illustrate the generality of the problem. First, however, it will be useful to describe the administrative and legal context in which the OPA sought to control evasion.

The danger from evasion was recognized from the founding of the OPA. In September 1943, Enforcement was made a separate department equivalent in the organizational hierarchy to the Price, Rent, and Rationing departments. Thus, it was one of the major divisions of the agency.[19] The staff of the Enforcement Department ranged from 2,000 to 5,000 investigators working under 500 to 1,000 attorneys. In 1945 the budget of the Enforcement Department was 11.6 percent of the OPA's total budget.[20] At the retail level, OPA could also count on local volunteers and, on occasion, local officials to monitor prices. Measured against the size of the economy it was trying to police, the Enforcement department was small, about one employee for every 9,000 civilian workers, but it nevertheless proved a force with which to be reckoned.

The Emergency Price Control Act (January 1942) provided OPA with four sanctions: injunctions (which could be obtained in state and Federal courts), license suspensions, treble damage suits, and criminal proceedings (which had to be instituted in Federal courts). The use of both the injunction and licensing provisions was never very important quantitatively. But the latter is of some interest because it was relied upon so heavily in World War I.

The power to revoke a license was potentially a powerful deterrent. Initially, the OPA issued licenses only to sellers of particular commodities. For example, in May 1942, the OPA licensed the sellers of scrap and salvage materials, one of the first markets to suffer from inflation, and when the inflation was arrested, from black markets. Then, under the General Maximum Price Regulation (April 1942) and a subsequent order, virtually all sellers of goods and services were in principle made subject to licensing. Finally, in an order issued in October 1943, the Administrator required a license for all sales subject to price control.[21] But license revocations were seldom used during World War II. Perhaps they were viewed as too blunt an instrument for achieving compliance in marginal cases. While licensing has become a commonplace feature of modern economic life, it is likely that many people would be alarmed by a similar extension and concentration of the licensing power in a peacetime version of OPA.[22] Given this experience, it would doubtless make sense to omit licensing from future control programs.

The treble damage suit was the basic enforcement weapon during World War II when a simple warning was ineffective. The relevant clause of the Emergency Price Control Act provided that either the victim of an overcharge or, under the appropriate conditions, the price administrator could sue for the larger of $50 or three times the overcharge. This clause was modified in the 1944 extension of the Act by the so-called Chandler Defense. If the violation was inadvertent, and if reasonable precautions had been taken to avoid it, the penalty was reduced to the larger of $25 or the amount of the overcharge.

The most severe penalty, criminal proceedings, was used infrequently. The main reason was administrative. Criminal prosecutions were handled by the United States Attorneys under the guidance of the Department of Justice. Often cases referred to Justice were held inactive for long periods and then returned to the OPA with the decision not to prosecute. It has been suggested by Ruth Duhl, an historian of the Enforcement Department, that there existed an undercurrent of opinion at Justice, and throughout the country, opposed to the use of criminal prosecution since many of the potential defendants were not from the "criminal classes."[23] Whatever the reason, sentences were often light in criminal cases, even when convictions could be obtained, and this was a further deterrent to the use of criminal proceedings from the OPA's point of view.

In addition to its powers under the price control acts, OPA could prosecute under certain other statutes. The Second War Powers Act was the authority for rationing. Under this statute criminal proceedings were more frequent, perhaps because the defendants were likely to be genuine racketeers rather than respectable businessmen. Peacetime laws were also used as the authority for enforcement. The counterfeiting statutes, for example, were employed successfully against counterfeiters of ration tickets. The criminal justice system had no reservations about dealing with violators in this class.

In some cases the OPA enforcement was also backed up by state and local laws that made price control violations subject to enforcement by local law enforcement agents. In general, however, the efforts made by local officials were not significant. The most important exception was in New York City, where, with the vigorous support of Mayor LaGuardia, numerous arrests were made.

Effective enforcement might have been seriously hampered if the constitutionality of each regulation issued by the OPA could have been challenged in the Federal courts. A defendant might have raised this defense in any one of the numerous district courts and severe economic dislocations might have followed an adverse ruling from a judge unsympathetic to the OPA. For this reason the Emergency Price Control Act set up a streamlined procedure for dealing with the constitutionality of OPA regulations. A special three-judge Emergency Court of Appeals was given exclusive jurisdiction over challenges based on constitutionality, with appeal directly to the Supreme Court. While the Emergency Court was far from a mere rubber stamp for the OPA, the limitation of appeal to this experienced and sympathetic court considerably eased the OPA's burden. A court of this sort would seem to be a feature worth incorporating in any future control programs.

How frequently did the OPA resort to legal sanctions? Table 5.4 provides an answer. It shows a count of the sanctions used by the OPA in 1944 and 1945, years of peak activity. In both years the OPA relied on milder forms of enforcement, saving the more severe forms for repeated or blatant offenders. In both years warning letters and informal adjustments were the most frequent forms of sanction, and settlements

Table 5.4. *Enforcement activities of OPA, 1944 and 1945 (cases)*

Activity	1944	1945
Investigations completed	333,151	193,348
Violations found	338,029	167,220
Warning letters and informal adjustments	205,779	29,096
License warning notices	14,300	14,275
Ration revocations by district offices	3,259	5,640
Suspension order proceedings	12,171	18,012
Administrator's consumer damage suits	1,529	10,684
Administrator's own damage suits	3,498	5,183
Injunction suits	16,649	33,756
License suspension suits	190	307
Pretrial monetary settlements of damage suits	22,702	27,204
Criminal prosecutions	9,260[a]	9,608

[a] Partially estimated.
Sources: 1944: OPA, *Twelfth Quarterly Report*, p. 75. 1945: OPA, *Seventeenth Quarterly Report*, p. 104.

of damage suits outnumbered cases actually brought to court. Altogether, the civil actions – damage suits, injunction suits, and license suspension suits – far outnumbered the criminal prosecutions.

The substantial decline in three categories between 1944 and 1945 – investigations, violations found, and warning letters and informal notices – might be accounted for by three factors. There may have been a genuine decline in the vigor of OPA enforcement. After VE day, the OPA began to have serious problems with staff turnover as employees began to think about permanent positions in the postwar economy. The decline in these categories may also have reflected the related removal of rationing and the consequent decrease in the OPA's formal duties. Finally, the possibility cannot be ruled out that it simply reflects an accounting change, a failure to count minor investigations and enforcement actions in 1945, perhaps because of the strain on the OPA's resources.

Enforcement policy passed through three distinct phases. Initially, the OPA simply responded to complaints as they came from the public. This policy made sense as a first try because it gave the agency time and provided the information with which to formulate a more energetic approach. The volume of complaints from different sectors of the economy signaled the areas which needed more systematic investigation. A passive policy may also have been based on the mistaken hope that voluntary compliance would make evasion a minor problem.

In late 1942 and early 1943 the Enforcement Department launched a series of about 20 "drives" in which all available resources were concentrated on a particular market in which violations appeared to be particularly bad. The drives secured a good deal of publicity for the agency, and may for that reason have had important deterrent effects. But for a variety of reasons this maneuver was not a good basis for a long-term policy. For one thing, investigators who were constantly being shifted from one line of activity to another could not build up the detailed knowledge necessary to detect subtle forms of evasion. For another, it appears that some of the targets were chosen without giving sufficient thought to the economic significance of the commodity. Drives were undertaken, for example, against violators in pickles and wolf fur.

What might be termed the mature phase of the Enforcement Department's policy evolved in the spring of 1943. The staff was divided along commodity lines, and investigators continuously monitored the markets under their jurisdiction. For example, about 37 percent of the investigative staff generally was devoted to food, a percentage that corresponded closely to the weight of food in the consumer price index. About 38 percent of the food investigators, about 14 percent of all investigators, were assigned, normally, to meat, one of the most troublesome markets, although this percentage was increased dramatically when meat black markets were particularly severe. By the time it organized along these lines, the Enforcement Department was accomplishing a good deal. By 1944, Enforcement, as Table 5.4 shows, was carrying out investigations at a rate of over 300,000 per year.

A portrait of the distribution of enforcement activity, by commodity, is given in Table 5.5. This table is on a defendant, rather than a case, basis (as was Table 5.4). A better feel for the meaning of the categories can be obtained by considering the most important problems within some of them. In groceries the most frequently violated regulations were the ones setting up community dollar-and-cents price ceilings. The category of agricultural commodities is actually a catchall which includes the frequently violated restaurant regulations. In apparel the most frequently violated regulation set prices for women's and children's outerwear. Among industrial materials the regulations fixing prices on Southern pine produced the most violations. In manufacturing it was the retail price of farm machinery.

Table 5.5. *The distribution of defendants in OPA
sanctions, 1944*

Activity	Total	Percentage
Meat and dairy	10,355	16.2
Groceries	7,055	11.2
Agricultural commodities	8,315	13.0
Apparel	4,271	6.7
Textile and leather	667	1.0
Industrial materials	1,836	2.9
Industrial manufacturing	2,032	3.2
Gasoline rationing	11,103	17.4
Automotive supplies	5,524	8.7
Heating fuel	787	1.2
Consumer durables	2,666	4.2
Rent	6,855	10.8
Services	2,298	3.6
Total	63,749	99.9

Source: Miller and Clinard (1945U).

The simplest hypothesis about the distribution of violators consistent with the crudely aggregated data in Table 5.5 is that the number of defendants was proportional to the importance of a particular area in the consumer's budget. In January 1944 food accounted for 41 percent of the consumer price index and 40.4 percent of the defendants were in Meat and Dairy, Groceries, and Agricultural Commodities. In January 1944 clothing accounted for 12.6 percent of the consumer price index, and Apparel and Textile and Leather accounted for 7.7 percent of the index, and 10.8 percent of the defendants. House furnishings accounted for 2.9 percent of the index and consumer durables, which included many house furnishings, accounted for 4.2 percent of the defendants. The largest discrepancy is in the area of gasoline rationing and this problem subsided, as OPA took measures to deal with the stealing and counterfeiting of ration coupons.

An association between amount of OPA enforcement activity and the importance of a sector for the consumer was not purely the result of a neutral response by OPA to the pattern of violations. The OPA was charged with keeping consumer prices in check. It therefore made sense for it to allocate its enforcement resources to "important" areas, as it did in the mature phase of its enforcement policy, and the volume of resources allocated undoubtedly had a substantial impact on the number of violations found. Indeed, although I have no direct confirmation, it is highly plausible that OPA used the shares of various goods and services in the consumer price index as a guide to the allocation of resources in the Enforcement Department.

Food

Let us look more closely at violations in some of the major sectors, and at the OPA's response. There were more violators in the food sector, as shown in Table 5.5, than in any other. Yet circumstances favored food price controls in many ways. Civilian supplies, as we have seen, were generally high by prewar standards. Food prices were allowed to rise longer than others, forestalling excess demand. Rationing, which tended to mitigate the worst fears of consumers, was introduced in 1943, and patriotism limited some of the worst abuses. At least some distributors ignored profit opportunities and allocated food "fairly."[24] Nevertheless, food was one of the areas in which evasion and black markets were widespread.

Many of the evasions in the food market were relatively mild. Weekend sales, for example, were frequently eliminated. This continued a prewar trend. But, since prices were frozen at levels which reflected midweek values, the elimination of the sales represented a real, if small, increase in the prices paid by people who had used the sales.

Simply charging more than the ceiling price was also a problem. A reporter for *Woman's Home Companion* traveled the country twice in search of black markets.[25] On both occasions she complained of paying above-ceiling prices on grocery items. This problem, however, tended to be self-limiting. Much as a driver will go 5 or 10 miles per hour above a speed limit, while being afraid to go 40 or 50 miles per hour above, a grocer would charge a small amount in excess of the legal ceiling but would be afraid to go too far. Overcharging, moreover, was more severe in the early days of controls. Under the General Maximum Price Regulation, each grocer set his own prices. As explicit dollar-and-cents prices applying to all stores in an area were introduced, the problem receded. Indeed, the transition to dollar-and-cents pricing was accelerated by surveys in the coal mining areas where there was considerable labor unrest. These surveys bore out labor's contention that the General

Maximum Price Regulation was not working, and that dollar-and-cents pricing was more effective.[26]

The tie-in sale was also ubiquitous in food markets. Wholesalers complained that meat packers forced them to take a variety of unwanted products along with more desirable cuts. Getting evidence was hard. Many wholesalers were afraid to testify against the packers out of fear that their supplies would be limited, and some wholesalers recanted their stories before grand juries. Eventually, however, the OPA gathered enough evidence to go after three of the Big Four packers.[27]

Quality deterioration became a problem in many foods where it sometimes went under the older name of "adulteration." Fat was added to hamburger, the butterfat content of milk was reduced, cornstarch was added to spices, and coffee was stretched with fillers.[28] The OPA tried various ways of meeting this problem. One regulation required butchers to grind hamburger in the presence of the customers. Other regulations specified the amount of fat that could be left to border a given cut of meat. In 1944, the OPA filed a number of injunction suits in cases of improper fat trim, an adumbration of what might be expected with a permanent system of controls on the World War II model.[29]

Upgrading (selling lower quality merchandise as if it were of a higher quality) and shortweighting were also used to evade controls. Butter, for example, was sometimes sold as ninety-three score, when it was not. Upgrading of meat was widespread. One partial solution was to have the grade stamped by Federal inspectors at very close intervals across the carcasses. Perhaps the most famous case of shortweighting was the shrinking candy bar. *Consumer Reports* surveyed candy bars in 1943.[30] They found that nineteen out of twenty bars had shrunk between 1939 and 1943, hiding a price increase of 23 percent. Not all of this shrinkage could be explained by price controls. But this was undoubtedly a major cause. In court the candy manufacturers argued that their bars were still on average above the weight specified on the wrapper. What had happened, as the cases revealed, was that the companies had reduced the gap between the mean weight and the weight claimed on the wrapper. While the average bar was still heavier than claimed, the *proportion* of underweight bars had risen. Candy makers also substituted inferior ingredients in ways not permitted by the OPA.

Above all, it was in poultry and beef that evasive practices and black markets were at their worst. The main reason for the severity of this black market was that the demand increased rapidly with increases in real income. Meat has, to use the economist's term, a high-income elasticity of demand. Thus, as wartime incomes increased, the gap between the market clearing price and the ceiling price, the reward to black marketeers, grew more rapidly for meat more than it did for other commodities. This process was exacerbated by the disappearance of consumer durables and certain other products from the market. The purchasing power that might have been spent on them was concentrated instead on other priorities such as meat.

In Delaware, Maryland, and Virginia, an important poultry producing region, the black market grew so severe that for a time virtually all poultry was moving through illegal channels. Even the army had trouble supplying its needs. Finally, the OPA and the army joined together in an enforcement drive. With the war raging in Europe, state police were used to intercept and requisition the payloads of trucks filled with black-market poultry. Apparently this effort broke the black market.[31]

The meat black market was also particularly severe in New York City. Part of the problem was created by the restaurants, especially the steakhouses. Since there was a limit on the amount of meat one could purchase in groceries and butcher shops, but no limit on the amount one could consume in restaurants, the demand for restaurant meals was high. Moreover, since prices inevitably varied from one restaurant to another, indeed from one dish to another, achieving effective control over restaurant prices was extremely difficult. Accordingly, the incentive for a restaurant to increase its meat supplies through black-market purchases was great. A number of nationally famous restaurants in New York City were charged with black marketeering. Pressed to estimate the extent of this black market in the city, Thomas I. Emerson, the deputy administrator of enforcement for the OPA, suggested 10 percent of the wholesale trade and perhaps 15 to 20 percent of the retail trade.[32]

In June 1946, on the eve of decontrol, a reporter for the *Wall Street Journal*, Berkley Hill, Jr., surveying the wartime increases in the price of living in New York City, gave the list of black-market prices contained in Table 5.6. The gap between the black-market price and the ceiling price seems to have been substantial for most of the items, ranging from about 104 percent for center-sliced ham to about 45 percent for sliced bacon. New York, however, was an extreme case. New York was more distant from illegal sources of supply and this raised the differential on the black market.

Table 5.6. *Prices of black-market meats in New York City, June 1946*

Cut of meat (best grade)	Black-market price (dollars per pound)	Ceiling price (dollars per pound)
Center-sliced ham	1.00	0.49
Beef steak	1.00	0.56
Roast beef	0.75–1.00	0.39
Pork tenderloin	0.90	0.52
Pork chops	0.80	0.40
Sliced bacon	0.60–0.65	0.43

Source: *Wall Street Journal*, June 27, 1946, p. 1.

It is also worth noting that the items in Table 5.6 are for good cuts of the best grades of meat. It is my impression that black marketeering was more common for "luxury" items – the best cuts of meat, shrimp, canned salmon, and so forth – than for lower-priced items. For the most part lower-quality items were available through conventional channels. Although the evidence is not definitive, this conclusion is, at least, highly plausible. For one thing the demand for luxury meats probably rose faster than that for meats as a whole, just as the demand for meat rose more rapidly than the demand for other commodities, so that in these markets the gap between the market clearing price and the ceiling price was larger. In addition, the high ratio of value per pound made luxuries relatively easy to distribute through clandestine channels.

How large was the black market for all foods? It is impossible to say precisely. In 1944 Chester Bowles suggested $1.2 billion, about 4 percent of the nation's food bill.[33] Bowles, of courses, was in as good a position as anyone to judge. He was not, however, an unbiased observer. By emphasizing the size of the black market, he might have hoped to win support for more resources and sterner measures. On the other hand, a large estimate was ammunition for the opponents of OPA who argued that price control was impossible. In any case, black-market activities do not leave good statistical records and any estimate must be viewed as having a wide margin of potential error.

Would greater regimentation have prevented the black market in meat? Or more to the point, how drastic would effective measures had to have been? The OPA had before it the example of Great Britain where stronger measures were used. In Britain the government was the sole purchaser of live cattle and imported beef, slaughtering was limited to a small number of plants, and each consumer had to register with one retailer. The United States never went that far. But the OPA consistently sought greater control over the flow of meat. Its attempts to control the industry, however, frequently were set aside because of objections from the meat producers and sometimes from the War Food Administration. Slaughter controls which limited the number of live animals that could be slaughtered in individual plants and, in some cases, specified the markets into which a slaughterer had to ship his meat, were imposed and removed several times before being abandoned. These controls were important because the slaughterer represented a narrowing in the flow between producers and consumers, a point at which control could be achieved. The main purpose of slaughter controls was to divert animals from the non-federally-inspected slaughterhouses that sprang up during the war, and which were the main source of black-market meat. But they were also introduced to give the OPA greater control over legitimate channels of distribution. Whether the full set of controls advocated by OPA, or even a more complete set on the British model, would have been sufficient to control the black market in meat cannot be known. But clearly, tight regulation of this market or substantial subsidies would have to be part of peacetime controls, especially if they were continued for long in a regime of high aggregate demand.

Clothing

The regulation of clothing prices may well have been the most difficult problem encountered by the OPA.[34] In January 1946 Chester Bowles was moved to write an article for *Colliers*, which he called "Crisis in Clothes," in order to defend OPA regulations then in effect and to shift the blame for current troubles to the industry. These troubles arose from two causes. The industry produced a highly diversified commodity in which style and seasonal changes were important, making it hard to specify prices. Also, the industry used cotton, and cotton had powerful friends in Congress. The OPA found that taking on the clothing industry was not an easy task, whether in the marketplace or in the political arena. Yet clothing could not be ignored if living costs were to be stabilized. Clothing constituted 11 percent of the consumer price index at prewar (1935–9) prices.

Evasion mainly took two forms: quality deterioration and forced uptrading. A variety of ways of reducing quality were shown in an exhibit prepared by the OPA for the Senate War Investigating Committee in July 1944. To quote an official history of apparel price control:

The items submitted included . . . a pair of men's shorts made of cheesecloth, with 50 percent added sizing to give it form until washed; a woman's slip made of practically unwearable coarse, heavily sized muslin; a pair of baby pants, allegedly water-resistant, which "allowed about a third of a glass of water through after being laundered once"; and a cotton sweater "too loosely knit to hold its shape."[35]

These examples were deliberately provocative, but more objective analyses confirmed that considerable quality deterioration had taken place, and consumer complaints were numerous.[36] Ironically, two years later, the National Retail Dry Good Association turned this tactic of choosing dramatic examples against OPA. The Association set up a series of "horror exhibits" to show the shoddy quality of merchandise reaching the market as a result of controls. The organization argued that terminating controls would restore quality garments, and the OPA issued a vigorous rebuttal challenging the authenticity of the exhibit.[37]

Perhaps even more serious than quality deterioration, at least toward the end of the period, was what was known as forced uptrading. Price controls tended to freeze profit margins on different lines of clothing. In peacetime, higher-priced lines typically had larger profit margins, due to the risk that, if fashions changed, a manufacturer might be stuck with unsalable merchandise. In the war economy, however, this risk disappeared. All markets were characterized by excess demand at the ceiling price. It made sense, therefore, for manufacturers to shift production to the high-priced lines. For many consumers this was not a problem. With higher incomes, and many of the normal channels of expenditure blocked, they wanted to trade up to higher-priced lines. But for low-income consumers the shift toward more expensive lines was a burden. They wanted to buy inexpensive clothing but found none. Moreover, by adding some cheap trim to a low-priced garment a manufacturer transformed it into another garment, which he could claim belonged to the high-style category. This combination of quality deterioration and forced uptrading was hard to defeat because style is such an elusive concept.

The extent of the clothing shortages, particularly in the lower-priced lines, was revealed in a number of surveys conducted by the Office of Civilian Requirements of the War Production Board. In the first quarter of 1945 a survey showed, for example, that only 44 percent of the demand for children's underwear, 53 percent of the demand for house dresses, and 72 percent of the demand for men's dress shirts were met.[38] The Bureau of Labor Statistics tried to take uptrading into account in computing the consumer price index. When the Bureau could no longer price a particular low-priced item, it substituted a higher quality (and hence higher priced) alternative. One-half of the price differential was taken as a pure price increase. These increases caused by forced uptrading explain much of the substantial measured increases in clothing prices. From August 1939 to January 1946 the consumer price index as a whole rose at an annual rate of 4.3 percent, while the clothing index rose at an annual rate of 6.3 percent.

Perhaps the most persuasive evidence of the extent of these problems lies in the drastic attempts the OPA made to bring clothing under control. The first was the so-called highest price line limitation. The idea was simple. If, during the base period, a manufacturer had produced suits in the $20, $30, and $40 ranges, then the maximum he could charge for a suit was $40, even though the suit might be entitled to a higher price on other grounds. This prevented some manufacturers from claiming that they were producing new, high-quality garments. But it was not a significant restraint on manufacturers who had produced a wide variety of lines in the base period. The highest price line limitation was introduced in the summer of 1942. It ran into considerable opposition from the clothing industry, particularly after the industry had become upset by other OPA programs. It was outlawed in the Price Control Extension Act of 1944 due to industry objections.

The next attempt by the OPA to solve the clothing crisis was the ambitious "new program" of 1943. Similar to a system used in Britain, the new program contemplated dollar-and-cents ceilings tied to specific quality levels, standardization and simplification of garments, emphasis on the production of low-end goods, development of war model clothing, and, if necessary, rationing.[39] But only part of the program was implemented. Maximum Price Regulation 304, issued in January 1943, established dollar-and-cents ceilings at the wholesale and manufacturing levels for a variety of garments, and specified the construction of the garments entitled to these prices in great detail – all the way down to the diameter of the buttons.[40] One war model program was introduced, in men's overalls.[41] But most elements of the program were abandoned. Partly this was because the program required the cooperation of the War Production Board which was not forthcoming, and partly because the program ran into a furious attack from the industry, a part of the larger attack on "professors" at the OPA. Congress eventually prohibited the OPA from completing the "new program" in clothing.

The OPA's final and most ambitious attempt to control the clothing industry was the Maximum Average Price (MAP) regulation. Unable to secure the War Production Board's cooperation, the OPA determined on MAP as a way of forcing manufacturers to maintain their output of low-end merchandise while OPA appeared to issue only price regulations. The agency did not legally have the right to regulate production, but MAP would have given it this power indirectly.[42] The basic idea was the following: Clothing output was divided into approximately 400 different categories – men's dress shirts, women's blouses, and so forth. In each category, of course, prices were already set on individual items by various regulations. What MAP added was the requirement that the average price of the items in that category not be higher than in a specified base period. The average referred to was a weighted average, calculated by multiplying each individual price by the share of that item in the total output in that category, and then adding these weighted prices. The concept is a natural one for economists; the consumer price index is calculated along similar lines. But it is not surprising that many clothing manufacturers had trouble with it, at least at first, and needed help in making their calculations. The point of the calculation is that if a manufacturer concentrates on his highest price lines, then the weight on those prices, and consequently the average price, will be higher than in the base period. While the manufacturer has some freedom, say to shift from mid-priced items to offsetting high and low-range items, the freedom to eliminate low-end merchandise would have been considerably reduced.

The enforcement mechanism was also clever, but contained a public relations hazard of major proportions. If the manufacturer's average price in each category at the end of a quarter was at or below his maximum average price, he was said to be in "balance." But if his average in a particular category was above his maximum, he was in "surcharge." The surcharge had to be made up in the next thirty days by selling items below the maximum average price. The manufacturer had to deliver enough makeup items to equal the dollar amount of the surcharge – the difference between the actual average price and the maximum average price multiplied by the total number of items delivered in the preceding quarter. If the surcharge was not made up in the thirty-day period, the manufacturer was prohibited from delivering any item in any category at a price higher than the maximum average price. With a smoothly running MAP program only a small proportion of manufacturers would be subject to this penalty. But if a substantial number of firms failed to make up their deficit, an artificial shortage could develop, and in some cases it did. The newspapers showed pictures of clothing waiting to be delivered to the public, but held back because of a complex OPA regulation. It was not an enviable situation for price administrators to explain.

The MAP regulation was issued on April 19, 1945, to go into effect on June 1, which as it turned out, was after VE day. This in itself stacked the cards heavily against MAP. The industry attacked MAP, as it had earlier measures, and was again successful. The OPA continually watered down the MAP regulations, and the mechanism was outlawed in the Price Control Extension Act of 1946.

It seems possible that the "new program" or a refined form of it, could have solved the quality deterioration and low-end merchandise problems that plagued the clothing field. But it is important to keep in mind that this was not required by any exigency of the war, but rather by the effort to control prices in a period of rising aggregate demand. Regimentation of this industry, and with it some reduction of the change and diversity which are at the heart of it, seems to be one of the inevitable costs of price control if continued in a period of high aggregate demand.

Shelter

Rent controls, in the view of most economists, are likely to cause fewer problems in the short run than other forms of price controls. The reason for this is that the supply of dwelling space cannot be decreased very much in a short period of time. Thus, while controls prevent price increases and help tenants (who in some cases are more "deserving" than their landlords), they have relatively few negative effects. This view, of course, is far from universal. Conservative economists have emphasized indirect changes in "supply" (doubling-up will be inhibited by controls, and decreases in maintenance expenditures will reduce the supply of a given quality of dwelling space) and the possibility of black markets that can occur fairly quickly.[43]

The tolerance for rent controls shown by most economists was matched by the enthusiasm of the general public. Even after public opinion turned against price regulation as a whole, support for rent controls remained strong, and rent controls were continued in many areas long after other controls were removed. When price controls were reimposed during the Korean War, many areas were still under the rent controls imposed during World War II. Rent control was especially urgent, in the public mind, in the new industrial centers where munitions were being turned out. Here the sudden increase in demand produced substantial rent increases, and the idea of making profits from war workers was roundly condemned.

Despite strong popular support for rent controls, however, evasion was widespread. One reason was that the price of owner-occupied housing was not controlled. This was the basis for several evasive schemes. The simplest was to evict the current tenants and sell the property to them, or anyone else who would buy it, at the market price. This could be varied by allowing the purchaser to pay in monthly installments in which the accumulation of equity was extremely slow. In effect the tenant was simply paying rent above the legal maximum.[44] Leaving owner-occupied housing uncontrolled also tended to divert construction resources into housing rather than apartments. But this tendency was offset, to some extent, by government construction and by allowing higher rents on new apartments.[45] The OPA sought authority to control the resale price of owner-occupied housing, but this was denied by Congress.

Other forms of evasion used more familiar techniques. Bribes and cash on the side were common. In a survey of wartime cost-of-living increases in Portland, Oregon, a busy war center, the *Wall Street Journal* reported that in June 1946, rents were then officially about $10 higher than they were in June 1941, when they ranged from $38 to $60 for five unfurnished rooms. But it was also reported that black-market bribes ranged from $5 to $500 to get an apartment, and that often $10 to $15 per month was paid on the side.[46] Leon Henderson, who you will recall was the first director of the OPA, called the must-buy-furniture requirement "the most common dodge." He gave an example of a six-room apartment in Chicago which the landlord was willing to let at

Table 5.7. *Wartime trends in rental income and expenditures for repair and maintenance (index numbers)*

Year	Apartment houses		Small structures	
	Rental income	Repair and maintenance	Rental income	Repair and maintenance
1939	100.0	100.0	100.0	100.0
1940	100.6	99.0	102.8	95.0
1941	104.4	102.8	108.0	93.7
1942	110.1	91.4	112.4	81.8
1943	112.0	79.9	113.3	74.3
1944	112.9	80.2	114.0	75.3
1945	113.4	81.9	114.2	75.1
1946[a]	113.7	84.3	114.3	78.9

[a] Year ending June 30, 1946.
Source: U.S. Congress, House, Banking and Currency Committee, *Hearings on H.R. 2549*, statement of Ivan D. Carson, 80th Cong., 1st sess., 1947, p. 170.

the OPA ceiling of $75 per month. There was, however, a small catch: the tenant must first buy the furniture for $1,500.[47]

The tendency for landlords to reduce maintenance expenditures followed a predictable course. This can be measured accurately because the OPA regularly surveyed the income and expenditures of a large sample of rented dwellings. Table 5.7 shows that substantial declines in outlays for repair and maintenance occurred in both apartments and small structures. If account were taken, moreover, of the increase in the cost of maintaining rental properties, the decline in real maintenance expenditures would be even greater than shown in Table 5.7. Some of the decline in these expenditures may have been deferred improvements. But this could not have been a substantial fraction of the decline. Deferred expenditures were estimated to be only 1.5 percent of rental income.[48]

How significant was the decline in maintenance expenditures? One approach is to view this as a hidden price increase. Suppose we define the true rent as what the tenant pays his landlord, plus what he would have to spend to make up for the landlord's neglect. Table 5.8 compares the rent component of the consumer price index that was published with an adjusted index corresponding to the true rent concept. Although the rate of increase is slow in both series, it is about twice as fast in

Table 5.8. *Adjustment of the rent index for changes in repair and maintenance expenditures*

Year	Standard rent index	Adjusted rent index[a]
1939	100	100
1940	100.3	100.8
1941	102.1	102.4
1942	104.4	106.6
1943	104.3	108
1944	104.6	108.2
1945	105.0	108.5
1946[b]	105.5	108.5

[a] Calculated from the formula $I^* = I + \phi(1 - M)$, where I^* is the adjusted rent index, I is the standard rent index, ϕ is the ratio of maintenance expenditures to rental income in the base period, and M is the average index of repair and maintenance for apartment houses and small structures.
[b] Year ending June 30, 1946.
Source: Historical Statistics (1960G, p. 125) and Table 5.7.

the adjusted series: 1.4 percent annually from 1941 to 1945 compared to 0.7 percent.

The OPA was aware, of course, of the maintenance problem and tried to meet it by mandating rent reductions or requiring various kinds of maintenance expenditures. After VJ Day (when landlords could not fall back on the excuse of wartime shortages), the New York district office of the OPA required that a maximum of three years could elapse between the redecorating of rented rooms, including painting and wall-papering.[49] In order to plug this loophole in a permanent system of price controls, a detailed code outlining the landlord's responsibilities would have to be written. It would not be enough to say that the rooms must be painted; the type of paints, number of coats, and so forth would have to be specified.

Equally comprehensive data are not available on other forms of evasion in the rented dwelling market. Fortunately, Marshall Clinard, the historian of the black market, reports three surveys of some breadth. One was described as a door-to-door survey in black neighborhoods on Chicago's South Side taken in 1944. Of 739 units, 310 were not registered with the OPA, and tenants in 125 (about 17 percent) were paying overcharges.[50] A survey of 122 cases in Brooklyn revealed 18 cases, about 15 percent, that warranted enforcement action.[51] And a Bureau of Labor Statistics survey conducted early in 1945 revealed that 10 to 20 percent of landlords failed to register their property; on registered property there was an average 8 to 9 percent overcharge, a good example of the general tendency to bend but not break the rules.[52]

Fuel

Within the fuel sector gasoline provided the most headaches for the OPA. Typically, a station would sell gasoline without receiving ration coupons in return. The station would then buy black market coupons, either stolen or counterfeited, to make up its deficit, although in the early days of the program, the station might have tried to get away with simply overstating the amount of coupons it was turning in.[53] Similar practices were used in the fuel oil market. Here the distributor, who had custody of the coupons, might remove coupons for more fuel than he had actually delivered to one customer, permitting excess deliveries to other customers at black-market prices.

The black market in gasoline ration currency resulted from the failure of the OPA, initially, to treat the ration currency with the same care as ordinary money is treated. Once efforts were made to prevent counterfeiting (the Treasury Department helped with this), to prevent the stealing of ration currency, and to bring the banking system into the counting and transferring of ration currency, the black market declined rapidly. While it lasted, however, this was probably the most important black market in the United States. Early in 1944 Chester Bowles estimated that about 5 percent of all gasoline was purchased without coupons or with stolen or counterfeit coupons.[54] Marshall Clinard has estimated that sanctions had been imposed on about one in sixteen service stations by January 1945, and that if stations that were simply debited in their ration accounts for stolen or counterfeit currency were included, that probably from one in five to one in two stations were in violation.[55]

Rationing was not always adequate to bring the supply of and demand for gasoline into equilibrium, particularly on the East Coast, where, as was noted above, supplies were especially tight. The major difficulty was that the basic ration could not be made sufficiently small to cover the available stocks without creating shortages for drivers with extraordinary "needs" for gasoline. The problem was compounded by the right of local boards to issue emergency rations in unlimited amounts. Some relief was possible through the issue of ration series that made gasoline available in larger amounts for doctors, clergymen, and so on. But it was not possible to tailor everyone's ration to their "needs." In principle, relief was also possible by creating a so-called white market, in which excess tickets could be sold.[56] This solution was not tried, perhaps because it appeared to redistribute income unfairly.

Earlier, when supplies had grown extremely tight on the East Coast, the OPA had announced a ban on pleasure driving. This episode is important for the light it sheds on the tolerance of the community for regimentation in a wartime emergency.[57] The ban, which limited driving in the East to essential activities, was first announced on January 7, 1943. Initially, it produced positive results. But as time wore on criticism began to mount, and enforcement by local police waned. Drivers began ignoring the ban. On March 3 the ban was made voluntary, and on March 22 it was revoked. On May 20, when supplies were again extremely short, with the summer driving season approaching, the ban was renewed. Sporadic efforts were made to enforce it, and on June 26 over 1,700 cars were stopped in the New York area.[58] But again the ban was widely disregarded and criticized. On July 15 it was modified to permit one trip to a summer home, an action which understandably outraged many people, including, of course, those who had forfeited earlier trips. From this time on the ban was a dead letter. It came to its official end on September 1.

Once the black market based on counterfeit and stolen coupons was successfully attacked, the major problem became evasion through quality deterioration. It might be thought that fuels would be one area free of this phenomenon. Indeed, gasoline and coal are two of the examples John Kenneth Galbraith cites (the others are electricity and numerous foods) in which quality deterioration is difficult for technical reasons.[59] It may have been difficult, but it was not impossible. In gasoline the main form of quality deterioration was accomplished through the addition of a substance called "Lubrigas" to regular gasoline, and the selling of the adulterated product as premium.[60] Of course it was difficult for a driver to tell when gas was being pumped whether it was regular or premium, and much gas was upgraded in this way without the benefit of Lubrigas. Quality deterioration was also a problem in bituminous coal, even though prices were fixed by grade and by mine. Coal was prepared less well, raising the ash content, more fine coal was included, and coal from less desirable portions of a given mine was sold.[61] The overall deterioration in quality of bituminous coal may have been from 5 to 10 percent.[62] Even fuel oil for home consumption deteriorated. The lighter hydrocarbons were removed from the standard distillate for use in military fuels. In unadjusted heating equipment this raised heating costs about 5 percent. Adjusted equipment might have actually used this fuel more efficiently, but the adjustment costs would have to be taken into account in figuring the "true" change in the price of fuel oil.

Upgrading, short-weighting, tie-in sales, and cash on the side all made their appearance in coal markets. Since coal is sold both by grade and size, upgrading took place along both dimensions. In addition, the sale of coal in highly prized sizes was tied to the sale of coal in other sizes. In some cases, however, still another tie-in sale was used: the purchaser was required to buy stock in the mine selling the coal![63] I do not mean to suggest that quality deterioration in these commodities was severe. It was often more a matter of bending the rules than of open defiance. Rather, the point is that the appearance of deterioration and related evasive schemes in relatively homogeneous commodities testifies to the ubiquity of evasion.

Consumer durables

Production of many consumer durables was stopped during World War II as plants that produced them were converted to munitions. During the War this greatly simplified OPA's enforcement problem. But during reconversion, when these durables were reintroduced to the market, the absence of a continuous production history created a problem: It was hard to calculate appropriate prices for the new models, and, of course, alert manufacturers quickly exploited this difficulty by claiming high prices. Those consumer durables, such as furniture, that stayed on the market during the war suffered from considerable quality deterioration. One indication of the severity of the problem is the number of specification changes made by the Bureau of Labor Statistics in compiling its consumer price index. The Bureau had its investigators price items that were defined by a list of characteristics: weight, thickness, composition, and so forth. The Bureau changed specifications only when it was impossible to find the old items. A committee appointed to examine the index found that the Bureau had been forced to change the specifications for 32 percent of the items in the house furnishings component of the consumer price index because of quality deterioration.[64] The committee, moreover, confined itself to changes that reflected a decrease in durability, ignoring changes that reflected only a deterioration in style.

As production of consumer durables returned to normal after the war, the problem became that of preventing manufacturers from receiving too large an increase in price for the improvements introduced in new models. The scope of this problem was revealed by a survey of consumer durables made by the OPA, a study that showed that approximately 30 percent of the manufacturers were selling at least some of their products at overceiling prices.[65] The OPA made a determined effort to enforce ceilings on durables, but how successful it would have been in the long run is not clear because the agency was just beginning to wrestle with the problem in its normal proportions when wage and price controls were removed.

No discussion of consumer durables during the war would be complete without consideration of automobiles; some of the most flagrant black markets evolved to evade controls on the price of automobiles. The issuance of the regulation controlling used automobile prices on July 10, 1944 was greeted almost immediately by evasions, which included forced trade-ins, forced financing, and cash on the side concealed by filing false certificates showing that the transaction had occurred at the ceiling price.[66] Enforcement drives, according to the OPA, cooled the black market in subsequent years, at least until 1946, but it was never eliminated.

John Kenneth Galbraith has argued that industries dominated by a few large producers (the automobile industry is a prototype), were relatively easy to police.[67] But this proposition glosses over one aspect of the problem. No matter how concentrated the manufacturing sector of an industry, the number of distributors must be large, and enforcement will still be difficult at this level. Ultimately, the consumer is indifferent to whether the excess he or she pays over the ceiling price ends up in the pockets of the owners of the manufacturing firms, the owners of the distributing firms, or the salesman, who is the last link in the chain. The total price, moreover, is likely to be greater than the free market price when effective control is exercised at the production level, discouraging production, while successful evasion takes place at the distributive level.

This is precisely what happened in the automobile industry in 1946 when pent-up wartime demands met new supplies in a controlled market. Cash-on-the-side deals were frequent. Sometimes the excuse was to ensure "priority" delivery. The most common evasion, according to the OPA, was for the dealership to require a trade-in, for which the market was very strong, and to pay less for it than the market price.[68] Many buyers cooperated willingly with these schemes. They also wanted to evade controls.

No other black market in 1946, with the possible exception of meat, got as much attention in the popular press as did the black market in automobiles.[69] The most notorious cases involved huge lots in which black-market cars, some newly purchased from franchise dealers, were brought from all over the country to be resold at black-market prices. One at Leesville, South Carolina, which was raided by the OPA, was operating at a one-hundred-million-dollar rate. To some extent the situation was temporary. Had the OPA been able to stay in business, it could have expected the problem to subside somewhat, but it is doubtful that it could have eliminated the black market at the distributive level while holding its low ceiling prices at the production level.

Given the foregoing catalog of evasions in markets ranging from chickens to used cars, and accepting the accuracy of the examples, one is still led to ask how extensive all this was. After all, the patriotic motive was strong. If that did not work, there was still the fear of being caught! Could it not be true that while rules were frequently bent, the aggregate importance of all this was limited? There is no way of answering this question satisfactorily to all. The question itself is somewhat ambiguous. By the "extent" of evasion does one mean the proportion of the public that engaged in such activities, the proportion of business firms, the proportion of total output, or some other measure? Clearly evasion could be considered extensive by some measures and insubstantial by others. Even if one definition of the extent of the black market could be agreed upon, it is unlikely that completely convincing data now exist. People engaged in illegal activities do not make accurate records available to the officials investigating them. Finally, even if a satisfactory definition could be devised, and unimpeachable evidence accumulated, it is unlikely that agreement could be reached on the adjective to be attached to the measure computed. What would appear "small" and "unimportant" to some would appear "large" and "of major proportions" to others. Nevertheless, such difficulties have not prevented economists from expressing opinions on the subject, and perhaps have encouraged them to do so. John Kenneth Galbraith, for example, has argued that "the proportion of actions in the black market was small even at the

Table 5.9. *Sanctions instituted by OPA*
February 11, 1941–May 31, 1947

Total sanctions instituted	259,966
Total proceedings closed	167,774
Suspension order proceedings	52,297
Determination proceedings	165
Recission of veterans' housing sale	1
Restitutions of sales control overcharge	10
Revocations of dealers' authorization	27
Voluntary contribution	8,213
Administrator's consumers' treble damages	
Monetary settlements	33,612
Suits filed	26,094
Administrator's own treble damages	
Monetary settlements	28,125
Suits filed	12,638
Injunction suits	78,081
License suspension suits	1,013
Local criminal prosecutions by OPA agents	5,127
Federal criminal prosecutions	13,999
Contempt proceedings	564

Note: These figures exclude revocations of consumer rations, most OPA price panel and informal rent violation settlements, debiting of dealers' ration bank accounts for stolen or counterfeit coupons or undercounts, prosecutions by state and local governments, and actions by other federal agencies and private individuals.
Source: Clinard (1952B, p. 33) from OPA, *Twenty-Second Quarterly Report*, p. 16.

end of the war."[70] Here I will survey three types of quantitative evidence on the extent of evasion: the number of sanctions imposed by the OPA, estimates of the evasion-linked error in the consumer price index, and surveys conducted among representative groups of consumers. Ultimately the reader must decide for himself whether he agrees with me that the adjective "large" is warranted.

Total sanctions

Table 5.9 lists the total volume of sanctions instituted by the OPA over its lifetime, providing an overall picture of enforcement activity. These sanctions represent, of course, only those activities that were detected by the OPA, that generated sufficient evidence to permit legal action, and that for some other reason – their size or possible deterrent effect – warranted action. In short, the number of sanctions is only a lower bound on the total volume of evasive activity. One way of judging the volume of sanctions is in relation to the number of businesses. In 1942 there were 3,185,800 firms in the United States (the wartime peak).[71] If only one sanction was applied to each firm, and if only firms existing in 1942 received sanctions, it follows that roughly 8.2 percent of all businesses were subjected to sanctions by the OPA. Of course, in practice, several sanctions were sometimes applied to the same firm; progressively more severe sanctions were applied to repeat violators. On the other hand, the OPA found many violations on which it chose not to act, and failed to find many others.

Annual violations detected were reported only from 1943 onward. There are several ways of utilizing these data to get an estimate of total violations discoverd by OPA. Since the definition of what constituted a "violation found" varied more than that of a sanction applied, the safest procedure is to tie the estimate of violations found to the estimate of total sanctions. In 1945, as shown in Table 5.4, OPA reported 167,220 violations found, about 1.51 times as many violations as sanctions of the type counted in Table 5.9. If this ratio applied for the whole period, and this is a rather conservative assumption (using the figure for 1944 would create a higher ratio), then the percentage of firms found in violation during the period would be 12.4 percent (8.2 × 1.51 = 12.38). This is a large figure, although it should be kept in mind that this cumulates violations over the entire lifetime of the OPA.

Another way to view the volume of enforcement activity is to contrast the judicial activity generated by the OPA with that being generated by other laws. Comparisons of this sort are carried out in Table 5.10. The top panel shows the breakdown between OPA and non-OPA cases in 84 Federal district courts. Obviously, the proportion of OPA cases was substantial, reaching 38 percent of all cases, and 54 percent of civil cases in 1946. The lower panel compares OPA cases with prohibition cases. Perhaps the best summary figure is total OPA cases as a percentage of total prohibition cases in the analogous year, the last line, since the distribution between civil and criminal cases was radically different in the two experiments. Again, the number of OPA cases appears substantial; in 1945 OPA cases amounted to about 50 percent of prohibition cases in 1930.

Table 5.10. *OPA cases commenced in 84 U.S. District Courts, 1943–7*

Type of case	Wartime[a]				
	1943	1944	1945	1946	1947
OPA cases					
Civil	2,219	6,524	28,283	31,094	15,169
Criminal	2,791[b]	4,524	4,753	2,520	1,454
Total	5,010	11,048	33,036	33,614	16,623
All cases					
Civil[c]	28,166	29,742	52,144	57,512	48,809
Criminal	n.a.	37,063	37,070	30,665	31,114
Total	n.a.	66,805	89,214	88,177	79,923
OPA cases as a percentage of					
Civil	7.9	21.9	54.2	54.1	31.1
Criminal	n.a.	12.2	12.8	8.2	4.7
Total	n.a.	16.5	37.0	38.1	20.8
	Key prohibition years				
	1920	1925	1930	1931	1932
Prohibition cases[d]					
Civil	92	5,927	12,938	12,103	15,490
Criminal	5,095	47,925	52,706	61,521	69,155
Total	5,187	53,852	65,644	73,624	84,645
OPA cases as a percentage of					
Civil	2,412.0	110.1	218.6	256.9	97.9
Criminal	54.8	9.4	9.0	4.1	2.1
Total	96.6	20.5	50.3	45.7	19.6

[a] Excludes the District of Columbia and the Territories.
[b] This is the number of defendants and is somewhat larger than the number of cases commenced.
[c] Includes private cases about 5 percent of which were OPA related.
[d] Cases terminated.
Source: Wartime cases: Mansfield (1947G, p. 271); or Clinard (1952B, p. 38). Prohibition cases: Wooddy (1934B, p. 86).

The message of Table 5.10 is that reinstituting OPA-type controls would impose a substantial new burden on the judicial system. It is likely, moreover, that in peacetime the Congress, in writing the price control law, and the courts, in enforcing it, would give greater weight to the rights of alleged violators, further increasing the volume of judicial resources that would have to be devoted to price control cases. During the war the American Bar Association expressed concern over what it

Table 5.11. *OPA's challenges to the 100 largest corporations*

Corporation	Rank (Assets, 1935)	Date	Issue
1. Carnegie–Illinois Steel (subsidiary of U.S. Steel)	2	5/1945	Payment of overceiling prices[a]
2. Gulf Refining (subsidiary of Gulf Oil)	12	6/1945	Overcharging[a]
3. Swift	19	7/1944	Payment of overceiling prices
4. Armour	20	5/1943	Tie-in sales
5. American Tobacco	23	8/1946	Elimination of special discounts
6. Sears Roebuck	27	3/1946	Overcharging[a]
7. F. W. Woolworth	35	11/1944	Highest priced line limitation
8. Jones & Laughlin Steel	40	4/1944	Reduction of quantity discounts[a]
9. Montgomery Ward	47	12/1943	Highest price line limitation
10. Pure Oil	54	8/1945	Overceiling prices, record keeping
11. S. S. Kresge	70	2/1945	Tie-in sales[a]
12. Wilson	93	12/1942	Price posting rules
	93	1/1946	Pricing of new product[a]
13. Cudahy Packing	97	1/1945	Tie-in sales
14. J. C. Penney	98	7/1943	Ration coupon rules[a]

[a] The court found in favor of the corporation.
Source: Rockoff (1981a, J).

deemed the "Kangaroo Courts" conducted on occasion by the OPA.[72] Whatever the intrinsic merit of this charge, it seems likely that such charges would receive a more sympathetic hearing in peacetime, and would produce a complex network of legal safeguards.

Since it has been suggested that large corporations were more willing to cooperate with controls, it will be useful to look separately at the performance of these firms. Table 5.11 shows all of the cases that I have been able to find that were brought against firms ranked in the top 100 (by assets). In terms of the number of cases, the large corporations were not out of line with the percentages calculated for all firms. Many of the cases brought against large firms, however, involved violations through inadvertence or through an attempt to bend the rules. On the whole, the giant corporations did not openly defy the OPA. The cost in terms of outright sanctions, and in terms of public image, would have been too high. Instead they resisted in more subtle ways. During the postwar wave of labor unrest, for example, they made it clear, as we have seen, that they would prolong strikes if price increases were not granted. The methods employed by the giant corporations to resist the OPA, thus, were often different from those employed by small firms. But large firms as well as small ones created headaches for the OPA. The large firm had not evolved into some new form of entity which willingly cooperated with controls.

Findings of the Mitchell Committee

Another way to judge the extent of evasion is to examine the impact of evasion on the consumer price index. How accurate was the index? Did the index measure all of the inflation that occurred, or was evasion so serious that considerable inflation went unmeasured? This issue became politically important during the war. Organized labor was upset by the National War Labor Board's policy of limiting wage increases to a percentage equal to the increase in the consumer price index – the Little Steel Formula. So labor attacked the index on the grounds that it seriously understated the extent of inflation.[73] President Roosevelt responded by appointing a committee to examine the accuracy of the index. That committee in turn called on a group of experts headed by Wesley C. Mitchell, one of America's most distinguished economists, to investigate the index.

The Mitchell Committee found that the index understated inflation, but not nearly to the extent claimed by the labor unions. The set of errors found by the Mitchell Committee is displayed in Table 5.12. For example, because of quality deterioration in food (more fat in hamburger, and so on) the true food index in December 1943 was probably from one to three percent higher than the index published by the Bureau of Labor Statistics. For the index as a whole, the Mitchell Committee found a probable error, after weighting the components in Table 5.12, of from 2.8 to 3.6 percent in December 1943, a relatively modest number.[74]

The Mitchell Committee's estimate, however, neglected the impact of many of the problems discussed above: forced uptrading in clothing, quality deterioration in fuel, and so on. Their reasons for neglecting these problems, as we will see below, were valid given the task set for

Table 5.12. *The Mitchell Committee's estimate of the potential errors in the Consumer Price Index, December 1943 (percentage)*

Component index	Source of error				
	Quality deterioration	Elimination of sales	Forced uptrading	Under-reporting	Miscellaneous
Food	1–3	0.5	0	0.5–1	0
Clothing	4–5	1	0	0	0
House furnishings	7–9	1	1–2	0	0
Rent	0	0	0	0	1.5[a]
Fuel, electricity, ice	0	0	0	0	0
Miscellaneous	0	0	0	0	0

[a] New-unit bias (1) and rooming rent bias (.5). See the Committee's report for details.
Source: Mitchell (1945G, pp. 316, 337, 355, 365–9).

the committee, but we will also see that these omissions mean that the Committee's estimates cannot be considered a complete measure of hidden inflation. They are better viewed as a lower bound.

In the first place, the consumer price index referred to a market basket purchased by workers and low-income, salaried employees in the latter part of the depression. Since the demand for higher quality goods grew more rapidly than for the items in this market basket, evasion and black markets were probably more severe outside the group of commodities that were covered by the consumer price index and subject to the committee's scrutiny. Other indexes would have to be adjusted by more.

Second, and this gets at the heart of the matter, the Mitchell Committee felt that certain burdens should be shared by labor during the war. Hence, it excluded some kinds of quality deterioration and other forms of evasion which it knew to be taking place – longer waiting times in service establishments, quality deterioration in clothing and certain other commodities other than deterioration in durability, and so on – from its estimate of the error in the index. These were burdens the committee felt should rightly be shared by labor. This is not a criticism of the Mitchell Committee. The question then at issue was whether the consumer price index was a fair basis for adjusting wages, and if not, what adjustments had to be made to the index to make it fair. It is a reason, however, for being cautious in using the Committee's findings for other purposes. This restriction has been missed by later users of the Committee's estimates.

Third, and perhaps equally important, the Committee estimated the error that had accumulated between January 1, 1941, and December 1943. December 1943 was still relatively early in the period of stringent control. Roosevelt's Hold-the-Line Order had come only eight months earlier. Stringent controls continued until February 1946, another twenty-six months. Since excess demand was accumulating during this period, evasion and black markets grew worse. In addition, patriotism was a less potent influence after the Allies had won the decisive battles. In December 1943, D-Day was still six months away.

I have attempted to overcome the timing problem by extrapolating the Mitchell Committee's estimates to June 1946 when controls expired. The methods used were simple, but I think they produced a conservative estimate in the spirit of the Committee's efforts. The extrapolations are given in Table 5.13. The idea behind the extrapolations in the first line

Table 5.13. *Summary of adjustments to the Consumer Price Index, December 1943 and June 1946 (percentages)*

Source	December 1943		June 1946	
	Lower bound	Upper bound	Lower bound	Upper bound
Concealed price increases (Mitchell Committee)	2.0	3.2	3.2	4.8
Quality deterioration in rented dwellings	1.0	1.3	1.0	1.3
Shortages of consumer durables	1.1	2.3	0.3	0.6
Shortages of meat	0	0	0.3	0.6
Total	4.1	6.8	4.8	7.3

Source: Rockoff (1978J, p. 417).

was to keep the same ratio between unmeasured and measured inflation for the two periods December 1943–June 1946 and January 1941–December 1943. It seems to me likely that the ratio was higher in the latter period, so that if anything, the errors were larger than indicated in the table. Overall these estimates imply an understatement of the price level of from 3.2 to 4.8 percent in June 1946, if the Mitchell Committee's definitions are strictly maintained.

An estimate that included an allowance for the burden of the shortages of meat and consumer durables which afflicted the economy in June 1946 and for the quality deterioration in rented dwellings, also shown in Table 5.13, put the total error at from 4.8 to 7.3 percent. All of these errors disappeared in the postwar period, and so should be subtracted from postwar price increases to get a more accurate picture of postwar price movements.

Public opinion polls

Finally, we can consider a form of evidence frequently neglected by economic historians: public opinion polls. During the war the National Opinion Research Center took six polls of cross sections of the American people and questioned them on whether they had observed violations of the price control laws. The results are presented in Table 5.14. Line one of the table, for example, can be interpreted as follows. Sometime close to May 5, 1943, the Center asked a large representative sample of American men and women whether they personally had ever observed a violation of the price control laws. In that poll 12 percent said they had, 75 percent said they had not, and 13 percent said they were not sure or gave qualified answers. Four of the five subsequent polls were restricted to women, because it was felt that the women did the shopping and would therefore be better informed. The polls show that a substantial number of people were familiar with evasions – perhaps around 30 percent, if one looks at the polls in June 1944 and February 1945.

There are, it is true, a number of problems with this evidence. No allowance is made for the number and type of evasions observed. A person who saw one can of tomato soup selling for one penny over the ceiling would have the same influence on the final percentage as someone who observed hundreds of cars being sold for hundreds of dollars over the ceiling. It is not clear, moreover, how broadly the interviewees interpreted the question. It seems likely that if someone had observed

Table 5.14. *National Opinion Research Center polls on price violations during World War II*

| | | | Have you observed violations?[a] | | |
| | | | | | |
Date	Group	Reference period	Yes (%)	No (%)	Other answers (%)
5/1943	Men and women	Ever	12	75	13
12/1943	Women	Ever	9	65	26
1/1944	Men and women	Last few weeks	11	89	—[b]
6/1944	Women	Ever	32	56	12
2/1945	Women	Ever	31	69	—[b]
8/1945	Women	Last six months	25	75	—[b]

[a] This is a paraphrase. The exact question changed from poll to poll.
[b] Less than 0.5 percent.
Sources: Line 1: Cantrill (1951B, 45). Line 2: Ibid., p. 659. Line 3: Ibid., pp. 659–60. Line 4: Ibid., p. 660. Line 5: National Opinion Research Center (1945A,U). Line 6: National Opinion Research Center (1945B,U).

an item subject to a dollar-and-cents ceiling with a larger price tag, they would have answered yes to the Opinion Research Center pollster. But what if they observed some evasive technique, too much fat on the margin of a steak, a tie-in sale, and so on?

A more serious problem stems from the possibility that some people may have been afraid to cooperate. It was unpatriotic to buy on the black market; millions of people had taken a pledge to fight the black market. Would people answer that they had observed violations if it could be construed that actively or passively they were cooperating with an unpatriotic activity? One way around this problem would be to use a concealed interview technique, to engage people in a discussion of the issues without letting them know that they are being polled by an "official" organization. Unfortunately, this was never tried on a national scale. One poll was taken in this manner in New York City by students from the City College of New York supervised by Seymour Lipset. This survey reported considerably more black market activity. Of the 300 shoppers interviewed, one-third said they bought on the black market regularly, and seventy percent said they sometimes violated OPA regulations.[75] There is no way of telling whether this poll was different primarily because the polling technique was different, or because New York was different.

Professor Galbraith has suggested that the social memory (to use his evocative phrase) of World War I is of inflation, while the social memory of World War II is not.[76] His point is that in the second war controls kept inflation to "acceptable" levels. But to what extent do memories of black markets and shortages still remain with people who lived through the experience?[77] In other words, was the black market also kept to acceptable levels by this criteria? The question is of sufficient importance to justify a careful study of a large representative sample of people from the war generation, the kind of project that has become popular under the rubric of "oral history." Until such a study is completed, any assertions about the social memory of the war must remain tentative. A plausible answer is suggested in Roy Hoopes's *Americans Remember the Home Front: An Oral Narrative.* Hoopes's sample is not representative in the statistician's sense; every American in the war generation did not have an equal chance of being chosen. But it is representative in the more colloquial sense that it includes people from "all walks of life." It is possible, moreover, that a sensitive journalist, such as Hoopes, may be able to develop a truer picture of the memory of the war than a technically more advanced, but less sensitive statistician.

About 66 percent of the people he interviewed mentioned rationing or shortages. About 31 percent mentioned the black market. And far more people remembered these aspects of the war than remembered any other feature of the homefront such as civil defense.[78] Evidently, the regimentation of economic life left an indelible imprint.

A summary

Now we can answer the four major questions which people ask about price and wage controls in World War II. (1) What was the effect on prices? Did controls work in the sense of keeping inflation to a tolerably low level? Was any temporary suppression of prices offset by a postwar price explosion? (2) Did controls require a huge administrative bureaucracy, one that employed a substantial share of the nation's resources? (3) How smoothly did rationing work? Were shortages few and far between or did controls damage the aggregate efficiency of the economy? (4) Did controls produce an extensive black market?

Controls did reduce inflation and protect the real value of vulnerable incomes, although this statement must be qualified by noting that it applies to only part of the period. When controls were maintained across the board and backed up by wage controls, vigorous enforcement and rationing, price increases, although not held to zero (particularly when evasion is taken into account), were clearly reduced to low levels. When controls were applied selectively and backed up solely by appeals to patriotism, and vague threats, they failed to prevent inflation from continuing at alarming levels. In the year before President Roosevelt's Hold-The-Line Order, consumer prices rose at an annual rate of 11.9 percent. After the hold-the-line policy was scrapped, the official index rose at an annual rate of 8.4 percent. In contrast, during the hold-the-line period itself, prices rose at a rate of only 1.6 percent per year, thus protecting fixed incomes. The hold-the-line period corresponded almost exactly to the maximum effort by the OPA in the areas of rationing and enforcement.

The limitation of success to the hold-the-line period was not accidental. With demand pressures strong, control over part of the price structure led people to shift expenditures to uncontrolled areas, forcing prices up even faster in those areas. Only across-the-board controls worked.

To be sure, the end of price controls witnessed a substantial surge of prices. But had there been no controls during the war, the government would have run larger deficits and created more money to cover them. Postwar prices would have been still higher than they actually were. There was, in other words, a postwar surge in prices, but prices did not reach the level they would have reached in the absence of controls.

The second question is how large a bureaucracy was created to administer controls during World War II? No precise answer can be given because the answer depends on arbitrary judgments about which agencies to include and how to evaluate the contribution of volunteers. But a fairly generous estimate suggests that about 150,000 people were involved with controlling the civilian economy in World War II. Was this a "large" bureaucracy – something to be shunned in a peacetime economy? Not really. The whole bureaucracy, even at the wartime peak, was smaller than the Post Office Department. Even making allowance for a large bureaucracy within the business sector would not substantially change this judgment.

The third question concerned the effects of controls on economic efficiency. It was clear from our examination of this issue that, while rationing created headaches and while individual examples of inefficiency could be given, any case that controls damaged the aggregate productive power of the economy would be built on slender reeds. Most of the available evidence goes the other way – it shows the wartime economy to have been highly productive.

Finally, having surveyed the evidence on the extent of evasion, what conclusion should be drawn, what adjective should be applied? Extensive? Insignificant? Marshall Clinard, the historian of the black market in World War II, wrote that

Such extensive conniving in the black market in illegal prices and rationed commodities took place among so many business men, ordinary criminals, and even average citizens that serious questions might be raised as to the moral fiber of the American people.[79]

The additional evidence surveyed here merely reinforces Clinard's judgment that the black market was extensive, although as an economic historian I am permitted few illusions about moral fiber. What I would add is that successful control of the black market always turned on an extension of governmental power that would be unacceptable to most Americans in a peacetime economy.

A final conclusion about the relevance of the World War II experience must wait until Chapter 8 when the full set of examples will be available from which to make comparisons and generalizations. But the World War II experience is so important to the general picture of controls that finally emerges, that it is useful here to anticipate the conclusions by asking what generalization could be produced from this one episode. The answer, it seems to me, is this: The modern state has the power to control prices even in the face of a vast expansion of aggregate demand relative to output, but it can do so only through a drastic regimentation of economic life. Such regimentation was appropriate in the war, when no other mechanism capable of protecting the real incomes of vulnerable groups such as monetary and fiscal austerity was politically feasible, when expectations of inflation were themselves a cause of inflation, and when the community was willing to cooperate in the effort. But when the termination of the war ended the balance of costs and benefits swung against controls, and they were removed. Sometimes democracies (despite their critics) make the right decisions and I believe we did so during and after the war with respect to controls. The lesson for the future is that a short-term application of controls might make sense as an emergency measure, but permanent controls, especially if combined with an expansionary monetary and fiscal policy, would be a mistake.

6. The Korean War

At the present time, we are beginning to impose price and wage controls. Extension of such controls now appears inescapable. To administer such controls, as well as to promote effective voluntary cooperation, price and wage specialists are being recruited and offices are being opened in various cities as rapidly as they can be manned.

Harry S. Truman, January 15, 1951

The crisis

On June 25, 1950 North Korea invaded South Korea. One of the consequences of this action, and of the American response, was a wave of inflation and speculative hoarding on the American home front that would soon produce a call for extensive wage and price controls. President Truman responded quickly to the invasion by authorizing the use of U.S. troops and ordering air strikes and a naval blockade. He did not, however, seek a declaration of war, or call for full mobilization, in part because such actions might have been misinterpreted by Russia and China. Instead, on July 19 he called for partial mobilization and asked Congress for an appropriation of $10 billion for the war. The reluctance to mobilize fully and to embrace across-the-board controls was reinforced by Leon Keyserling of the newly formed Council of Economic Advisors, who argued that price controls at that time would interfere with the expansion of production, the only real hope, as he saw it, for avoiding inflation.[1]

Military events also delayed imposition of across-the-board controls. The Inchon landing and related actions undertaken in the latter half of September created the expectation of an early end to the war. As a result, the wave of speculative buying (focusing on goods which had been in short supply during World War II, particularly consumer durables) came to a temporary halt. With some reason, the hope developed, particularly in the government, that the inflation would soon abate.

Popular sentiment for across-the-board controls, however, was strong throughout the period. A Gallup Poll taken on June 30, 1950, just after the North Korean invasion, showed that 55 percent of the public thought a wage–price freeze was a good idea. By October the percentage who favored a freeze had risen to 63 percent.[2] Popular support for controls flowed partly from some simple economic ideas. Frequently, people see that inflation reduces the value of the increments in income they earn, but not that their income grows, in part, as a result of inflation. The favorable attitude toward controls also reflected favorable memories of how well controls worked during the hold-the-line phase in World War II. The public's willingness to embrace them again, after such a short period of time, is testimony to at least the surface effectiveness of controls in World War II. The popularity of price controls was reflected in the Congress. Particularly influential was the testimony of Bernard Baruch, who argued, as he had in the early days of World War II, that an across-the-board freeze was crucial to effective mobilization.[3]

Even in the business community there was strong support in certain quarters for controls. As early as July the major steel producers said they favored a government-administered program of rationing and price control in the event that the Korean conflict turned into a major war. At first glance this may seem an unusual stance. Would they not be likely to gain more in an uncontrolled market? Perhaps, in the short run. But the steel makers had longer term interests in mind, a concern they voiced in public statements. In an uncontrolled market they would constantly be faced with the awkward task of turning away long-term customers in order to take the profitable wartime contracts, thus damaging relationships that would be important after the war. The presence of a governmental allocator would allow the steelmakers to tell a long-term customer that they were *forced* to turn down their request.[4]

In response to public and business pressure Congress passed the Defense Production Act in September 1950. The law gave the President a wide range of options, including the imposition of selective or of across-the-board controls. There were few limitations to his potential powers. He was required, however, to control wages in any industry where prices were controlled, and to provide protection for individual firms against arbitrary decisions by the price authority. The statute, moreover, included a specific termination date for the program: June 30, 1951.

Truman decided not to exercise his drastic options immediately. Instead, he chose to urge voluntary restraint, while stabilizing selected wages and prices. He also began filling posts in the bureaucracy that would eventually administer controls. In mid-September, following a declaration of a national emergency, Truman appointed Charles Edward Wilson of General Electric to head the Office of Defense Mobilization. In October he appointed Alan Valentine to head the Economic Stabilization Agency, to oversee the whole effort, and Cyrus Ching to head the Wage Stabilization Board. About a month later he appointed Michael V. DiSalle, the energetic mayor of Toledo, Ohio, to the position of Price Stabilization Director. Eventually, DiSalle came to play a role similar to the one played by Chester Bowles in World War II. Both men believed passionately in the value of tough wartime price controls, and both had a gift for communicating their enthusiasm. DiSalle soon became the rallying point for administration forces that wanted an across-the-board freeze. His boss, Valentine, demurred, citing among other factors the absence of a bureaucracy to administer the freeze.

The tide of events, however, lay with DiSalle. MacArthur's forces were in retreat in Korea, after the Chinese intervention, prices were rising rapidly at home, and the limited measures for controlling them that had been taken did not seem to be enough. The President had ordered a rollback of automobile prices, had imposed controls on raw materials prices, and had promised that similar controls would follow in similar situations. But for other sectors there was only the Economic Stabilization Agency's warning that "unjustified" increases would be rolled back, and its call (on December 19) for a voluntary freeze. The latter initiative, in particular, seems to have had little effect. On January 19, 1951, Valentine resigned. On January 23, the Office of Price Stabilization (OPS) was formed, analogous to the Office of Price Administration in World War II. This gave greater authority to DiSalle, the most determined advocate of a freeze. DiSalle had explained his position to Senator Taft by likening price control to "bobbing a cat's tail." It was better to do it close to the body all at once. If you did it an inch at a time you always had a mad cat with a sore tail.[5] On January 26 DiSalle saw his philosophy prevail. The Economic Stabilization Agency ordered a freeze on most wages at their current level and most prices at the maximum level at which there had been transactions during the period December 19 to January 25.

DiSalle and his staff recognized that the freeze would only be effective for a short period. They anticipated that a major problem would be created by firms squeezed by rising costs. Retailers, for example, might be caught as they replenished inventories at higher prices while their selling prices were fixed. In addition, the administration had been calling for voluntary restraint, and it hardly seemed fair to punish those firms that had acted in the public interest. The OPS, therefore, planned a series of "roll-forwards" which provided price increases for firms caught in a cost–price squeeze. The Office hoped to balance these, at least to some extent, by ordering rollbacks where prices had been raised to "unreasonable" levels in anticipation of the freeze. As it turned out, however, squeezes were not as widespread as anticipated.[6] Most businesses had anticipated the freeze and were not caught in an untenable position. This is in sharp contrast with the situation in the early days of World War II in which some firms, because of their inexperience with inflation and controls, had been slow to adjust.

After imposing the freeze and dealing with the few squeezes that did develop, the OPS set out to write regulations "tailored" to the peculiarities of particular industries. For retailers and wholesalers this meant setting maximum margins. Initially, margin regulations issued in World War II were reissued. Later, margin regulations consistent with an amendment to the Defense Production Act, which required pre–Korean War retail and wholesale margins to be met, were issued. For industrial concerns "tailored" regulations involved the development of a complex earnings standard under which price increases could be granted. Eventually, the OPS was able to summarize its policy in a set of four tests for the adequacy of an existing price ceiling. First, an industry had to be earning at least 85 percent of its average for the best three years of the 1946–9 period. If not, price increases were justified. Second, on any particular product line the average producer had to be at least breaking even. If not, increases in that line were justified. Third, individual sellers were allowed increases to avoid losses. Finally, without regard to any earnings standard, prices could be raised to protect the supply of an item vital to the defense effort.[7]

Numerous exemptions from control had been stipulated in the original Defense Production Act: real property; professional services; publications of press associations, books, magazines, motion pictures and newspapers, radio, television, theaters, and outdoor advertising; insurance rates, rates of public utilities and terminal warehouses; commodity exchange requirements; and sales by states and other political subdivisions – all of these were exempt from control. The justifications for most of these exemptions were clear. In the case of professional services, there was a fear of interfering with prices that were part of a sensitive interpersonal relationship, and that formed the income of powerful interest groups. In the cases of prices already regulated by government agencies or directly charged by them, constitutional scruples played a role. And in the case of prices charged by the news and entertainment media, the desire was to avoid censorship. Had an expansionary monetary policy been followed, it is likely that price increases in the exempt sectors would have posed a serious problem for the stabilization effort.

Weakening amendments

Across-the-board controls had just been instituted when a barrage of amendments were added to the initial legislation which further reduced the ability of the OPS to control prices. The administration, and liberal members of Congress, fought these amendments bitterly, blaming them on the power of special interests. There was, to be sure, an element of self-preservation in liberal complaints, since any later failures could then be blamed on the weakening amendments rather than the original law or its administrators. But there is no doubt that the amendments made the administration of controls more difficult, and might have been damaging if controls had been forced to contend with considerable excess demand. The failure of the President, and his Congressional allies, to resist these amendments can be traced, in part, to the rapid erosion of public confidence in the program. The evidence is that by mid-June of 1952 there was widespread dissatisfaction with the controls. The Gallup Poll asked whether the price control laws had worked well or not, and only 31 percent answered yes. Forty-five percent answered no, and 24 percent fell into the no-opinion category.[8] In part this disappointing result reflected the nature of the question. People are inherently skeptical about the performance of government bureaucrats. In part, however, it reflected the contrast between the reality of the controls and people's expectations that prices would not only be held in check but that they would also be rolled back.

The amendments that limited the scope of meat price controls were particularly troubling for the OPS because of the crucial role of this market in forming public attitudes toward the whole program. In mid-

June Gallup asked the following question: Considering the items you buy from day to day, which one annoys you most because of the high price you have to pay for it? Fully 60 percent of the respondents answered meat. No other commodity came close.[9] DiSalle was acutely aware both of the general attitude toward the administration of controls and of the extent to which the price of meat, particularly beef, shaped those opinions. Gardner Ackley, an economic adviser to the Office of Price Stabilization who later wrote the fullest account of the episode, described the relationship in this way: "The cost of living is high when hamburgers, or T-bone steak, is expensive. Price control works well if beef is available, of good quality, and low in price."[10] DiSalle was determined to meet the public's demand for lower beef prices. Against the advice of his economists, who were concerned with the effect of lower prices on supply, he ordered a rollback of beef prices when dollar-and-cents ceilings were issued late in April. Further rollbacks were contemplated.[11]

But the beef producers were adamantly opposed to this policy, and perhaps emboldened by the success they had achieved in getting Truman to remove controls in 1946, they pressed their case on Congress. The result was the antirollback amendment included in the Defense Production Act Amendments of 1951. This amendment prohibited the OPS from setting any ceiling on any agricultural product below 90 percent of the price prevailing on May 19, 1951 (as determined by the Secretary of Agriculture). This formula had, of course, been chosen deliberately to prevent further reductions in beef prices.[12] The Secretary of Agriculture, who was sympathetic to the producers, was likely to resolve uncertainties in their favor. The law was also amended to prohibit any restriction on the amount of livestock that could be handled by a particular slaughterer.[13] This prohibition significantly reduced the chance of preventing shortages or a black market. The President and Congressional liberals challenged these amendments, but to no avail.

There had already been some complaints of shortages of meat, for example, by the Division of Standards and Purchase of New York State, and by the fall of 1951 violations of cattle ceilings appeared widespread.[14] But with no method for rationing supplies, there was little that the OPS could do. Only an early end to controls, and a restrictive monetary policy, prevented this market from becoming the disaster that it had been in the closing days of World War II.

The Capehart Amendment created analogous difficulties for the OPS

in the manufacturing sector. This amendment provided that a manufacturer could apply for an increase in the ceiling on a particular item
to a level equal to the highest price received for that item in the period
January 1, 1950 to June 24, 1950, the preemergency period, plus increased costs incurred prior to July 26, 1951.[15] This formula considerably
reduced the ability of the OPS to hold down the general price level: it
prevented offsetting rollforwards with rollbacks. And since many costs
were weakly controlled even after the "freeze" – these included certain
wages, the prices of imported raw materials, and so on – this formula
meant granting many substantial increases. The amendment was also
hard to implement, as the administration's opponents of the measure
argued forcefully.

The greatest problem for the amendment was posed by large corporations. Costs are notoriously difficult to allocate in the multiproduct
firm. In practice there is no unambiguous answer to what the costs of
production are for a particular product. Since application for an increase
under the Capehart formula was at the discretion of the manufacturers,
it was likely that they would load overhead costs on those products for
which they were challenging the price ceilings. The defense for the
Capehart formula rested on an equity argument. The amendment protected individual firms from capricious decisions, and provided only
for the maintenance of profit levels, perhaps even a lowering of the real
value of profits after adjusting for inflation.

A related amendment provided retailers and wholesalers with their
customary markup during the period May 24 to June 24, 1950.[16] It was
open to similar objections and could be justified with similar arguments.
Different retailers would sell the same item for different prices, dependent
on their own, somewhat arbitrary, cost calculations. Again, the OPS
would be forced to ratify price increases that began with costs that
were in part beyond its control. The defense, once again, was that it
protected the small businessman from discriminatory decisions, and
protected his nominal (if not his real) profits. The greater weight given
to protection of the individual business, and to special interests, in the
Korean War compared with most of World War II is accounted for
partly by the changed political makeup of the Congress and partly by
the limited nature of the war. There was less reason in the Korean War
to abandon "politics as usual." The clear implication of this experience,
along with that in World War II toward the end of controls, is that
any peacetime controls program, particularly one continued long after

the inflationary emergency has passed, is likely to be riddled with exemptions that considerably limit the ability of the price authority to carry out its mandate.

Outright exemptions from price control were also multiplied in subsequent legislation.[17] In 1951 wage exemptions were expanded to include the wages of workers in agriculture, small businesses, and bowling alleys, as well as the wages of barbers and beauticians. The professional exemption was narrowed somewhat the first time around, but in 1952 it was expanded to include the fees charged by engineers, architects, and CPAs. Perhaps most alarming to the OPS was the exemption of fresh fruits and vegetables in 1952. This action was prompted primarily by a shortage and black market in potatoes.[18] But the exemption covered all fruits and vegetables, which together accounted for about one-fifth of the consumer's food dollar.

Decontrol

Whether the controls, weakened in this way, would have been effective against a new round of inflation turned out to be a moot question. Inflationary pressures abated in 1952. Indeed, demand was so weak in many sectors that prices were below their ceilings. This state of affairs naturally aroused sentiment for decontrol. Why maintain a bureaucracy and all of its petty annoyances, people reasoned, if there was no pressing need for it?

In fact, the OPS had, almost from its inception, followed a policy of decontrolling certain items. But this policy at first was largely cosmetic. The proportion of the wholesale price index covered by controls fell steadily but slowly from 87.3 percent in January 1951 to 70.2 in December 1952.[19] Part of this change, moreover, was mandated by law. Many of the items that the OPS voluntarily decontrolled were of trivial significance, and many that were not were decontrolled with the threat that they would be recontrolled if the price rose to some predetermined level, and with the new ceiling no higher than before. While the latter items had technically been decontrolled, the situation was far removed from what we ordinarily think of as a free market. Thus, while the OPS's policy served to disarm critics of the agency – for example, those who claimed that DiSalle wanted to fasten a permanent system of controls on the country – it is clear that the OPS's basic philosophy was reminiscent of the hold-the-line policy in World War II.

The real end to controls was a product of the change in the Presidency. At first General Eisenhower's views concerning controls were not well known. One report in January 1952 suggested that he might support some kinds of controls.[20] Later statements seemed opposed to controls. In January of 1952 DiSalle, responding in part to what he perceived as the trend in the General's thinking, announced his intention to resign from the OPS and to run for the Senate from Ohio, a race he ultimately lost.[21] President Eisenhower's State of the Union address in February 1953 left no doubt about his position; it called for an immediate end to most of the regulations. A series of sweeping decontrol orders issued soon after ended controls in March 1953. Although there were some price increases after controls were removed, there was nothing to compare with the price explosion that had followed the removal of controls in 1946; the Korean War controls ended not with a bang but a whimper. This is an important but neglected fact. It shows that a temporary control program need not be followed, as some have argued, by a post-control price explosion.

The effect on prices

Table 6.1 shows the rate of growth of prices, wages, and money per unit of real output before, during, and after the Korean controls. It is clear, first of all, that monetary pressure does not explain the rapid increase in prices that began with the outbreak of the war. Money per unit of real output actually *fell* at an annual rate of 6.4 percent while prices *rose* at a rate of 11.1 percent per year. The real reason for the inflation was the anticipation of still more inflation and shortages once expenditures for war began to make themselves felt. With these antic-ipations widely held, businesses could easily raise prices and find willing buyers. Wages, moreover, did not lag behind consumer prices. Labor demanded higher wages and the increases were granted because businesses knew they could afford them, and knew that it was crucial to pay them to keep their labor force intact during the coming boom. Inflation, in short, was based on fears about the future: Price controls quickly arrested this inflationary spiral. The consumer price index rose at an annual rate of only 2.1 percent per year under controls. With the anticipated rate of inflation much reduced, the actual demand pressure on prices declined.

Table 6.1. *Prices, wages, and money per unit of real output during the Korean War*

Period	Annual percentage rates of change		
	Prices	Wages	Money per unit of real output
June 1950–Jan. 1951 (outbreak of war–price freeze)	11.1	11.8	−6.4
Jan. 1951–Feb. 1953 (price freeze – termination of controls)	2.1	5.6	−0.4
Feb. 1953–Oct. 1953 (termination of controls – postwar price peak)	2.6	3.4	4.1
June 1950–Oct. 1953 (total period)	3.8	6.3	−0.6

Notes: Prices: The Consumer Price Index. Wages: Production Worker Average Hourly Earnings in Dollars. Money Per Unit Real Output: M_2 divided by Real GNP. Quarterly real GNP was interpolated linearly to estimate real GNP for the appropriate month. These series are not adjusted for the effects of evasion. Subsequent sections show, however, that evasion during the Korean War was far more limited than in World War II. It is therefore unlikely that adjusting for evasion would materially change the inferences drawn from the table.
Sources: Prices: various issues of the *Monthly Labor Review.* Wages: U.S. Department of Labor, Bureau of Labor Statistics (1976G, p. 40). Money: Friedman and Schwartz (1970B, Table 1, column 9, pp 41–43). Real output: various issues of the *Survey of Current Business.*

It is true that if the restrictive monetary policy which prevailed during the precontrol and control periods had been maintained in the face of rising prices it would have eventually arrested the inflation without controls. But it is likely that the restrictive monetary policy itself would have been abandoned before it had taken effect. Rising prices would have meant larger arms bills, larger government deficits, and more money created to finance those deficits.

Milton Friedman and Anna J. Schwartz in their *Monetary History* ignored controls, arguing that other events dampened the inflation.[22] In particular, they singled out the Treasury–Federal Reserve Accord of March 1951, noting that the upward surge of prices ended at about the same time. The Accord freed the Federal Reserve from the obligation of fixing bond prices, a policy that had been followed since the beginning of World War II. It was feared that if the Federal Reserve tried to preserve bond prices in a market in which economic pressures were forcing interest rates up, it would become a mere engine of inflation, buying up far more bonds than it wanted. The announcement of the Accord tended to dampen inflation in two ways. First, it put the public on notice that the Federal Reserve was now free to fight inflation through a more restrictive monetary policy; this would cause knowledgeable observers to revise their expectation of future inflation. In addition, by reducing the liquidity of government bonds it encouraged the public to hold more cash, which may have reduced the willingness to spend. But both effects, intuitively at least, seem small and uncertain compared with the dramatic announcement of a mandatory freeze on wages and prices, particularly when it is considered that many professional economists at this time argued that monetary policy was of minor importance in determining the rate of inflation.

Two other events occurring at the beginning of the period also served to dampen inflation: Taxes were raised, clearly an action that would quiet fears of a runaway inflation. And Bert Hickman has argued that the demand for many products, particularly durables, decreased as consumers worked down stocks purchased in the speculative buying sprees which occurred in the early months of the war.[23] But again it would seem intuitively that these factors must be ranked after controls as forces which halted the inflationary spiral. Inflationary expectations, the driving force behind the inflation, were changed most by the evidence people had directly before their senses, not by long and controversial chains of reasoning accepted by a minority of experts, nor by events limited to a few markets.

Where the Accord and a conservative fiscal policy were important, however, was in making possible the remarkably slow growth in money per unit of output during the control period. This measure of monetary policy actually *fell* at an annual rate of 0.4 percent per year, a performance that undoubtedly eased the problems of the price controllers. More important, it meant that strong inflationary pressures were not built up during the War. This is the reason why a price explosion of the type which had followed World War II did not occur when controls were removed in early 1953. As Table 6.1 shows, the consumer price index rose at a gentle rate of 2.6 percent from the end of controls to the postwar price peak.

On the whole then, controls during the Korean War, although the product of a rough melange of political forces, were coordinated almost perfectly with monetary policy. They were imposed to halt an inflation that was the product of inflationary expectations rather than an over-

Table 6.2. *The cost of administering controls in the Korean War*

Fiscal year	ESA (millions of dollars)[a]	Related agencies[b] (millions of dollars)	ESA as a percentage of Postal Service expenditures	ESA and related agencies as a percentage of Postal Service expenditures[c]
1952	91	6	3.4	3.6
1953	64	7	2.3	2.6
1954	1.5	0.4	0.06	0.07

[a] Check-issued basis. ESA, Economic Stabilization Agency.
[b] Office of Defense Mobilization, Defense Materials Procurement Agency, Defense Production Administration, Defense Transport Administration.
[c] Postal Service Expenditures are on a net obligation basis.
Sources: U.S. Treasury (1952–54G); U.S. Bureau of the Budget (1953–55G).

expansive monetary and fiscal policy. At the same time a restrictive monetary policy for the duration of the period was assured through the Accord and subsequent actions by the Federal Reserve. Inflation was arrested. Finally, controls were lifted, and because restrictive policies had been in effect, no postcontrol explosion in prices occurred. The benefits from this policy were the protections afforded those living on fixed incomes and those who for other reasons could not win quick adjustments in their incomes. Average real annual earnings in public education, for example, fell (although only slightly) from 1950 to 1951, but then rose, under controls, from 1951 to 1952 and from 1952 to 1953.

The size of the bureaucracy

A restrictive monetary policy, and a short-term application of controls, made it possible to carry out the program of price controls with a much smaller volume of real resources than was employed in World War II. One is tempted to say, in fact, an almost trivial volume of resources. Table 6.2 shows the costs of administering the Korean War Controls.[24] In 1952 the relevant agencies – the Office of Price Stabilization, other agencies under the general umbrella of the Economic Stabilization Agency, and more distantly related agencies that undertook functions ordinarily performed by the market – together spent less than 4 percent as much as the Post Office. Surely no one would argue that increasing the budget of the Post Office 4 percent, say by raising the price of stamps, would crush the economy under an intolerable weight.

The Korean War bureaucracies made some use of volunteers from the private sector. But there is no reason to think that greater use was made of them in the Korean War than in World War II. Hence, the conclusion reached concerning the use of volunteers in the latter war, that they played a minor role, also applies here. It is true that businesses incurred considerable costs in dealing with the regulations. Unfortunately there do not appear to be data available on the extent of these costs during the Korean War. During the Vietnam War, the most reliable survey put these costs at from 7½ to 21 times as much as the visible costs incurred by government. While such high ratios were probably not the case during the Korean War (because rules were changed less frequently, and because monetary policy was more favorable), these figures nevertheless suggest that compliance costs on the business side were much in excess of the figures shown in Table 6.2. Still, these costs were small in comparison with the inequities of sudden and rapid inflation. It should also be noted that estimates of business costs ignore the savings which accrue to business under controls because fewer resources are devoted to monitoring the prices charged by rivals.

Efficiency

It is possible to assemble some dramatic examples from the Korean period that illustrate the tendency of price controls, particularly when not accompanied by rationing, to produce shortages or other manifestations of inefficiency. One, discussed above, is the rolling back of beef prices. This action, undertaken for political purposes, and over the objections of the economists at the OPS, produced troublesome shortages. A second example, discussed in the next section, was the "gray" market in steel. The steel rationing program sometimes denied steel to the users with the strongest demands. In a free market these users would have bid steel away from those with less pressing needs; the market would have assured that steel was employed where it would produce the most output as valued by consumers. To be sure, in some cases rationing was shifting steel from producers of consumer goods to producers of war goods, a useful process. But in some cases rationing was merely shifting steel (in comparison with the free market allocation) from one producer of civilian goods to another, with a net loss in total output.

Table 6.3. *Year-to-year percentage changes in productivity, 1948–1958*

Year	Total factor productivity (Kendrick)	Expected total factor productivity (Kendrick)	Total factor productivity (Denison)	Adjusted total factor productivity (Denison)
1948–49	2.48	0.65	−0.75	0.53
1949–50	6.65	3.73	6.85	3.29
1950–51	0.80	2.67	0.73	2.29
1951–52	0.11	2.10	0.13	1.38
1952–53	3.25	2.79	2.61	2.89
1953–54	2.18	0.63	−0.05	1.36
1954–55	4.43	3.34	6.14	2.25
1955–56	−0.41	2.02	0.59	1.63
1956–57	1.23	1.74	0.35	1.65
1957–58	2.22	0.61	−0.45	0.90

Sources and methods: Column 1: U.S. Bureau of Economic Analysis (1973G, series A161, p. 209). Column 2: the predicted values from the equation $P = 2.16 + 0.14C$, where P is the percentage change in productivity and C is the percentage change in the Federal Reserve Board's estimate of capacity utilization. This series is from various issues of the *Federal Reserve Bulletin*. The equation was fitted over the years 1948–9 to 1968–9. The t statistics are 6.88 and 2.71, respectively, and the R^2 was .24. Capacity utilization produced the best fit of several measures of aggregate demand. Omitting the war years from the regression does not change things significantly. Columns 3 and 4: Denison (1974B, Table 6-1, columns 1–3, 9, p. 62).

The gray market greatly ameliorated this problem. But the resources employed in running the gray market were used inefficiently.

These examples do not show, as was emphasized in preceding chapters, that on average the controllers made more mistakes in setting relative prices than the free market would have, although critics of controls are quick to point to examples of this sort. Neither the markets for beef nor steel nor the myriad of markets which did not experience difficulties during the war function perfectly in the absence of controls. Only aggregate measures of productivity change, such as those given in Table 6.3, can provide potentially convincing evidence on whether controls damaged efficiency. The first column gives the percentage change in Kendrick's measure of aggregate productivity, the ratio of real output in the economy to a geometrically weighted index of factor inputs. This measure shows that controls did not reduce aggregate productivity. During the crucial period 1951–2, however, productivity growth was slow, the second slowest rate of increase for the decade, so it can be argued that growth was slower during this period than it otherwise would have been.

This interpretation is strengthened by an examination of column 2, which shows "expected" productivity growth, based on a simple regression. Since productivity growth generally accelerates during a period of high aggregate demand, one wants to compare actual productivity growth with what would be expected given the level of aggregate demand. One estimate of a demand adjusted rate of productivity growth is shown in column 2. Thus, the gap between columns 1 and 2 may be a better indicator of the effect of controls than the difference between growth in a year when controls were in place and in the average year. A comparison of columns 1 and 2 reveals that both 1950–51 and 1951–2 were years in which productivity growth was unusually low. In only one other year is actual growth so much smaller than the expected growth.

Column 3 shows the percentage changes in Denison's independently computed estimates of productivity. Here the percentage change during 1950–1 was below the median, although not so strikingly below as in Kendrick's measure. The last column is productivity change, according to Denison, after deducting the part which can be attributed to changes in aggregate demand, economies of scale, weather, and similar extraneous factors. It includes the effect of certain reallocations of resources to more productive uses and the "residual," the increase in productivity that is frequently attributed to the increase in knowledge. The latter sources of growth are the ones likely to be influenced by controls. The reallocation of resources, for example, is likely to be hindered because controls would block the appropriate changes in relative prices. Thus, this column should reveal the effects of controls on productivity more clearly than column 3. As in the previous cases, this measure of productivity change was below the median, but by no means the lowest of the decade, during the year 1951–2.

What all this means is that there is some evidence of a slight retardation in productivity growth. But even if this could all be attributed to controls, and the other dislocations of the war (drafting of experienced workers and so on) ignored, it would not constitute a very strong case against temporary controls. Similar slowdowns have occurred in peacetime without causing undue alarm. The loss, moreover, was offset by a vigorous rebound when controls were removed.[25]

Resistance and evasion

Evasion and outright resistance were not as ubiquitous in the Korean War as in World War II. But, in certain markets, where demand was particularly strong, troublesome problems developed. Because of the crucial role of steel in the military effort there was excess demand at the ceiling price in most markets for raw or fabricated steel. This industry, then, provides an interesting opportunity to contrast the response of large and small firms to binding price ceilings. The small firms downstream from the mills – the fabricators, warehouses, brokers, and so forth – evaded controls by entering the so-called gray market, which will be discussed below. The large primary producers, on the other hand, while not entering the gray market, were far from the compliant technocracies sometimes depicted in the literature on the large firm. By refusing to come to terms with their unions they put considerable pressure on the government to come across with a substantial price increase. A small firm could hardly hope to succeed through such a policy since most of the costs of a strike would fall on the firm itself and on its work force. An industry-wide shutdown of primary producers, however, could not easily be ignored. In World War I, as we have seen, the mere threat of seizure seems to have been sufficient to bring the steel producers around. In World War II, during the demobilization phase, the government came through with sufficient price increases to satisfy the industry, increases larger than the Office of Price Administration thought justified. But this compromise weakened the stabilization program. During the Korean War the Truman Administration used its ultimate weapon: It seized the steel mills.[26]

The steel problem was anticipated some months in advance of the December 31, 1951 expiration date of the contract between the CIO and the steel companies. Truman referred the demands of the steel workers to the Wage Stabilization Board, and the union agreed to work under the old contract while the Board deliberated. On March 29, 1952 the Board announced its recommendations: a 26¢-an-hour increase in wages and fringe benefits, and the institution of the union shop. While these were considered generous terms, the OPS did not think they justified a price increase under its standards (beyond those already due the industry under the Capehart formula, about two to three dollars per ton). The industry, however, refused to settle with the union unless a substantially larger price increase was granted. In this case, the dangers in separating wage control from price control were particularly clear. The government would have been in a much stronger position if it could have negotiated the wage and price decisions simultaneously – and in secret.

As it was, Truman felt that the steelmakers had left him few alternatives. Permitting a strike, and letting labor and management reach a solution through collective bargaining, might endanger the war effort. Granting sufficient price relief to the industry to reconcile it to the Wage Stabilization Board's package would wreck the stabilization program. Utilizing the emergency cooling-off period in the Taft–Hartley Act was anathema to Truman, whose sympathies and political fortunes lay with labor. The only acceptable alternative appeared to be to take over the steel mills. Truman announced the seizure on April 8, 1952, accompanying his announcement with a vitriolic attack on the steelmakers.

The seizure touched off a national debate on whether Truman had overstepped his constitutional authority. The industry took the issue to court and had the seizure enjoined. On its part, the administration did a poor job in defending its action; at one point in a press conference Truman managed to create the impression that he saw no particular problem with seizing newspapers, in other words with abrogating freedom of the press, in an "emergency." In a dramatic decision issued on June 2, 1952, the Supreme Court upheld the lower court's decision. The exact meaning of the Supreme Court's decision has been much debated because of the number of concurring opinions, but a common thread was provided by the idea that since Taft–Hartley and other legislation existed for dealing with emergency situations, the President could not ignore them and rely instead on his general constitutional powers. The Supreme Court's decision (*Youngstown Sheet & Tube* v. *Sawyer*) triggered a strike. Truman responded by asking Congress either to pass seizure legislation or order him to invoke Taft–Hartley. When it would do neither, only suggesting he invoke Taft–Hartley, Truman refused to take further action. The strike dragged on for fifty-three days. The final settlement involved a 21½¢ wage and fringe benefit package and a union shop formula. A price increase of $5.20 per ton was granted simultaneously. Together this was something of a victory for the steelmakers, compared with what the stabilization agencies were willing to grant when the entire controversy began.

Truman's refusal to invoke Taft–Hartley once the strike was on is explained primarily by his unwillingness to antagonize organized labor.

But it is also true that the dire consequences predicted did not materialize. Steel users evidently had laid in heavy inventories. It is not so clear, however, when they laid them in. Had the strike occurred earlier, say, in January when the old contract expired, the pinch might have been more severe. Still, in the light of his own unwillingness to invoke Taft–Hartley, Truman's assertion in his *Memoirs* that the strike harmed the war effort appears overstated.[27]

The industry's unwillingness to settle after the Supreme Court decision might have been due in part to a simple desire for revenge, a possibility hinted at by Marcus, one of the historians of the steel seizure.[28] But it also made economic sense. The industry may have felt that Truman, trapped by his own predictions of disaster, would have to invoke Taft–Hartley. If he did, the industry would gain several months of production at the old cost–price relationship and the possibility of a more favorable settlement. Only when Truman did not invoke Taft–Hartley, and when he began to threaten seizure through a lengthy process provided for in the Selective Service Act, did Big Steel finally decide to settle. The larger point illustrated by this example is that the concentration of production in a small number of firms does not make price control easy. It changes the nature of the battle between the industry and the stabilization authorities but not the fact of conflict.

The smaller firms in the steel industry were in no position to threaten the stabilization agencies with prolonged strikes. They could, however, evade them in other ways. In this sector of the steel industry, as well as in similar sectors of the aluminum and nickel industries, the so-called gray market developed.[29] It was gray rather than black because the prices charged were not strict violations of OPS regulations, or so the operators claimed. On this there was some dispute. Operators in the gray market were notoriously vague about whether they were selling at legal prices.

Typically, metal in the gray market moved through a series of brokers, the "petals" of a "daisy chain," from the initial producer to the end-user. In one daisy chain traced by the Senate Select Committee on Small Business, and illustrated in Figure 6.1, steel passed through as many as seven brokers before reaching its final destination. The steel left the mill, Wierton or Fort Pitt, at a price set by the OPS of from $5.20 to $5.80 per hundred pounds, and passed through a series of brokers who steadily marked up the price. The fifth broker in the chain divided the steel into two approximately equal lots. One was bought by the Daisy

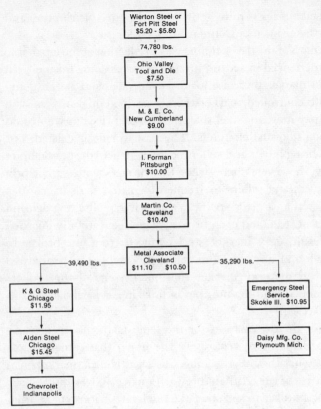

Figure 6.1. A typical "daisy chain" of gray market steel, 1951. (Source: U.S. Senate, the Select Committee on Small Business, *Steel Gray Market*, p. 137 [1951B, G].)

Mfg. Co., the BB gun maker, for $10.95 after passing through a sixth broker. The other lot passed through two other brokers and was finally bought by a Chevrolet plant in Indianapolis for $15.45, a price almost three times the ceiling at the mill.

Why did gray market steel move through so many hands? One reason was that intermediaries were needed for concealment. Suppose, to take a typical example, a metal fabricator with a "legitimate" need for steel decided it was more profitable to cut back production and sell his raw material on the gray market. Selling it under his own name would be risky because his supplier might find out and cut his allotment. It was possible, however, to sell the surplus to a dummy corporation which would then resell it on the gray market. At most, however, this explains only a four "petal" chain – mill, fabricator, dummy distributor, and end-user – and the chain was frequently much longer.

In part, the length of the daisy chains was a reflection of the inevitable inefficiencies experienced in setting up new ways of doing business. In the normal steel market there is no unsatisfied demand at the going price. But in the controlled market there were potential buyers who were willing to pay more for steel than the market price but who could not buy it through normal channels. The basis for deals existed, but someone had to bring buyer and seller together, hence, the gray market broker. Initially, however, there were few brokers with sufficiently long lists of buyers and sellers to frequently match the surplus of a particular supplier at a particular point in time with an offsetting demand from a consumer of steel, and each broker, of course, carefully guarded his list. As a result, gray market steel bounced from one broker to another until it found its way from the producer of steel to the end user. In time, had the gray market continued, some of the brokers would have expanded, and the number of links in a typical daisy chain would have decreased.

A third part of the explanation for the long daisy chains turns on the belief (or perhaps more accurately the hope) that some brokers entertained that what they were doing was legal if their markup was "moderate," that is, based on their prewar practice. Given this belief, it made sense for a broker to sell steel at a moderate markup to another broker (perhaps in the expectation that the favor would be returned) rather than to charge an end-user a much higher price.

The gray market was stifled, to some extent, by the imposition of a controlled materials plan similar to World War II's and a ceiling price on premium steel that did not permit additional markups for brokerage services. The former measure, by doing a better job of rationing steel, reduced excess demand. The latter eliminated any pretense to legitimacy in gray-market operations. Still, the distribution of steel would have been smoother had some legitimate method existed for manufacturers who were not allocated sufficient steel to meet their most pressing needs to buy part of the ration of other users. This "white" market in ration "tickets" would have eliminated the economic function of the gray market.

Examples, as was argued in previous chapters, do not necessarily provide an accurate picture of the overall extent of evasion; some form of quantitative measure is needed. The best surviving evidence is the amount

Table 6.4. *Price and rent control cases commenced in the Federal District Courts during the Korean War*[a]

Year (fiscal)	Rent control	Defense production act	Total cases	Rent and Production Act cases as a percentage of the total
Civil cases				
1951	4295	26	43,591	9.91
1952	3789	2141	50,263	11.80
1953	3197	1103	55,462	7.75
1954	304	46	51,103	0.68
Criminal cases				
1951	0	3	36,860	0.01
1952	2	108	36,236	0.30
1953	3	70	35,344	0.21
1954	0	23	40,098	0.06

[a] Excluding the District of Columbia.
Source: U.S. Administrative Office of the U.S. Courts, *Annual Report 1952* (1953G, Table C2, pp. 126–127, Table D2, pp. 154–156); *Annual Report 1954* (1955G, Table C2, pp. 152–154, Table D2, pp. 186–188).

of legal activity generated by controls. The number of cases begun in Federal Courts, the measure used here, of course, is a function of a large number of variables, including both the intensity of enforcement and the skill of the evaders (who had the experience of World War II behind them), as well as the size of the pool of evasive activity. Nevertheless, if one is willing to assume approximate comparability in the levels of these variables for different kinds of illegal activities, the ratio of price control cases to other cases provides a rough measure of the extent of evasion.

The appropriate data are presented in Table 6.4. Examination of the table reveals that evasive activity was not nearly as extensive as during World War II. In the peak year, 1952, only 11.8 percent of the total new civil cases in Federal District Courts consisted of price control cases, compared with over 50 percent in 1946. (The number of criminal cases, as the table shows, was trivial.) When compared with the percentage accounted for by other regulatory measures, the burden generated by controls appears somewhat greater. In 1952 tax suits accounted for only

2.3 percent of all civil cases; food and drug laws accounted for only 3.6 percent; and liquor laws, only 1.4 percent. Controls quickly took their place as a source of legal activity alongside other major regulations.

But, I would argue that the expansion of legal activity that resulted from the imposition of controls in the Korean War was not the sort of burden (even when added to some of the other costs examined above) that would make people say, in retrospect, that controls were not worth the effort that went into enforcing them. Suppose the same increase in legal activity had occurred because of a greater use of more familiar suits, say something between a tripling and a quadrupling of suits brought under the food and drug laws. Would most people view that increase as an intolerable burden on the judicial system if there were clear health benefits that could be set against it? The correct conclusion, I believe, is that a short-term application of controls in the appropriate monetary and fiscal environment did not produce an unmanageable black market. The contrast with the latter years of World War II when the judicial burden was 5½ times the Korean War peak suggests that if we want the level of evasion to be of the same order as that generated by comparable forms of regulation, then controls must be used the way they were in the Korean War, to deal with a temporary inflationary emergency, not the way they were in the latter days of World War II, to hold the general price level below the level dictated by aggregate supply and demand.

Korea as a model

Milton Friedman, perhaps the best-known opponent of controls, has conceded as we noted in Chapter 1 that there is, in principle, a situation in which controls would be appropriate: if the government imposed price controls during an inflation while at the same time it cut the rate of growth of the money supply, the root cause of the inflation. Controls would then ease the transition to a lower rate of inflation by forcing price expectations into line with the new rate of growth of the money supply. If controls were not imposed, businesses might continue to raise prices and accede to higher wages for a time, even though higher prices and wages were not consistent with the growth of demand. The result would be unsold goods, falling production, and unemployment.

Friedman's example of a successful use of controls was based on the situation in Argentina in the early 1950s. The inflation rate there was

running from 20 to 30 percent per year.[30] He probably would not accept
the Korean War example as a correct use of controls because of the
lower rate of inflation. Yet it corresponds roughly with the scenario he
accepts. Controls were imposed when inflation was clearly the product
of the anticipation of still higher prices. At approximately the same
time, taxes were increased and a conservative monetary policy was
assured through the Treasury–Federal Reserve Accord. Once price
stability was achieved, controls were removed. This sequence resulted
from a variety of fortuitous circumstances, but in my judgment it
nonetheless represented something close to a model use of controls.

A price was paid for the stability achieved through controls. Some
shortages were experienced. Black markets developed in the distribution
of certain strategic resources and a few other commodities. Powerful
economic interests evaded the price controllers indirectly by pressuring
the Congress to amend the law in their favor, and in the case of the
steel industry they did so directly by refusing to bargain over wages
until their price demands were met. These forms of evasion clearly
portended a state of affairs which would have made permanent controls
a net loss. But they did not offset the immediate benefits achieved
during the emergency.

If temporary controls were a success in the Korean War, as I have
argued, why do so many economists and politicians claim that they
have never worked? Part of the answer is that few economists or politicians
have studied closely the history of controls. Instead, references are
made to historical experiences as a way of reinforcing a point already
held for theoretical or ideological reasons. Perhaps even more important,
economists and politicians tend to think implicitly of the case in which
controls are used to force prices below the level dictated by the long-
run growth of money and real output. They fail to consider the case
in which prices are driven by fears of future shortages to a level higher
than that consistent with the growth of money per unit output (or the
analogous case in which the rate of growth of the money supply is
suddenly reduced). In other words, they consider only the case in which
price controls and monetary policy are used at cross purposes, and
neglect the case in which the two are used together. By avoiding this
sort of reasoning, we can, I think, come to a much sounder conclusion
about the desirability of controls in the future.

7. The Vietnam War

> The time has come for decisive action – action that will break the vicious circle of spiraling prices and costs. I am today ordering a freeze on all prices and wages throughout the United States for a period of 90 days. In addition, I call upon corporations to extend the wage–price freeze to all dividends.
>
> Richard Nixon, August 15, 1971

The controls imposed by President Nixon on August 15, 1971 are sometimes referred to as the nation's first peacetime controls. But this statement (which, incidentally, ignores the Revolutionary War experiments) is true only in a legal sense. Undeclared war still raged in Vietnam; the treaty was not signed until January 1973, some 17 months later. From an economic point of view these were wartime controls designed to stem an inflation that had its origins in expenditures for war and the attempt to finance those expenditures through the creation of money. By the summer of 1971 the economy appeared, from the perspective of the times, to be deeply troubled. The rate of unemployment was close to 6 percent, up sharply from the levels reached in the late 1960s. This was partly the result of a tight money policy imposed by the Federal Reserve in 1969, which in turn was a response to the high rates of growth in the money supply and the large deficits run up in 1967 and 1968. The rate of inflation had responded to tight money: The consumer price index, which had risen 6.1 percent in 1969 and 5.5 percent in 1970, rose at an annual rate of only 3.6 percent in the first eight months of 1971. This result, moveover, was not produced solely by a decrease in the normally volatile food index, which sometimes distorts the interpretation of long-term trends. The increase in the consumer price index for all items other than food was 3.4 percent in the first eight months of 1971, compared with 6.5 percent in 1970, and 5.7 percent in 1969.

Table 7.1. *Public attitudes toward price controls*
in the period prior to August 15, 1971

Gallup: It has been suggested that prices and wages be frozen as
long as the war in Vietnam lasts. Do you think it is a good idea or
a poor idea?

Date	Good idea	Poor idea	No opinion
12/1965	45	42	13
4/1966	42	44	14
10/1966	33	51	16
1/1968	46	43	11
6/1969	47	41	12
5/1970	48	41	11
2/1971	49	38	13
6/1971	50	39	11

Harris: Would you favor or oppose the government's setting up a
system of wage and price controls?

Date	Favor	Oppose	Not sure
7/1970	49	32	19
1/1971	62	25	13

Note: The questions as stated are paraphrases of the longer ones
actually asked.
Sources: Gallup (1972B, pp. 1987, 2005, 2037, 2103, 2203, 2251–
2252, 2292, and 2315); Harris (1971B, p. 160), (1972B, p. 174).

But the public found this rate of progress agonizingly slow and
yearned for more authoritative action in the form of wage and price
controls. Some of the public opinion polls which documented the growing
impatience with inflation are summarized in Table 7.1. The Gallup Poll
asked people simply whether they favored a wage–price freeze, and
this percentage grew moderately from 46 percent in January 1968 to 50
percent in June 1971. The Harris Poll, however, used a more ambiguous
question and the results showed a more dramatic shift in attitude. The
percentage favoring "a system of wage and price controls" rose from
49 percent in July 1970 to an overwhelming 62 percent in January 1971.
The shift in the Nixon administration's attitude toward controls was
produced by this change in public opinion. In fact, Michael Wheeler
reports Charles Colson's claim that the decision to impose a freeze was
based largely on telephone polls taken by Albert Sindlinger.[1] These

polls showed that Nixon's popularity was suffering primarily because he had not taken decisive action to halt inflation.

While public support for a freeze was growing, professional opinion was also moving, perhaps even faster, toward the conclusion that some form of wage and price controls was necessary. The most visible advocate of controls was Arthur Burns, chairman of the Federal Reserve Board. But men closer to the President were also arguing that the time for wage and price regulations had arrived. Even within the business community, there was considerable support for controls.[2] With a Republican in the White House, business leaders had little to fear, and perhaps much to gain, or so they thought, if the government moved to control wages and prices.

The program that finally emerged, however, did not favor the business community as much as its leaders had imagined it would. What business hoped for, I believe, was simply the existing market system with a more stable wage and price structure, particularly more stable wages. Had the program worked in this way, it would undoubtedly have strengthened profits and the earnings of managers and entrepreneurs. But what business failed to consider is that price regulation inevitably transfers control of the machinery that determines the earnings of executives from the market to less friendly hands. Government bureaucrats are likely to view skeptically any increases in earnings that are already much higher than their own, and this is what happened. Business executives were later to complain bitterly about rules designed to keep increases in their compensation within the limits the government thought consistent with the stabilization program.[3] Perhaps if the business community had foreseen this implication of controls more clearly, its enthusiasm would have been more restrained.

Widespread public support for controls, particularly in influential quarters, was the main reason why controls were finally imposed, but not the only reason. The growing realization among international holders of dollars that the U.S. currency was overvalued also contributed a strong push toward controls. A devaluation of the dollar seemed inevitable. But if this action had been taken by itself, it would not have ended speculation against the dollar, and it would have been widely viewed as an overwhelming defeat for the administration. Other policies were needed to make devaluation effective and palatable. Controls were the answer. Congress, moreover, had previously given the President the power to impose mandatory controls. If the President failed to use this power, and inflation worsened, the blame would fall squarely on his shoulders.

The Nixon Administration's turn toward wage and price controls was closely associated with the rise to power of John Connally. Nixon admired Connally. In his *Memoirs*, Nixon writes that "I believed that John Connally was the only man in either party who clearly had the potential to be a great President."[4] Connally had become Secretary of the Treasury on December 9, 1970, replacing David Kennedy. From there events moved swiftly. On June 26, 1971, Nixon made Connally the administration's sole spokesman on economic policy. On June 29, Connally announced the "four noes": no wage and price review board, no mandatory wage and price controls, no tax cut, and no increase in government spending. I do not know whether Connally then knew that six weeks later he would be the architect of a wage and price freeze. But clearly even if he did, he could not have taken another course on the 29th. Even an evasive statement such as "all options are being considered" would have run the risk that prices would have been advanced substantially by businesses that feared being caught in a freeze. Nixon asked for, and received on August 6, a report from Connally on the appropriate actions to cure the economy. Nixon, again according to his *Memoirs*, had expected "something bold," but was not prepared for the "total war on all economic fronts" proposed by Connally.[5]

Phase I

Nixon announced the comprehensive ninety-day freeze of wages and prices on August 15, along with other measures designed to improve the balance of payments. The freeze, it was hoped, would serve two purposes. First, it was a form of shock therapy for the economy. Much of the inflationary pressure in the summer of 1971 was expectational. Even though demand was weak at the moment, businesses were raising prices because they anticipated that labor would be demanding large wage increases and because they were secure in their assumption that their rivals were taking similar actions. It was hoped that the freeze would convince decision makers that the government was now putting a stop to inflation. If foreign dollar holders were also convinced that the dollar would maintain its value, and stopped their efforts to reduce their holdings, so much the better.

The second purpose of the freeze was to buy time. Once it became clear that the government was going to apply some form of wage and price controls many firms, as noted above, would start putting up their prices simply to be in the most favorable position when controls came. The freeze forestalled those increases, buying time with which to plan a flexible program of controls and to elicit public support. That the freeze also won the President enormous, if ultimately transitory, public acclaim was no doubt also a welcome outcome.

The freeze was intended to cover virtually the entire economy. It was believed that an across-the-board policy would have the greatest appearance of equity and would have the greatest chance of reversing expectations of future inflation. Only two substantial sectors were excluded from control: raw agricultural products and finished imports. The former was excluded because the volatile nature of supply in this sector raised the possibility that shortages might emerge even in the brief period contemplated for the freeze; the latter sector was excluded simply because there was no easy way of controlling the prices of imports.

In one respect the coverage of the freeze was even more comprehensive than it was during similar phases in World War II and the Korean War. In these previous experiments prices charged by the news and entertainment media had been excluded because of the danger to the freedom of the press, but under the Vietnam controls these sectors were included. To see the potential conflict, consider the advertising rates charged by the television networks. These ordinarily reflected expected audience size, a function of the time slot and the attractiveness of the individual program. The freeze came shortly before the beginning of the new television season and the controllers had to decide how new advertising rates would be set. Their decision left the networks with some discretion: For established programs the rate could be what was charged for that program or that time slot in the previous season, but for new programs the time slot alone was decisive. While this rule followed a common-sense approach, it is clear that in the long run the price controllers would have had considerable leverage over what was presented on television.[6] By altering their rules they could have substantially altered the impact of the ratings on advertising charges and hence on the programs networks chose to show.

Due both to President Nixon's admonition to avoid a "huge bureaucracy" and to the absence of any controls before the freeze, the controllers had to rely on a small, hastily assembled bureaucracy. Providing overall policy guidelines was the cabinet level Cost of Living Council.[7] Directing the day-to-day operations was the Office of Emergency Preparedness, an obscure agency originally established to deal with the aftermath of a nuclear attack. Because of the latter's limited labor power, however, the Internal Revenue Service was used as the agency dealing directly with the public. The choice of the Internal Revenue Service was a logical one. It was the "off-season" for the Service so considerable resources could be spared. And the trepidation that many people feel in dealing with the Service undoubtedly encouraged compliance, even if in fact there was little likelihood that violators of the freeze would have their taxes audited. The staff of the Service, moreover, understood the business practices that would be the focal point of the freeze. A third agency, the Agricultural Stabilization and Conservation Service, part of the Department of Agriculture, was called on to distribute information in rural areas.

The word "freeze" suggests a relatively simple formula for determining prices, one that should create relatively few problems. Nonetheless, a number of definitional knots had to be untangled. Basic was the problem of defining the base period price. This was done by defining the ceiling price as a price which had prevailed in at least 10 percent of actual transactions during the preceding thirty-day period. While some exceptions were made, for example, for prices that varied seasonally, this formula was adhered to with some fervor during the remainder of the freeze.

Voluntary cooperation was relied upon as the main tool for achieving compliance. If expressions of support for the program are taken as evidence of a willingness to comply (an assumption, to be sure, that requires a certain faith in human nature), reliance on voluntary compliance was well placed. Public approval of the freeze was overwhelming. A Gallup Poll taken immediately after the President's announcement showed 68 percent of the public approved of the freeze, compared with only 11 percent who disapproved, and 12 percent who expressed no opinion.[8] A Harris Poll taken at about the same time showed 73 percent in favor. This percentage rose to 75 in September, and then dropped a few points to a still overwhelming level of 67 percent in November.[9] Even among the dyed-in-the-wool Republicans, enthusiasm for the freeze was widespread. Barton polled a group of American leaders, completing about one-half of his interviews before the August 15 announcement. He found support for the controls among the Republicans in his sample increasing from 22 to 70 percent with the announcement; support among Democrats and Independents, already high, went up a few percentage points.[10] With such widespread support for the program, it seems in retrospect that the time was ripe for fundamental reforms of our monetary and fiscal system, reforms designed to alter the inflationary bias of our economy. One of the tragedies of the Vietnam era controls is that this opportunity was lost.

Evasion of the freeze

Despite the short duration of the freeze, and the support for it from the public, problems developed that hinted at serious difficulties that would have to be dealt with by a long-continued program of severe restraint. The most difficult area to control was the clothing sector, the same one that had proved to be such a headache during World War II. The new fall and winter fashions were coming on the market continuously during the freeze. Under a seasonality rule, prices were not supposed to be increased over what they had been for the same fashion in the same season the year before. But the problem of locating the price of an analogous garment precluded rigorous control. The advance of the apparel component of the consumer price index and the large volume of consumer complaints testified to the weakness of the freeze in this area.[11] Apparel prices increased at an annual rate of 3 percent during the freeze, compared with 2 percent during the preceding six months; perhaps even more to the point, wages increased 4.7 percent faster than clothing prices before the freeze, while they lagged behind clothing prices at the rate of 0.8 percent during the freeze. In this sector the freeze was simply ineffective.

While evasion was most pervasive in the clothing sector, the controllers actually ran into evasion in a wide variety of other circumstances. For example, trading stamps were dropped by a number of retailers. The Cost of Living Council held that in such cases prices had to be cut by the market value of the stamps that would ordinarily have been provided. Steel fabricators were caught when an increase in the price of finished products was prohibited that traditionally had followed an increase in the price of raw steel. Some tried to escape the squeeze by requiring their customers to buy the raw steel and charging only for the fabrication. The Cost of Living Council refused to sanction this change in what was, for many fabricators, the normal pricing system. The meat packing industry, a sore spot in earlier episodes, also provided an example of evasion. Many packers traditionally sold meat by the cut, pricing steaks relatively high compared with roasts during the summer when demand was strongest, and then pricing steaks relatively lower during the winter. The freeze interfered with this adjustment, so some of the packers switched to selling beef by the carcass. This change was also forbidden.[12]

In only one case did the government go all the way to court to reverse what it considered an evasion of the freeze through quality deterioration. The Cincinnati Transit Corporation, which provided bus service, had been authorized by the city's public utilities director to reduce service in order to avoid losses. The government filed suit to prevent further cuts and was upheld in the federal district court.[13]

Phase II

During the freeze an administration task force outlined the basic structure of Phase II, which began on November 14. The main elements were the Price Commission and the Pay Board. The former was composed entirely of "public" members, a number of them from the academic community, while the latter had a "tripartite" structure, with representatives drawn from business, labor, and the public.[14] In addition, separate committees were set up to deal with interest and dividends, rent, health services, and state and local governments. Either by conscious imitation, or simply responding to similar pressures, the administration had come up with a structure very similar to the ones that had emerged in earlier experiments. The basic idea behind the Price Commission, for example, was almost the same as that behind the Price Committee established in World War I: to achieve at least the appearance and ideally the reality of an impartial, judicial process of price setting.

The Price Commission was given considerable freedom in setting standards and handling individual cases. The reason was that a crisis atmosphere prevailed in which the forces ordinarily shaping public policy were temporarily suspended. According to C. Jackson Grayson, the Chairman of the Price Commission, he was told by Paul McCracken and Herbert Stein of the Council of Economic Advisors in effect that "Not much in classical economics seems to be working, why don't you come up with something on your own rather than be prejudiced by our views" – a remarkable admission from men who ordinarily have strong opinions on economic matters.[15] Freedom of this sort creates a favorable environment for controls, for as we have seen in earlier episodes, the assertion of power by special interests tends to produce exemptions where excess demand can make itself felt. Freedom of this sort, of course, is also likely to be short-lived.

As in the Freeze, the coverage was broad. There were, however, a number of important exemptions. Raw food products were again exempt, as were exports and imports after the first sale. Small domestic rental units were exempt, as well as farm, industrial, and nonresidential property. The latter exemptions made sense for a program designed to be temporary since most renters are protected by contracts in the short run. In January 1972 the Cost of Living Council exempted retail firms with sales under $100,000, and in May firms with sixty or fewer employees, except in health or construction. Even among the larger firms formally subject to control there was a division into various "tiers," with the tier containing the largest firms subject to the closest scrutiny.

In a broad sense, then, the Phase II system corresponded to Professor Galbraith's concept of confining controls to those sectors of the economy in which firms have market power while leaving more competitive sectors exempt. The assumption that underlies such a framework, unfortunately, is that the inflation stems from the exercise of monopoly power. If inflation is produced by excessive aggregate demand, then as we have seen, selective controls will produce a shift of demand toward the uncontrolled sector. Monetary policy was extremely expansionary during Phase II, so whatever the short-run logic of selective controls, the economy was changing rapidly into an environment in which only across-the-board controls would have been effective. This process is not inevitable. But the theory that inflation is the result of market power – the theory that makes selective controls so attractive – when widely held, makes it more likely that selective controls will be undermined by an expansionary monetary policy. If the real cause of inflation has been dealt with, policymakers will reason, why not expand the money supply to reduce unemployment and lower interest rates? This may not be the whole story of monetary growth in Phase II (the issue is dealt with below), but it is, nevertheless, a plausible scenario for future experiments with controls.

The most divisive issue before the Price Commission was whether firms could only pass through costs only dollar for dollar or would be allowed to add their customary markups. A numerical example will illustrate the distinction. Suppose a company manufactures soup at a cost per can (for foodstuffs, labor, the can itself, and so on) of one dollar, and that it then customarily marks up the price 10 percent, so the final selling price is $1.10. Suppose further that controls are introduced, and that because of increases in certain imperfectly controlled costs, say labor and raw materials, the cost per can goes up to $1.50. There are two alternatives open to controllers: (1) Dollar-for-dollar pass through. This would allow the manufacturer to raise his price only by the additional 50¢ to $1.60. Or (2) The addition of a customary markup to the cost increase. In this case the manufacturer could add an additional 5¢ (10% × 50¢) to the cost increase, for a total of $1.65. Formula (1) keeps total profits constant, while (2) keeps the ratio of profits to the total income of the firm constant.

The debate over these alternatives has a long history. In the colonial period and the Revolutionary War, markup formulas such as (2) were used. The issue was considered in World War I when markup pricing, first on the basis of customary markups, and later on the basis of official industry markups calculated by the authorities, was used. In World War II the appropriate formula was at issue in the debate over the Taft Amendment to the 1946 renewal of the legislation, which would have applied markup pricing to every good separately. The Office of Price Administration feared that with wages uncontrolled the Taft Amendment would leave the agency with no authority, except to validate inflation. If wages and other costs rose 5 percent, then prices would have to rise 5 percent. If wages and other costs rose 10 percent, then prices would rise 10 percent. How could an agency control prices without controlling wages or profits?

This fear undoubtedly affected those members of Nixon's Price Commission who opposed markup pricing. But there was also a split along political lines. The first formula seems to keep profits constant, at 10¢ per can in the example, while the second allows profits to increase to 15¢ per can. The liberal members of the Commission were undoubtedly concerned about adopting a formula that produced increased profits. But it should be noted that typically the second formula keeps profits constant in *real* terms, while the first reduces real profits. Suppose, to return to the example, that all prices rose at the same rate as the costs for this particular product; then, in real terms there would be no increase in the level of real profits under the second formula. Prices and profits would both have risen 50 percent. A large part of profits, it should also be noted, are reinvested to maintain and increase productivity. If dollar-for-dollar pass through had won out, if controls had remained in place for a long period of time, and if cost increases had been substantial, formula (1) would have reduced the real level of investment in the economy and slowed the rate of growth.

During Phase II this debate was resolved in favor of the customary markup as it had been in most of the earlier debates, although increases in labor productivity were deducted from the cost-justified increase in computing the maximum price. But the Price Commission was almost evenly split. It was hoped that productivity increases would be in the neighborhood of 3 percent, a figure justifiable on the basis of historical trends. This assumption, when combined with the Pay Board's standard of a 6.2 percent increase in wages and qualified fringe benefits, suggested that price increases would fall in the neighborhood of 3.2 percent. By the latter part of Phase II, the controllers could make the case that they were reaching this goal.

Mention should also be made of another option made available to large multiproduct firms: term limit pricing. Under this system a firm which kept its average price increase below a certain maximum was permitted to distribute its increase across products, for the most part, as it saw fit. This was an administrative device designed to conserve resources. Eventually, the commission was criticized on the grounds that the firms under these agreements made larger profits than if they had been under the main system. But of course, only those firms which found this option profitable chose it.

Phase III

Consumer prices were relatively stable in the latter part of 1972; from June to December the increase was only 1.8 percent. The stabilization program seemed, at that time, to have reached its goal. President Nixon, partly as a result of the popularity of his economic initiatives, had overwhelmingly won reelection. Thus the time seemed propitious for a start on Nixon's pledge to remove controls before they became a permanent feature of the economy. The result was Phase III, inaugurated in January 1973. The Price Commission and Pay Board were disbanded, and the Cost of Living Council assumed direct responsibility for administration of the program. John Dunlop, who had been Chairman of the Construction Industry Stabilization Committee (the earliest stabilization agency, and a survivor in Phase II), became director of the council. It has been charged that the administrators of the Vietnam controls were philosophically opposed to controls and, therefore, subtle saboteurs of them. But the choice of Dunlop belies the charge. The administration picked one of the most experienced price controllers in the nation.

There were surprisingly few changes in coverage or the formulas for controlling prices, but the changes made were in the direction of allowing larger increases. For one thing, a profit margin limitation, which had served as a second line of defense in Phase II, was eliminated. On the wage side the rules were eased to allow greater flexibility in individual cases, and to exempt workers earning less than $3.50 per hour. The exempt sector was also extended to include all rental properties. The major change in the program, however, was in the form of administration: Controls were to be largely self-administered, businesses were to interpret the general rules themselves. Rules on prenotification and reporting were also eased.

In the first months under Phase III prices increased rapidly. The food index, pushed by meats, led the way, increasing 4.5 percent between January and March, a 30.2 percent annual rate! The remainder of the index increased 0.7 percent between January and March, a 4.3 percent annual rate, moderate but higher than in Phase I. Not surprisingly, the controllers began retreating from the position that the regulations could soon be eliminated. Meat price ceilings were imposed in March, and prenotification rules were tightened to delay major increases. Finally, in June, a new price freeze was imposed.

Freeze II and Phase IV

The second freeze was greeted with considerably less enthusiasm than the first, and with good reason. The second freeze produced many of the distortions that had been predicted for the first freeze but had not developed on a significant scale. The difference was in the extent of demand pressure. The Federal Reserve Board's index of capacity utilization, which had stood at 73.9 when the first freeze was introduced, was up to 83.3 by the time the second freeze started. The second freeze, which was limited to sixty days (although some prices were thawed more quickly), marked the beginning of the end of the Vietnam controls, rather than an attempt to buy time with which to establish still another program. The administration had decided that it was time to remove controls, and the shortages experienced during the second freeze only served to reinforce that belief, and to ready the public for a return to free markets.

Phase IV, the final one, replaced the second freeze in August 1973. Paradoxically, even though the economy was being decontrolled sector by sector, the wage and price standards in those areas still under control were tougher, in certain ways, than they had been in Phase III. On the price side the most important change was the substitution of dollar-for-dollar pass-through of costs, formula (1) above, for customary mark-ups. On the wage side, there were no major changes, although the rules for limiting increases in executive compensation were tightened. The uncontrolled sector was expanded at the outset to include public utilities, long-term coal contracts, and lumber and copper scrap (the latter two had experienced considerable difficulties). Decontrol gathered steam as Phase IV progressed. Throughout there was an emphasis on decontrolling relatively unimportant markets, the "dogs and cats" as the controllers knew them, as quickly and with as little fuss as possible. But in more significant industries, automobiles for example, the controllers tried to work out agreements in which the firms promised price restraint, or other actions such as investment spending, in exchange for early decontrol. With controls coming to an end, however, the officials had little leverage with which to bargain and no effective mechanism to force businesses to live up to their promises.

In April 1974 controls, except on petroleum prices, came to an end. For some observers the experience was a sobering one. For others, it was simply evidence that even a good program could fail if not given sufficient support. In the following sections I will examine in detail the benefits and the costs of the Vietnam era controls, and the reasons why they were less successful than in some of the earlier experiments.

The effect on prices

Table 7.2 shows the behavior of prices, wages, and money per unit of real output, before, during, and after the imposition of controls. The impression that the public derived by concentrating on prices and wages was straightforward. Inflation had been reduced by Phase I and Phase II. But then, as a result of the weakening of the program in Phase III, inflation had accelerated. The public's interpretation of the effect on real wages was similar. Increases in wages had outpaced increases in

Table 7.2. *Prices, wages, and money per unit of real output during the Vietnam War*

Period	Annual rates of change		
	Prices	Wages	Money per unit of real output
12/70–8/71 (8 mo. before)	3.6	6.1	5.1
8/71–11/71 (Phase I)	1.3	4.5	2.8
11/71–1/73 (Phase II)	3.5	8.8	4.1
1/73–6/73 (Phase III)	8.7	3.6	2.4
6/73–8/73 (Freeze II)	12.1[a]	3.0	1.6
8/73–4/74 (Phase IV)	9.6	6.8	13.2
8/71–4/74 (total period)	6.2	6.7	5.8
4/74–12/74 (8 mo. after)	12.2	8.7	10.4

[a] Food prices were freed in July. This explains the large increase during the "freeze."
Notes: Prices: The Consumer Price Index. Wages: Production Worker Average Hourly Earnings. Money Per Unit of Real Output: M_2 divided by real GNP. Quarterly real GNP was interpolated linearly to estimate real GNP for the appropriate month.
Sources: Various issues of the *Monthly Labor Review* (Prices and wages); the *Federal Reserve Bulletin* (Money); and the *Survey of Current Business* (GNP).

prices during Phase I and Phase II, but then had lagged behind. Over the period as a whole, there had been little change in real wages. The lesson was clear: Strong controls reduced inflation and raised real wages.

Some economists shared the public's interpretation, but others worried about suppressed inflation. Were the high rates of inflation observed in the latter phases of controls the result of unleashing inflation that had been kept in check by strict controls in Phases I and II? If so, the public was focusing on the wrong part of the program. Rather than blaming the weakness of Phase III controls for the acceleration of inflation, the public should have been condemning the strength of the Phase I and II controls. The concern with suppressed inflation naturally led economists to think about the role of monetary policy. Had the Federal Reserve added to the problem of suppressed inflation by expanding the money supply too rapidly during the early phases of the program?

The third column of Table 7.2 shows the rate of growth of money per unit of real output during the various phases of the program. It provides a simple way of addressing the question of suppressed inflation. This is the same measure used in the examination of the earlier experiments with controls. The behavior of this variable suggests that the concern with suppressed inflation was justified. The growth of money per unit of real output was faster than prices in the eight months before controls were imposed, in Phase I and again in Phase II. It is not surprising then that inflation proceeded more rapidly than the growth of money per unit of real output when controls were relaxed in Phase III. Phase III was, to use another term, a period of catchup inflation. Over the whole period, from August 1971 to April 1974, prices, wages, and money per unit of real output grew at similar rates. This implies that in the absence both of controls and of any change in monetary policy, the rate of inflation would not have been very different over the period as a whole. The main effect of controls was to turn a steady inflation into a fluctuating inflation, clearly a disappointing result.

My analysis suggests that much of the inflationary pressure accumulated in the early months of the program was released during the latter phases, so catchup inflation was probably not a major explanation for the double-digit inflation which hit the economy in late 1974. This acceleration of the inflation rate probably had its origin in the "supply side" shocks which hit the economy at that time. These were well understood. First, there was the run-up in oil prices in late 1973 in the aftermath of the Arab Oil Embargo. Second, there was the substantial rise in world food prices that has been attributed to crop failures in several countries, and even to a shortage of those famous Peruvian anchovies, which are a close substitute for American soybeans. In effect, these shocks raised the ratio of money to real output by reducing the resources available for producing goods and services.

The central conclusion for policy that follows from an examination of this episode is that the Vietnamese controls were a lost opportunity. If a restrictive monetary policy had been imposed at the same time that controls were used, we could have avoided both the vacillating nature of the program and the disappointment we experienced when controls were lifted and we discovered that inflation was as much a problem as ever. Think for a moment about the contrast between monetary policy in the Korean and Vietnamese Wars. During the Korean War, money per unit of real output was kept virtually stable from the time controls were imposed until they were removed. In fact, money per unit of real output actually fell at an annual rate of −0.6 percent per year. During the Vietnamese War, by contrast, money per unit of real output grew at an annual rate of 5.8 percent from the time controls were imposed until they were removed. Is it any wonder that in retrospect the Korean controls appear to have been a success and the Vietnamese controls a failure?

A considerable number of econometric studies have been made of the Vietnamese episode. In a general way these analyses support the historical treatment sketched above. They differ with it, however, and differ among each other, with respect to many significant details. A survey of the more important of these studies will serve to establish the limits of what we know and do not know about the Vietnamese experience.

The logic underlying most of the econometric studies can be better appreciated by exploring a simple version of the model that underlies them. The simplest interpretation of this model is based on the markup pricing approach to predicting inflation. In this approach the debate over whether monetary forces or fiscal forces are the ultimate cause of inflation is put to one side. Instead, inflation is related to the behavior of costs, particularly wages, and a measure of aggregate demand, such as the level of unemployment. Presumably, monetary policy influences prices through its effect on the aggregate demand variable. This approach follows naturally from a consideration of the pricing policies of a typical firm. In any particular period a firm may experience some increase in costs. Part of this increase may be offset by increased productivity. But the rest will have to be passed on in the form of higher prices. In addition, the firm will want to maintain or if possible increase its profit. This will also mean price increases. Whether the firm can maintain or increase its profits, whether it can maintain or increase its "markup" on its costs, will depend in turn on the state of demand for its product. Thus, it would appear that a regression that explained inflation in terms of the behavior of costs, productivity, and a demand variable, might do a good job of predicting inflation even if the fundamental causes of inflation are ignored. This is the way that most of the investigations of controls have proceeded. Once the regression is estimated, the path of inflation in the absence of controls can be derived from the coefficients of the regression and the actual or assumed values of the independent variables.

Typically, the equation estimated can also be interpreted as a Phillips curve. The Phillips curve is the economist's term for the relationship between inflation (or in some formulations, unanticipated inflation) and the level of unemployment (or some closely related variable). For our purposes, however, the simpler interpretation, markup pricing, is adequate.

The markup pricing approach, unfortunately, is not entirely satisfactory for estimating the effects of controls. The problem is that the equations have no way of representing suppressed inflation. Suppose that a markup pricing equation were estimated for an economy at full employment. Suppose further that the money supply were then expanded rapidly while controls kept prices and wages constant. We know from our experience after World War II, if from nothing else, that prices would rise rapidly once controls were removed. But a markup pricing model would fail to predict the inflation. None of the terms of the equation would reflect the growth of suppressed inflation. Thus, the attempt to quantify the effects of controls during the period when controls were in place would lead to underestimates of the effects of the policy. Nevertheless, the markup pricing model was widely used to analyze the Vietnam controls, mainly because models that attempt to incorporate fundamental determinants of the price levels, such as the money supply, have not always done a good job of explaining inflation in periods when there are no controls. Many of the investigators of controls thus chose to use the markup pricing model on the grounds that it gave the best results when applied to precontrol or postcontrol data.

Table 7.3 shows the portrait of controls derived from a bare bones markup pricing or Phillips curve model. First, the rate of inflation was regressed on the trend rate of inflation, assumed to be the determinant of wages and other costs over which firms have little short-run influence, and the gap between real GNP and its trend value, assumed to be a good proxy for aggregate demand. The constant term was expected to capture the effects of productivity growth. Next the path of inflation in the absence of controls was generated from the coefficients of the regression, the actual gap in real GNP, and the actual and predicted rates of inflation as appropriate. Finally, the simulated rates of inflation were deducted from the actual rates and the results cumulated so the effect on the price level could be observed.[16]

In general Table 7.3 is consistent with the monetary analysis developed above. Controls, according to the regression, held prices down, with the effect reaching a maxiumum of −1.5 percent during Phase III. In other words, prices were −1.5 percent lower in the first quarter of 1973 than they would have been had controls never been imposed.

Table 7.3. *The impact of controls on the measured price level 1971 (3)–1975 (4) percentage difference between actual and simulated prices)*

Year	Quarter			
	1	2	3	4
1971	—	—	−0.3	−0.6
1972	−0.4	−1.0	−1.3	−1.4
1973	−1.5	−1.3	−1.2	−0.9
1974	−0.9	−0.2	0.7	2.0
1975	3.3	3.4	3.9	4.4

Notes: The table is derived from the equation

$$p = \underset{(.91)}{.37} + \underset{(10.71)}{.94L(p)} + \underset{(2.66)}{.30g}$$

where p is the percentage change in the GNP deflator, $L(p)$ is the rate of change in the GNP deflator from the year before, and g is the gap between real GNP and an average of real GNP one year before and after. The equation was estimated for the period from the fourth quarter of 1957 to the fourth quarter of 1978 by the Cochrane Orcutt method. The R^2 was .91; t statistics are in parentheses below the appropriate coefficient.
Source: Various issues of the *Survey of Current Business.*

This effect – which was significant when compared with the rate of inflation prevailing when controls were introduced – dissipated quickly. Indeed, it was gone by the end of Phase IV. The absence of suppressed inflation in the last phase means that the large run-up in prices in 1974 and 1975 comes as a "surprise" to the model, and cannot be accounted for by a return of the price level to an equilibrium. Again, the explanation seems to be the supply-side shocks described above.

Table 7.4 summarizes most of the econometric studies of the Vietnam episode with which I am familiar. These studies focused explicitly on the control period. There are many other studies, of course, that include dummy variables for this period and thus provide some evidence on the effect of controls. But here I have decided to stick with analyses in which the main concern was controls. Of these studies the one by Alan Blinder and another by Blinder and William Newton are among the most recent and the most sophisticated. The underlying model of inflation

Table 7.4. *Econometric studies of the Vietnam controls*

Investigator	Method	Maximum gap (percent)	Timing of maximum (by quarter)	Catch-up (full or partial)
Lanzillotti, Hamilton, & Roberts				
Model A	Markup	-2.4^a	1972–4	n.a.
Model B	Markup	-4.5^a	1972–4	n.a.
Model C	Markup	$-.2^a$	1972–4	n.a.
Adams, Green, & Rowe	Large-scale Keynesian	-1.0^b	1973–4	n.a.
Darby	Monetarist reduced form	-4.2^c	1973–1	n.a.
McGuire	Rational expectations	-1.4^c	1972–2	Yes
Gordon (1975)	Markup	-3.5^d	1973–3	n.a.
Gordon (1977)	Markup	-2.4^d	1972–4	n.a.
Blinder	Markup	-1.7^b	1974–1	n.a.
Blinder & Newton				
Model A	Markup	-3.1^d	1974–1	n.a.
Model B	Markup	-4.2^d	1974–1	n.a.
Eckstein	Large-scale Keynesian	-1.4^c	1973–4	n.a.

[a] Private nonfarm deflator.
[b] Consumer Price Index.
[c] GNP deflator.
[d] An index of nonfood, nonenergy prices.
Sources: References for all of these studies can be found in the Bibliography. With the exception of Adams, Green, and Rowe, which was apparently unpublished. For the latter, the entry in the table is based on a report in Dunlop (1974G, pp. A-99–A-102). The table omits a study by Fiege and Pierce (1976B) which eschewed economic modeling.

in these discussions is the markup pricing model just illustrated, but it is worked out in considerably more detail. Since the two investigations were quite similar, it is only necessary to consider the second in order to understand their underlying logic.

Two equations were estimated. The price equation related the rate of change in the consumer price index, net of food and energy prices, to the share of the economy under controls, to the rate of change of labor productivity, to the rate of change of unit labor costs, to a demand variable (several were tried) and to a special variable designed to catch the inflationary impact of decontrol. The latter was based on the fraction of the consumer price index decontrolled in a particular month. The share of the economy under controls was expected to be negatively related to the rate of inflation, and the share decontrolled in a particular month was expected to be positively related to the rate of inflation. Lags were introduced where this seemed appropriate. A second equation related wages, one of the independent variables in the price equation, to consumer prices and the rate of unemployment. The estimated regressions were then used to generate two hypothetical price paths: one with controls on and one with controls off. The advantage of this procedure over one that compares actual prices with simulated prices, as I did above, is that the comparison of two hypothetical price paths does not attribute the effect of random disturbances to controls.

Three experiments with this approach – they would seem to differ primarily in the choice of different proxies for aggregate demand – yielded similar results with respect to the point in time at which the repression of the price level reached a maximum. All three models put this in February 1974. This is plausible, although somewhat later than is suggested by some of the other investigators. The three models differed somewhat, however, with respect to the issue of catchup inflation. The earlier study (by date of publication) showed prices catching up with and then exceeding the level that would have prevailed had controls never been imposed. By 1977, according to this model, consumer prices were about one percent higher than they would have been had controls not been used. This is a somewhat surprising finding although it could be rationalized by appealing to the argument that controls had interfered with the way new capital had been invested. In the later formulations, however, this anomaly disappeared. One of these experiments showed the consumer price index (excluding food and energy prices) returning, after controls were removed, to about where it would have been anyway. The other of the later experiments showed prices remaining below what they would have been without controls. As late as December 1975 the consumer price index (again excluding food and energy prices), according to this model, was still some 2½ percent below what it would have been had controls not been imposed.

Robert Gordon's 1977 study is the one closest in spirit to the analyses discussed immediately above; although Gordon did not use a variable to measure the extent of the economy controlled. His results, a maximum repression of the consumer price index (excluding food and energy prices) of about 2.4 percent, are similar to those presented by Alan Blinder and William Newton. But Gordon finds the maximum effect coming earlier, at the end of Phase II, and he does not find a permanent effect on the price level.

A later date for the maximum repression is supported, however, by simulations using large-scale econometric models. It is difficult to give a simple description of these models. They are based, in general, on the Keynesian model of income determination, and prices are calculated through a markup–pricing equation. The most recent results based on this methodology are presented by a group headed by Otto Eckstein. Using a giant 900-equation model and dummy variables for the control periods, they found that the maximum repression of the GNP deflator was about 1.4 percent in the first quarter in 1974.

Thus, if one is willing to forgo the attempt to get a precise picture of the effects of controls, and to rely on the most recent estimates using the markup–pricing approach, one can develop a general outline of the effects of the Vietnamese War policy that commands general agreement. Controls appear to have suppressed the price level for a time by an amount that was significant given the rates of inflation prevailing when controls were imposed. This effect dissipated as controls were weakened and removed. But both the initial depression of the price level and the subsequent catchup were small compared with the inflationary shocks which subsequently hit the economy.

The range of results reported in Table 7.4, however, warns against putting too much faith in any one particular set of numerical results.[17] Michael Darby's study, for example, used a different methodology (a monetarist reduced-form equation) and came to the conclusion that controls had a much larger impact – reaching 4.2 percent in the first quarter of 1973. Darby regressed the real stock of money on lagged nominal stocks and used this regression to simulate prices in the absence of controls, in the last respect following a procedure similar to the one I used with the markup pricing equation underlying Table 7.3. Professional opinion remains sharply divided on the theoretically correct method for modeling inflation, so it would be presumptuous for me to single out one model as best. Nevertheless, the very general conclusion drawn from an historical analysis, that controls suppressed inflation for a time, but that some or all of these gains were offset as controls were weakened and removed, seems consistent with almost all of the econometric studies.

Table 7.5. *The administrative costs of the Vietnam era controls*

Sector	Annual cost (millions of dollars)	As a percentage of Postal Service expenditures in fiscal 1971
Government		
Phase II	107.6	1.2
Phase III	78.4	.9
Phase IV	99.9	1.1
Average	95.3	1.1
Business[a]		
Minimum	721.4	8.0
Maximum	2,024.4	22.4
Total[b]		
Minimum	799.8	8.8
Maximum	2,132.0	23.6

[a] The Cost of Living Council reported these estimates with the warning that they might be biased by being too heavily weighted by industrial firms.
[b] The total minimum adds the Phase III estimate for government and the minimum for business; Phase II is used for the total maximum.
Sources: Costs: Dunlop (1974G, Appendix O, annualized cost, p. A-106; Appendix P, Estimated Total Annual Cost to Business, p. A-109). Postal Service: U.S. Dept. of Commerce, Bureau of the Census (1972G, p. 489).

Professor Blinder concluded in his earlier treatment that the decision to embark on controls was a mistake. The small and temporary depression in the price level was not worth the costs, particularly the catchup inflation which resulted from their removal. He also suggests that this may be inherent in peacetime controls.[18] But looking at a broader set of examples leads to a less pessimistic view. The significance of the wartime periods earlier in the century is that in those cases prices were driven by fears of shortages to levels higher than consistent with the long-run determinants of aggregate demand. Controls served an equilibrating function. It is conceivable that peacetime emergencies analogous to these wartime situations might occur, even if the Vietnam episode was not one of them.

The size of the bureaucracy

President Nixon was adamant that his controls would not be administered by a "huge bureaucracy." He claimed, referring at times to his own experience at the Office of Price Administration in World War II, which he served for a time as an attorney, that this was one of the great dangers of controls.[19] As Table 7.5 shows, his wishes were carried out. Annual expenditures by the government (and the figures seem to include most of the expenses associated with controls) never amounted to as much as two percent of the annual expenses of the Postal Service, the basis of comparison used in earlier chapters. To be sure, the Postal Service is the largest civilian bureaucracy, but it is obvious that increasing the budget of the Service by two percent would not pose a noticeable burden.

On the other hand, the cost to the government was only the most visible part of the administrative costs. Businesses incurred costs in complying with controls. Several surveys were taken by business groups which purported to show large costs in this area. But the respondents to these surveys had an incentive to overstate costs, since the purpose of the surveys was to win sympathy for business. A more reliable study was conducted by the Internal Revenue Service. The incentive to exaggerate remained, but in this case it was tempered by an unwillingness to lie to a powerful agency. This survey, the results of which are also shown in Table 7.5, indicated that business expenses were considerably larger than government costs. The maximum estimate of business costs is nearly twenty times those incurred by the government. But even including business costs leaves the total in the affordable range, a bit less than 24 percent of Postal Service expenditures.

Distortions

"Distortion" was the term of choice by economists and government administrators during the Vietnam War episode for a misallocation of resources produced by price controls. Numerous allegations of distortions surfaced during the period, but for a number of reasons many of these charges must be viewed skeptically. It was tempting for businesses to lay their own failures at the door of government; a business that simply failed to anticipate the changing structure of the demand for its product, for example, might well blame its failure on price controls. Critics of the controls frequently tended, moreover, to consider the problems in one market at a time. They failed to see that granting a price increase, while easing a shortage in one market, would aggravate shortages in others. The real problem was with the general level of prices and wages, a problem that could be solved only by abandoning controls or adopting a more restrictive monetary policy.

We can be surest of those distortions acknowledged by the price controllers. Here we have the testimony of a hostile witness; it is unlikely that the controllers will concede more mistakes than absolutely necessary.

The closest thing to a final report issued by the Vietnam controllers was a statement John Dunlop made before the Senate Banking, Housing and Urban Affairs Committee. In Appendix Q he discussed the distortions alleged to have been caused by controls, dividing them into proven and unproven cases. Four cases were conceded: excessive exports of copper, shortages of beef, excessive production of heavier weight paper, and to a very limited extent, the disappearance of low-end textiles. Two of these, those involving textiles and beef, were also problems near the termination of controls in 1946. The recurrence of these problems resulted partly from structural characteristics of the industries, which will be discussed below. One cannot rule out the hypothesis, however, that an element of memory was involved. People in these industries may have remembered that the shortages were successful in 1946 in winning concessions from the government.

The evidence that controls produced a beef shortage in 1973 is still familiar. Ceiling prices were imposed on March 29, 1973. The rate of cattle slaughter abruptly fell below the levels recorded in 1972, but then recovered in May and June. On July 19 it was announced that price ceilings would be lifted on September 10. This was clearly the key action. From this point on it was foolish to send animals to market because once controls were lifted prices would inevitably be higher. Domestic slaughter rates plummeted. Stories about shortages being faced in the stores filled the press. When ceilings were terminated on schedule, slaughter rates abruptly returned to normal, and the shortages disappeared.

The beef shortages were undoubtedly the fault of controls in the sense that had there never been any controls there would never have been any shortages. But it could well be argued that it was not so much the control of beef prices but the decision to lift control, and especially the decision to announce in advance the date when control would be terminated, which really aggravated the problem. Had that announcement not been made, slaughter might have continued at close to a normal rate, as it had for the two months before the announcement.

The beef shortages quickly reversed public opinion concerning price controls in this sector. In April 1973, after meat prices had been frozen (with other food prices still free to vary), the Harris Poll asked a nation-wide sample whether they favored or opposed placing all foods under federal price controls. The results were 46 percent in favor, 41 percent opposed, and 13 percent not sure. In July 1973, during the period when controls were in effect, the Harris Poll asked various questions about what should be included in the Phase IV controls. Asked whether they favored a rollback and freezing of food prices, 76 percent of the respondents said they favored it, only 16 percent were opposed, and 8 percent were not sure. But in August, when the shortages were in full bloom, the results were very different. The Harris Poll asked whether "all price controls should be dropped on beef so that farmers will produce more beef, and that will bring the price of beef down": 64 percent agreed.[20]

The last statement, incidentally, contains the kind of fallacy that students in elementary economics are continually warned against. Lifting controls might have produced additional supplies because prices would be higher. But those additional supplies would not then operate to produce lower prices. Increased supplies would be forthcoming, by assumption, only as long as the price remained higher.

Whether controls on beef and the resulting shortages had a similar dramatic effect on attitudes toward the entire control program is difficult to tell because the questions asked by the pollsters changed over time. The clearest evidence comes from a series of Harris Polls which asked people to choose between a price and wage freeze on the one hand, and the existing system, whatever it might be, on the other. The per-centage favoring a freeze appears to have turned upward in the first half of 1973. It then fell well below 40 percent in the second half of 1973, as a result, I would argue, of the beef shortages. But the evidence is ambiguous since the fall in the second half of 1973 could be interpreted as a return to a downward trend observed earlier. The Gallup Polls, moreover, failed to document the change. In June 1973 the Gallup Poll asked people whether they wanted to go back to Phase I controls after Freeze II. Fifty-two percent favored returning to Phase I, 32 percent were opposed, and 16 percent had no opinion. But in August 1974, after the termination of controls, and presumably after a large shift in public opinion, a similar 50 percent still favored bringing back wage and price controls.[21]

Another problem reminiscent of World War II was the disappearance of low-end textiles. The price controllers, however, investigated four firms pointed out by the American Textile Manufacturers Institute and failed to document (to their satisfaction) the extent of the shift or any link with controls.[22] Instead, Dunlop attributed the problem (if it existed!) to rising input prices and increased capacity utilization. The complete logic behind his arguments, however, is far from clear. Rising input prices would have produced a larger fall in the output of low-end merchandise if demand in this part of the market were more elastic. But it is far from obvious that this was the case. Increased capacity utilization, because it reflected rising demand, may explain, to some extent, the disappearance of low-end merchandise if demand was increasing more rapidly for high-quality items. But again it is far from obvious that this was true.

A similar problem, but one where Dunlop concedes a clear link with controls, occurred in the market for printing paper. A buyer's market in 1970 had led to considerable emphasis by producers on lighter weight papers. As markets tightened, producers shifted toward the heavier weights. If prices were free to vary, buyers with a strong preference for lighter weight papers would have bid these prices up and maintained production. But price controls – particularly the "cap," a regulation which limited the amount by which the price of a given item could be increased above that of the product line as a whole – prevented this adjustment. The result was the disappearance of the preferred lighter weight papers.

The most dramatic cases of inefficiency occurred in those markets in which producers had the alternative to selling in an uncontrolled world market. This is a familiar problem. One of the main difficulties faced by controllers during the Revolutionary War was that the controls were regional and local efforts; there always existed an incentive to divert desperately needed supplies to uncontrolled markets. What was true in 1776 was also true in 1973. Dunlop discussed the cases of copper and copper scrap.[23] In early 1973 copper scrap exports were running at rates similar to those that had prevailed in 1972. But when the freeze was announced in June, exports jumped, producing a domestic shortage.

Exports then fell back to normal levels when the price was freed on July 19. A similar experience was recorded in the market for new copper from domestic producers.

There are three ways out of the dilemma posed by the existence of uncontrolled world markets: letting the domestic price rise to the world level; subsidizing domestic sales, or imposing quotas on exports. The Vietnam era controllers chose the first alternative. But during the late 1960s, when the Johnson administration was trying to hold these same prices down through a combination of "jawboning" and the release of stockpiled copper, quotas were imposed. The lesson is simply that free trade and domestic price controls do not mix.

Table 7.6 shows the three measures of efficiency familiar from previous chapters. As before, it is clear that the imposition of controls did not cause a dramatic decrease in productivity. In fact, through Phases II and III productivity gains were what might have been expected on the basis of the 1960s. Over the period 1960–70 real output per labor hour had grown 2.9 percent per year, Kendrick's measure of total factor productivity has gone up 2.4 percent per year, and Denison's, 2.0 percent per year. Productivity did decline in 1973–5 as controls were removed. But this is probably better attributed to the supply shocks that hit the economy, the recession, and perhaps the onset of what appears to be a secular decline in productivity growth. It is conceivable that the measures of output were distorted to some extent during Phases II and III because of unmeasured price increases, but as the discussion in the next section will show, the number of sectors where this was widespread was too small for this effect to be concealing a decline in productivity.

The early 1970s were, however, years of strong aggregate demand, although the economy had weakened in comparison with the late 1960s. (The NBER reference cycles show a trough in the fourth quarter of 1970 and a peak in the fourth quarter of 1973.) Could the relatively strong performance of aggregate productivity be the result simply of strong demand or other extraneous influences? Denison's partition of productivity growth by source provides one answer. The contribution of his categories which would appear to be most sensitive to controls – gains from the reallocation of labor and residual growth – are shown in the last column of Table 7.6.[24] In other words this column shows that, if high aggregate demand, favorable farm weather, and so forth had made no contribution to growth, productivity would still have grown by these percentages.

Table 7.6. *Productivity growth, 1970–5*

Years	Real output per labor hour (% change)	Kendrick's measure of total factor productivity (% change)	Denison's measure of total factor productivity (% change)	Denison's measure of total factor productivity (sources sensitive to controls) (% change)
1970–71	3.1	2.2	2.0	1.4
1971–2	2.8	3.2	4.0	3.0
1972–3	2.0	2.0	1.5	1.4
1973–4	−3.5	−2.9	−4.8	−0.8
1974–5	2.1	0.6	−2.0	−3.7

Sources: Column 1: various issues of the *Monthly Labor Review.* Column 2: Kendrick and Grossman (1980B, p. 114). Column 3: Denison (1979B, Table 5-1, Column 1, p. 65). Column 4: Denison (1979B, Table 5-1, columns 2, 3, and 12, p. 65).

But the contribution from the sources especially sensitive to controls was about what could have been expected on the basis of experience during the 1960s. Over the interval 1960 to 1970 the average contribution from these sources had been 1.7 percent per year. Thus, neither the qualitative evidence, nor the aggregate productivity measures, show a strongly negative imprint from controls. As usual, the brevity of the episode, and the ability of businesses badly affected to modify or evade the rules, combined to preserve the productive efficiency of the economy.

Evasion

The following example illustrates some of the problems, and some of the fun, of administering price controls in an age of electronic journalism. But it contains more important lessons as well. George Meany had charged on television that the number of matzoh balls in Mrs. Adler's matzoh ball soup had been reduced from four to three, with no corresponding change in price. C. Jackson Grayson, the head of the Price Commission, checked with the executives at Mrs. Adler's and, on learning that they denied the charge, sent his staff out to buy matzoh ball soup. Some thirty cans were opened to reveal four matzoh balls in each. The following Sunday, on the program "Face the Nation," Grayson waited for the appropriate moment and then, holding aloft a can of soup he had been concealing, he proclaimed the truth about Mrs. Adler's matzoh balls! The story verges on the surreal. Yet it clearly illustrates the ultimate difficulty with controls: the tendency of the administrators to become involved in every aspect of the production process.[25]

Even when an allegation of evasion appears to have some validity, in the sense that prices were, in fact, being raised indirectly, price controls may not have been the cause. Frequently, the practices referred to are the sort that would have developed in an uncontrolled economy that was rapidly approaching full employment. There were reports, for example, that fertilizer dealers were cutting off their slow-paying customers.[26] This process was undoubtedly aggravated by the tremendous demand for fertilizer produced by the widening gap between uncontrolled agricultural prices and controlled fertilizer prices. But even in an uncontrolled market, buoyant demand would probably have led fertilizer dealers to pressure their slow-paying customers, while trying to maintain the price to valuable long-term customers.

Reports of evasion were most frequent in the same competitive industries that had created problems in earlier episodes. The lumber industry produced numerous reports of quality deterioration (altered dimensions and specifications for plywood) and daisy chains with multiplied markups.[27] The beef industry, one of the problem areas in earlier episodes, also generated a substantial share of the allegations. Special sales were reduced.[28] And there was an increase in custom slaughtering, as there had been in World War II, partially for the purpose of assuring supply, but also for the purpose of hiding the buyer's ability to dispose of the beef at over the ceiling prices. It was also alleged that cattle were exported to Canada and then reimported into the United States, a scheme that was perfectly legal, and one that might have been profitable because the price of imported beef was not controlled.[29]

Evasion also occurred in concentrated sectors. In part this happened among the dealers and brokers who distributed products manufactured by oligopolies. A drive against auto dealers, for example, netted numerous cases of overcharging on parts.[30] Similarly in the oil industry, a drive against service stations which catered to truckers, undertaken as a result of complaints by the truckers, also caught numerous violators, although in some cases it was only the price posting rules that were violated.[31] Small brokers and sellers of fuel oil found it profitable to evade the controls, especially after the Arab oil boycott led to a substantial increase in price. Oil was bought and then resold, often in swap agreements, not because such sales were necessary to distribute the product, but simply because each dealer was allowed to add his normal markup. Thus daisy chains were created, where ordinarily the fuel would have changed hands only a few times.[32]

Evasion in the concentrated manufacturing industries also occurred in labor markets. The Chrysler contract with the United Auto Workers was alleged to have been a "controls contract." Numerous benefits were increased so that the total package exceeded the government's guidelines, even though it seemed to go along with the rules if evaluated solely on the basis of the visible costs.[33] The reason was that the contract included changes in pension benefits, supplemental unemployment benefits, and contributions to a dental insurance plan whose ultimate effect on costs would depend on how frequently workers became eligible for them. Ex ante, these costs could be estimated only on the bases of certain assumptions. It was relatively simple, then, to claim that the contract fell within the guidelines by making "conservative" assumptions.

This example suggests an intriguing idea: In labor markets just the opposite of Galbraith's hypothesis about cooperation with controls holds true. Professor Galbraith argued, as I have had occasion to note in previous chapters, that in product markets it was the concentrated industries that were easier to control. It appears, however, that in labor markets the situation is reversed; it is the markets characterized by a few large employers bargaining with a few large unions that are harder to control. The reason is that in competitive labor markets contracts are generally simple. Since the worker may be moving on after a short time, and since employers do not have the resources with which to administer a complicated program of "fringes," benefits that will accrue in the future are too uncertain to negotiate. the costs, moreover, of negotiating separate contracts that involve contingent benefits are prohibitive. On the other hand, in concentrated labor markets a single complex contract involving contingent and future benefits is likely to be the norm and to provide considerable opportunities for evading controls.

Evasion, however, was not confined to distributors or to the labor market side of concentrated sectors. The steel makers allegedly evaded controls through forced uptrading.[34] Traditionally they had manufactured three grades of sheet. In order to comply with the price controls they restricted their increase to the lowest grade; but they eliminated the middle grade, forcing buyers who normally bought this material to purchase the most expensive sheet. If price controls were made permanent, some form of control would have to be applied to the quantities of each product, perhaps something analogous to the MAP program for textiles tried at the end of World War II. It was also alleged at the end of the program that the auto makers violated agreements reached with the government to keep postcontrol price increases small.[35]

But these examples, while useful in creating a sense of the reality of controls, as we know from previous chapters, cannot be used to determine whether evasion deserves to be labeled "serious," "widespread," or "substantial," as opposed to "minor," "limited," or "insignificant." One could easily put together a long list of evasions for virtually any law which seriously interferes with what people want to do and which is seriously enforced. But such a list would not ordinarily imply that the law should be abandoned. Table 7.7 shows the number of court cases generated by controls, the measure we have relied on previously to create a quantitative picture of evasion.

Table 7.7. *Civil cases commenced in U.S. District Courts under the Vietnam controls, fiscal 1972–fiscal 1974*[a]

	1972	1973	1974
Economic Stabilization Act	376	283	175
Antitrust	1379	1206	1270
Total cases	96,173	98,560	103,530
Line 1 as a percentage of Line 2	27.3	23.5	13.8
Line 1 as a percentage of Line 3	0.4	0.3	0.2

[a] Includes the District of Columbia and territories.
Sources: U.S. Administrative Office of the United States Courts *Annual Report, 1973*, (1974G, Table C2, pp. 324–327); *Annual Report, 1974* (1975G, Table C2, pp. 389–390).

As a fraction of all activity in Federal District Courts, the increment created by the Economic Stabilization Program was small, never reaching 0.5 percent. (Remember that at its peak in World War II the same measure stood at over 50 percent.) To a limited extent the smallness of this figure during the Vietnam War reflects the heavy reliance on voluntary compliance by the stabilization program in the 1970s. Cases were taken to court to make examples of flagrant or strategic violators and to demonstrate the ultimate penalty for noncompliance. But even when the volume of cases generated by controls is compared with the number of antitrust cases, where the enforcement philosophy was similar, the burden generated by controls does not appear to have been substantial. At its peak, as line 4 of Table 7.7 shows, controls cases were only 27.3 percent of antitrust cases. The fundamental reason for the small burden placed on the judicial system, when compared with World War II, is that under the Vietnam controls a small volume of suppressed inflation was built up and then quickly dissipated while in World War II excess demand continued to grow until controls were removed. The incentive to violate the regulations, in other words, never became acute during the Vietnamese experience.

Vietnam as an antimodel

Economists from a surprisingly wide segment of the political spectrum agree that the Vietnam controls were a failure. If the impact on production and distribution were not as disastrous as some predicted, the effects on inflation also appear to have been small. A temporary reduction in inflation was traded for a higher rate of inflation as controls were removed, an even bargain at best. Contrasting the Vietnam experience with earlier episodes clarifies the reasons for the failure of the Vietnam controls. In the earlier episodes in the twentieth century, controls were imposed when fears of inflation and shortages had driven prices above the level consistent with underlying monetary forces. Controls were then an equilibrating force, although this conclusion must be qualified for the latter days of World War II. The Vietnam controls were used to depress prices below the level determined by fundamental economic variables. They were a disequilibrating force. Once the Vietnam controls were imposed, moreover, monetary policy took exactly the wrong tack; the money stock was allowed to expand rapidly. In the Korean War, by way of contrast, monetary policy, as a result of the Treasury–Federal Reserve Accord, followed a conservative path.

Why monetary policy was so expansionary during the Vietnam episode is not clear. The timing of the largest increases has given rise to considerable speculation. The money stock (M_2) increased 2.4 percent from December 1968 to December 1969 and 7.7 percent from 1969 to 1970. The rate of growth then accelerated to 10.8 percent in both 1970 to 1971 and 1971 to 1972. It then decelerated to 8.4 percent in 1972 to 1973, and to 6.9 percent in 1973 to 1974. One interpretation of these figures is that the Federal Reserve, under chairman Arthur Burns, was acting to reinforce the election chances of Richard Nixon. A second interpretation, which has more relevance to our concerns, is that the Federal Reserve was reacting to the imposition of controls. With the responsibility for inflation now in the hands of the price controllers, the Federal Reserve was free to get credit for lower interest rates or higher employment without worrying about being blamed for inflation.

Neither of these explanations, however, fits the facts all that well. Paul McCracken has noted that the expansion of the money supply in the early 1970s was a worldwide phenomenon which could hardly be attributed solely to the efforts of Arthur Burns to reelect Richard Nixon, or to American price controls, for that matter.[36] He might also have pointed to evidence closer to home. The rate of monetary increase clearly accelerated well before controls were imposed and before the election campaign. The rate of growth of total bank reserves, a variable subject to greater control by the Federal Reserve than the money supply, actually decelerated to 0.1 percent from December 1971 to December

1972. An equally plausible case could be made that in increasing the growth rate of the money supply in the early 1970s, the Federal Reserve was simply allowing the money supply to rise in response to an alarming increase in unemployment, an explanation that might apply to other countries whose business cycle was moving in synchrony with ours.[37]

What is clear, however, is that the opportunity provided by controls to adjust the rate of growth of the money stock to a rate consistent with long-term price stability was lost. The failure to coordinate monetary and price policy was thus a crucial factor in the failure of the Vietnam controls to alter the long-term path of inflation. It helps explain why so many professional economists have agreed that the Vietnam episode with controls was especially unsuccessful, a judgment with which I heartily concur.

8. Lessons for the recent crisis

It is, however, undoubtedly the fact that price fixing and propaganda against price raising are much more *à la mode* today than old-fashioned inflation. The political advantages of this policy are obvious. The objection to it is that, unlike old-fashioned inflation, it does nothing to bring about equilibrium, indeed on the contrary.

John Maynard Keynes, 1940

Taming the whirlwind

Can controls help in the fight against inflation? The answer is yes. In certain circumstances, a temporary application of controls can substantially reduce inflation at a reasonable cost. Controls can thus provide a breathing spell in which monetary and fiscal reforms can be introduced. The evidence for this comes from balancing the benefits and costs for those episodes in the past when controls have been used. History in this case is useful, a valuable tool for policymakers.

The record is particularly clear in the twentieth century. Strong inflationary surges originating in the fear of wartime inflation and shortages have been arrested. During World War I the rate of inflation measured by the wholesale price index was reduced from a figure of 32.4 percent per year in the fifteen months preceding controls to an annual rate of 7.1 percent in the fifteen months that were under controls. During World War II from April 1943, when President Roosevelt issued his Hold-the-Line Order, until June 1946, when price controls were suspended, the consumer price index increased at a rate of only 2.3 percent per year, a remarkable performance in a fully employed economy with heavy deficit spending. During the Korean War the rate of increase in the consumer price index was 11.1 percent per year from June 1950, when the war began, to January 1951, when a price freeze was imposed, but only 2.1 percent per year under controls. Even during the Vietnam War, when the emergency was less extreme, a slowing of the rate of inflation was observed.

To be sure, price indexes tended to understate the true rate of inflation when controls were in force. Producers found various ways of raising prices indirectly. They reduced quality, eliminated lower priced lines of merchandise, tied the sale of desirable goods to the purchase of unwanted goods, and so forth. Some sales, moreover, took place in black markets at overceiling prices. Indirect and clandestine price increases naturally did not find their way into the price indexes. During World War II, when this problem was most severe, a Presidential Committee was given the task of examining the effect of indirect increases on the consumer price index. An expert subcommittee, chaired by Wesley C. Mitchell, reported that by December 1943 the true consumer price index was potentially from 2 to 3.2 percent higher than the published index. By 1946 the situation had deteriorated further. I estimated that an extrapolation of the Mitchell Committee's estimate to June 1946 showed that the true index was then from 4.8 to 7.3 percent higher than the published index. Since my additions were incomplete, it is likely that the true index was still somewhat higher.[1] But the higher of these two numbers still suggests raising the estimate of the rate of inflation during the hold-the-line era only to, say, 5 percent per year. It is unlikely that even a perfect accounting of the neglected increases would overturn the finding that the price of a limited but crucial market basket was held relatively stable during World War II.

It has also been argued that price increases were only postponed by wartime controls. Controls were thus pictured as a dam holding back a flood; once the dam gave way, the water flowed with even greater force than before. Indeed, from June 1946, when the World War II controls were removed, to March 1947, when the pent-up inflation seems to have spent most of its force, prices rose at a 21.4 percent annual rate. But as high as this rate was, the price level would probably have reached still higher levels during the war, or shortly after, had controls not been used. The entire argument is too complex to repeat here, but its essence is that during the major wars the amount of money created was limited by controls. The government printed money in order to acquire the resources it desperately needed to prosecute the war. By holding down the cost of those resources, controls limited the total expansion of the money supply. The dam, to return to the analogy, need not burst. It can be used to hold back a sudden flood, and protect the cities downstream, while the excess water is slowly drawn off, and the river returns to its normal ways.

In summary, controls reduced the rate of inflation in the short run and in some cases in the long run. At times the reductions were substantial. The benefits of this to those individuals and institutions whose income could not adjust quickly to price increases is obvious. It occurred in situations, moreover, remarkably similar to our present crisis.

The costs of controls

The costs of controls were not as obvious as their benefits (a fact, incidentally, which explains a good deal of their popularity), but the economic historian must nevertheless estimate how great they were. There are four major costs to consider: (1) the size of the bureaucracies that had to be created to administer controls, (2) the damage they caused to economic efficiency, (3) the black markets that arose in response to controls, and (4) the additional burdens placed on our political institutions and labor relations. In the experiences we have examined, costs in all of these areas were heavy, but in the short run they were manageable.

The government bureaucracies were not large, except in World War II. The peak annual employment at the Office of Price Administration, which was reached in 1945, was a total of approximately 64,000. To this number it is necessary to add an estimate of the full-time equivalent of the volunteers who worked for the Office of Price controls and an estimate of the personnel who worked for other agencies whose primary function was price control or rationing. These additions raise the total involved in price regulation in 1945 to about 150,000 persons. To put this number in a comparative context, the total was about 40 percent of contemporaneous employment at the Post Office, our largest and perhaps most familiar civilian bureaucracy. If the comparison was carried out in terms of expenditures, the corresponding figure would be 35 percent.

Opposite the government bureaucracy there stood a bureaucracy of considerable magnitude within the private sector. Estimates are either absent or unreliable for earlier episodes, but a credible survey was taken during the Vietnam War. This survey put the annual costs of complying with the controls at from $700 million to $2 billion per year. Again, using the postal system as a reference, this figure ranges from 8 to 22 percent of the annual budget of the system. Since the Vietnam controls were designed with an eye to minimizing business costs, it is likely that in earlier episodes, particularly World War II, the costs were heavier.

Thus, the administrative costs of controls were far from trivial. But, an expansion of the postal system by 40 percent, or even 60 or 70 percent (to include an allowance for business costs), seems not too high a price to pay for arresting a dangerous inflationary spiral. After all, even this level of costs would have amounted to only 0.4 percent of GNP at the peak in World War II.

Added to this, of course, are the costs stemming from reduced economic efficiency. Bureaucrats, it is argued, cannot set relative prices with the same sensitivity to the nuances of supply and demand as the market. Certainly the history of controls provides numerous examples in which knowledgeable and sympathetic observers conceded that controls produced shortages or other symptoms of inefficiency. During the Revolutionary War, the main problem was that controls were typically local, and at most regional. There was an obvious incentive to divert supplies to areas where the price was uncontrolled. In World War I a shortage of sugar in the Northeast, manifested in long lines, was exacerbated by the inept policies of the controllers. In World War II gasoline shortages on the East Coast were apparently made worse by the unwillingness of the controllers to disturb standing commercial relationships; and the severe and controversial shortages of meat which attended the demise of controls in World War II are further evidence that controllers can make costly allocative mistakes. During the Korean War, too, the controllers created problems when they attempted to roll back the price of beef for purely political reasons. Finally, during the Vietnam war, shortages of copper developed because the domestic price was controlled while the world market price was free to fluctuate.

These examples, and others examined in the preceding chapters, are drawn from the writings of the controllers themselves. Since the controllers were, for the most part, both well informed and sympathetic to their own programs, their allegations are immune to the criticism that they come from a source biased against the regulations. These examples, however, even if they could be substantiated beyond a shadow of a doubt, would not prove that the total volume of mistakes was greater in the controlled economies than it had been under the free market. Mistakes are constantly being made in market economies. Every unprofitable investment is testimony to the existence of such mistakes. Only an index of aggregate productivity is capable of showing whether, on the whole, the controlled economies were less efficient than the market economies they replaced.

The most commonly used measures of aggregate productivity show that controls did not damage the allocative mechanism in the short run. Quite to the contrary. During the twentieth century aggregate productivity rose in every full year of price controls. These gains, particularly the large ones recorded during the hold-the-line period in World War II, do not prove that controls had no negative effects or that they enhanced productivity. Virtually all of the experience with controls is from wartime economies, and this imparts a significant upward bias to the productivity indexes. War goods were produced under conditions of rapidly increasing economies of scale, so the measured performance of the economy was improved even though no real change had taken place in the system's technical or organizational efficiency. It is instructive to note that productivity increases were larger under the World War I and II controls, when this effect was stronger, than under the Korean and Vietnam War controls. In addition, price indexes tend to be biased downward during periods of price control. This led to an overstatement of real output, and hence to an overstatement of productivity (since the measurement of inputs was usually less affected). These episodes, moreover, were too short for us to form a clear idea of what the course of productivity change would have been in the long run under controls.

What these reservations mean is that we cannot rule out a cautious restatement of the efficiency criticism. One can still argue that productivity change was less than it would otherwise have been, or that productivity change would have slowed in the long run. The qualitative evidence suggests that such a restatement would be near the truth. But the available evidence establishes rather clearly that the sudden and dramatic *decrease* in productivity envisioned by some critics of controls is a myth.

A more important cost of controls in the short run was the black market. Qualitative evidence of the black market abounds. During the Revolution, Benjamin Rush charged in the debate over controls that merchants had evaded local restrictions on the prices of rum, sugar, and molasses by raising the prices of the containers. During World War I, wheat price controls were evaded by selling inferior grain at the price fixed for the best grade. During World War II, the black market was even more extensive. In meat production tie-in sales, forcing customers to buy unwanted merchandise to get what they really wanted, were common. Eventually, the Office of Price Administration charged three of the big four packers with such activities. For a time an open black market flourished in poultry in the Delaware–Maryland–Virginia area, and the state police had to be used to intercept trucks laden with black-market chickens. In the clothing field the elimination of lower priced lines of merchandise was a severe problem that the OPA wrestled with repeatedly and unsuccessfully. In the housing market, landlords raised rents indirectly by reducing the amounts spent on maintenance. This list could easily be lengthened.

In the Korean War, black markets were restricted primarily to the strategic war materials, but here the black market was extensive. In steel, for example, the product sometimes moved from the mill to a "respectable" end-user through a long daisy chain of gray marketeers. The Vietnam War provides fewer examples of evasion, but even during this episode important examples can be adduced, typically from industries that had been particularly troublesome in earlier periods of control. Reports of violations were especially frequent, for example, in the lumber industry.

As in the efficiency case, however, quantitative evidence is needed and the best available measure of the black market is the number of cases reaching the courts. This measure is not fully satisfactory since it depends on the vigor of enforcement, the attitudes of the courts, and other extraneous factors. But, if one is careful to compare controls with laws backed by similar enforcement efforts, and aimed at similar ranges of activity, some useful judgments can be made. Approached in this spirit, the evidence points to an "extensive" black market in World War II, the most prolonged experiment. Office of Price Administration cases amounted to about 54 pecent of the civil cases in federal district courts by 1946. Or, to take another view, they amounted to a bit more than 45 percent of the cases generated by the prohibition laws in a comparable year. In other episodes, the volume of cases eventually reaching the courts was much smaller. During the Korean War, control cases at the peak were 11.8 percent of the total. The logical conclusion seems to be that temporary controls, especially if combined with a restrictive monetary policy, will produce a moderate black market, but if controls are used to permanently suppress a substantial inflation, the black market will become burdensome.

Powerful economic interests, moreover, had means of evading controls which did not reveal themselves in conventional statistics. In the Korean

War, for example, while small steel distributors frequently engaged in stereotypic black-market transactions, the steelmakers found a very different way of fighting controls, one they had used in earlier episodes. By refusing to complete wage negotiations (thus making a strike inevitable), until price increases were assured, they were able to put considerable pressure on the price controllers. The steelmakers eventually won some price relief, after a controversy which involved the seizure of the industry, a long strike, and a historic legal confrontation with the government.

Other interest groups were able to pressure the Congress into amending the price control laws in their favor through conventional lobbying. During most of World War II, the price controllers were given a fairly clean grant of power. But, after VJ Day (and in the latter stages of the Korean War), the guiding legislation was amended in ways which seriously interfered with effective price control. Indeed, it was the orgy of amendments in the final days of the World War II experiment which led John Kenneth Galbraith, perhaps the best known advocate of controls, to express a yearning for a world without such regulations.[2] I will return to these neglected forms of evasion, and some possible ways of dealing with them, in the section on "The Keys to Success."

Assessing the costs of evasion is not easy. Indeed, the purely economic effects may well be positive. A price increase that occurs in an open black market, or through quality deterioration, or that is won through political pressure, will serve an equilibrating function similar to that produced by a price increase in a free market. The extent of evasion probably explains much of the successful record on productivity; evasion took the rough edge off of controls. Nevertheless, there is a very real, if hard to measure, erosion of the social fabric when a substantial segment of the population expends considerable effort in evading the law. Prohibition is the classic example, but wartime black markets are a close second.

The attempt by the controllers to suppress evasion led to a progressive regimentation of economic life. It is axiomatic that when price is not used as a rationing device, some form of physical rationing must be substituted or evasion will be severe and the economy far less efficient. But rationing was adopted only slowly and reluctantly, because while price control was popular, rationing was not. A good example was provided by developments in the clothing industry during World War II. Although reluctant, the OPA was gradually moved to propose programs which specified the exact amounts of particular styles individual manufacturers could produce. In wartime these restrictions were accepted, in part because they were not attributed directly to price control. Even the seizure of firms in disputes arising out of the stabilization program met public acceptance in the world wars (although not in the Korean conflict). But most Americans would count the irksomeness of such regimentation as a heavy cost of peacetime controls.

What all this shows is clear. In the short run, twentieth-century wartime controls were generally worth the costs, heavy though they were. Controls made a positive contribution to the stabilization process. It appears, however, that controls were a wasting asset. The costs grew heavier while the benefits shrank and eventually became problematic. My conclusion is, therefore, that during the first three episodes in this century, although not in the most recent one, both the decisions to impose controls and the decisions to remove them were correct. The lesson for our day is that temporary controls can be employed profitably in peacetime to solve a similar emergency so long as they are terminated at the right time.

Voluntary or selective controls

Many of the cases we have referred to so far are ones in which controls were imposed across the board. Virtually all prices and wages were subject to legal restraint. It is sometimes argued that the benefits of controls, a reduction of inflationary expectations, could be achieved and the costs avoided by using less comprehensive controls. One suggestion is to make controls voluntary. Simply asking civic-minded business and labor leaders to forego price or wage increases or to follow some guidelines, it is held, will work – at least for a time. The lesson of history, here, is particularly clear. Voluntary controls will not work. In the early days of World War II and the Korean War, the government repeatedly called for voluntary restraint. Its call was backed by the authority of patriotism, a moral force that no peacetime government could hope to match. Yet the call went unheeded. Prices continued their upward surge. Eventually, stronger measures had to be adopted.

A second suggestion, which on the surface appears to be more realistic, is to make controls selective. Apply legal restraint only to those prices which are "leading" the inflation, or only to those prices which are set in markets dominated by large corporations and labor unions, runs the argument; thus the benefits of controls can be achieved without the regimentation of economic life which makes across-the-board controls so unpalatable. Again the lesson of history is clear. Selective controls may work for a short time, but then they are likely to fail. The reason is that demand will quickly shift from controlled to uncontrolled markets so that prices in the latter will rise even more rapidly. Eventually, this problem will lead to the abandonment of controls, or to the adoption of across-the-board controls. The selective controls imposed in World War I were in place for too short a time for this problem to become unmanageable. But in World War II selective controls could not stop the inflation. They were replaced by across-the-board controls early in 1942, and this time the controllers themselves recognized that the shift of demand to uncontrolled markets had made selective controls unworkable.

The keys to success

The first lesson to be drawn from America's experience with controls, then, is that across-the-board controls can make a positive short-term contribution to the stabilization effort. Whether they do so depends on how well the government can deal with a number of recurring problems. On one of these problems nearly all observers of controls, myself among them, are agreed: Controls will prove excessively costly if monetary and fiscal restraints are not maintained. If aggregate demand outruns aggregate supply, the black market will be almost impossible to control without regimenting society, and if controls are removed, a significant postcontrol price inflation will follow.

It is tempting to argue that restraining aggregate demand is bound to be impossible under controls. With one government agency directly responsible for prices, the monetary and fiscal authorities will have little incentive to keep aggregate demand in check. They are likely to be blamed for unemployment if aggregate demand is weak, but not for evasion of controls if aggregate demand is too strong. During the Vietnam period these considerations may have influenced the monetary authorities who failed to control aggregate demand once controls were in place, although the evidence is ambiguous.

But the experience during the Korean War shows that controls can be combined effectively with monetary and fiscal restraints. The rate of growth of money per unit of real output was close to zero (actually negative) during the control period. By the end of this period a number of prices were below their legal ceilings, and while some increases occurred after controls were removed, there was no postwar price explosion. This record was not an accident. At the beginning of the Korean War, Congress raised taxes to provide a secure source of revenues for the increased spending that lay ahead. Perhaps even more important was the famous "accord" between the Treasury and the Federal Reserve. This agreement ended the policy of maintaining low interest rates which had been followed in World War II and the immediate postwar years. It permitted the Federal Reserve to follow a conservative policy.[3] Thus, the Korean War experience shows that restraint can be maintained during controls, and that if this is done, controls can be removed without causing a surge in prices.

The question is how a similar policy could be assured in peacetime. There is no certain way of doing it, but we can see now that it would be useful to institutionalize a close working relationship between the monetary and price authorities. This could be done by creating a Board of Overseers to supervise the entire stabilization effort. This Board could include the head of the price control agency, the Chairman of the Federal Reserve Board, the Secretaries of Treasury, Labor, and Commerce, and representatives of the public. The Board would provide a basis for coordinating policies and could put pressure on the monetary and fiscal officials to support the price authority. Some further uses of the Board will be discussed below.

The history of price controls also shows that there are certain sectors of the economy that invariably become trouble spots. Success requires that the controllers deal aggressively with these sectors or the program itself will falter. Perhaps the single most troublesome area has been in the production and distribution of beef. As we noted in Chapter 5, shortages of beef and other meats may have been the single most important factor in turning public opinion against controls at the end of World War II. Beef seems to be one of those commodities to which the public attaches much greater importance than its weight in the consumer price index would seem to warrant; the consumer's surplus in beef consumption, to use the technical jargon, is substantial. Two courses lay open to the controllers: to ration beef and other meats, or to subsidize their production. The path of least resistance is to subsidize, and the wise course would be to anticipate the need for subsidies from the outset of controls. Provision should be made in the legislation establishing controls for subsidizing crucial areas and the subsidies should be applied as soon as shortages and black markets develop. Similar problems are likely to arise in wearing apparel. Here, the experience in World War II provides elegant testimony that rationing and other physical controls are likely to be unworkable. Again, subsidies would appear to be the right answer.

Subsidizing these and similar trouble spots will make control in other areas more difficult; inducing more resources to enter the troublesome sectors will exacerbate shortages elsewhere. But this is a price that should be paid – at least in the short term. Once the decision to control prices is made, no useful purpose is served by allowing shortages in strategic sectors to undermine public confidence in the program.[4]

Labor relations become more complex in a controlled economy and can easily become the rock upon which controls run aground. In effect, each strike becomes a two-way negotiation between labor and management, on the one hand, and the price and wage authorities, on the other. Strikes may drag on, irritating the public, while labor and management press the price and wage authorities for increases in excess of those already granted. As we have seen, this tactic was held in abeyance during World War II by the no-strike and no-lock-out pledges, but it came to full flower after VJ Day, and recurred during the Korean War.

The Board of Overseers, which we suggested above, could play an important role in blunting this potential hazard. Wage and price decisions in the case of major strikes could be passed through to the Board. It could overrule the price and wage agencies, if a face-saving concession was in order, or it could reaffirm their decision and place the authority of the whole government behind the decisions. It could also supply information from other agencies in the formulation of policy, which might make it possible to avoid confrontations.

History shows that one of the greatest dangers to controls lies in the tendency of legislators to make exemptions for favored constituents. Controls were most effective when they were applied across the board. When key prices were omitted, demand shifted to those areas, leading to substantial price increases and a distortion of production. Yet, the potential profits provided an enormous incentive for legislators to reward pressure groups with exemptions. Even during the Revolutionary War, a key problem in getting states to join in price controls was the benefit which any legislature could gain for its constituents by keeping them out of the controlled sector: Commodities would be diverted to their markets. In the early days of World War II, the special considerations for agricultural products built into the legislation were a constant headache to administrators. This problem was held in abeyance during the hold-the-line period but reemerged with vehemence when the legislation came up for renewal in June 1946. The latticework of exemptions and special privileges built into the renewal legislation was an important consideration in President Truman's veto. Again, during the Korean War, exemptions were the order of the day.

Obviously, in a democratic society there is no sure way of protecting the legislation from the machinations of special interest groups. But the Board of Overseers suggested above could play a modest role in protecting the ability of the controllers to apply regulations in an even-handed manner. An important function of the Board's staff would be that of reviewing and commenting on proposed changes in the law. The Board's claim to represent the broader interests of society would provide perhaps some counterweight to the legislature's claim to represent its constituents.

A short-run palliative

Controls, the record suggests, have frequently been effective in dealing with wartime inflationary emergencies. In recent years, we have witnessed a similar emergency developing in peacetime. Two similarities are striking: First, in both the wartime emergencies and the current crisis, huge government outlays financed by monetary expansion fueled the inflation, and more important, created the expectation that still further inflation lay ahead. In recent years, both the actual government budget and the full employment budget have remained in deficit year after year. In both the wartime emergencies and the present crisis inflation fed in part upon itself. The expectation of inflation led people to borrow and buy in the hopes of avoiding higher prices, and profiting by repaying debts with cheaper dollars, tomorrow. The wartime crises were brought on by forces outside the government's control, while today's crisis owes much to the failure of the government to manage its own affairs prudently. Nevertheless, the outcome of domestic mismanagement has been similar to that of wartime defense expenditures; the result has been a strong inflationary momentum that traditional monetary and fiscal policies could cure by themselves – but only if the government had the courage to use them and to risk a severe recession.

The second similarity with the wartime emergencies has been the role played by disruption of the flow of raw materials from abroad. In wartime, particularly at the start of World War II, this was brought about by enemy action. The analogy today is the series of price increases imposed by OPEC. In both cases, the disruption of the flow of raw materials contributed to the inflation directly by reducing the real resources available to the economy and indirectly by contributing to the expectation of still more inflation. These similarities suggest that the remedy for an inflationary emergency which worked in wartime would also work in peacetime.

But this analogy also reminds us not to lose sight of the other lessons of the wartime experience. The first is that without monetary restraint, controls will fail. If there is not an immediate breakdown, there will be evasion and a postcontrol inflationary surge. The second lesson is that controls are a wasting asset; after the emergency has passed, the controls must be removed with dispatch. To maintain controls permanently once reasonable expectations for price stability have been established would saddle the economy with a burdensome bureaucracy, an extensive black market, reduced economic efficiency, more acrimonious labor relations, greater incentives to corrupt the legislature, and an irksome regimentation of economic life.[5]

With what kind of medicine should we compare controls? In the debate over controls in the Continental Congress, two centuries ago, Richard Henry Lee came closest to the truth. He compared controls to a palliative. They are a medicine to be used to dull the pain and tranquilize the patient while monetary restraint and reform of our fiscal affairs work the fundamental cure. To renounce controls completely would subject the patient to needless pain, assuming that he would subject himself to the treatment at all. But to rely on controls to work the whole cure, or to continue their use after health was restored, would create more problems than it would solve. Thus, the extremists on both sides of the debate over controls are wrong. Controls are more than a mere placebo. But they will never be a wonder drug for an ailing, inflationary economy.[6]

Notes

The letters after dates in reference citations refer to divisions of the Bibliography: B, books; J, journal articles; G, government documents; and U, unpublished materials.

1. The debate over controls

1 Goodwin's *Exhortation and Controls – The Search for a Wage–Price Policy, 1945–1971* (1975B) traces these attempts from the end of World War II to 1971.
2 The original suggestion was made by Wallich and Weintruab (1971J). Since that time this proposal has been debated at length, and has inspired numerous additional proposals. These proposals are carefully explored in *Curing Chronic Inflation*, a conference volume edited by Okun and Perry (1978B).
3 Most of the arguments in the debate will seem familiar to the reader once attention is drawn to them. A perusal of my bibliography will lead the reader to a number of essays in which aspects of the debate are argued in detail. The essays by Friedman (1966B), Galbraith (1952B), and Solow (1966B) are particularly rewarding.
4 This story, as monetary economists will realize, makes two common but controversial assumptions. First, it assumes that inflation is largely a monetary phenomenon, and second, that, at least in the short run, the private sector can make repeated errors in its predictions. These assumptions will be maintained in the narratives that follow.
5 Friedman (1974B, pp. 86–7).
6 Friedman (1966B, p. 34). This is separate from the disequilibrium effects stressed by Barro and Grossman (1974). These seem unimportant for the wartime experiments.
7 See Schuettinger and Butler, *Forty Centuries of Wages and Price Controls* (1979B) for an entertaining, if one-sided account, of these and similar episodes.
8 See Fite (1910B, pp. 136–7) for an example of this attitude.

2. Forgotten experiments

1 See Hughes (1976B) for a stimulating discussion of economic controls of a wide variety, not simply price controls, and their relationships to colonial society.
2 Morris (1946B, pp. 86–90) is the source of statements in this section when no explicit reference is given.
3 Bruce (1935B, vol. 2, p. 289). Of course, even if the price had been free the planters would have had an incentive to pass the bad tobacco, but planters would have found it hard to unload bad tobacco without cutting the price on it.

4 "Wyatt Manuscripts" (1927J, 250–1). For the most part the interpretation of this proclamation is straightforward, but one aspect requires some clarification. Tobacco served as a medium of exchange during this period, as it did throughout the colonial period. For most goods on the schedule, money was supposed to exchange at the rate of one and one-half units of tobacco money to one unit of English money. But for three the ratio was different: for sherry it was 2.25, for Newfoundland fish it was 1.6 and for Canada fish, 1.75. This might be simply a misprint. If not, it seems likely that a varying exchange rate between tobacco money and English money would have proved unworkable. In principle, for example, one could have bought a gallon of sherry for nine shillings in tobacco, used the tobacco to buy a gallon of Malaga, and then sold the Malaga for six shillings in English money. The result would have been a profit of two shillings. Clearly, something would have to give. I have no proven explanation for why these unworkable ratios were incorporated. One potential explanation is that Governor Wyatt was paid in English money and was rather fond of fish and sherry! The general rule to cover other imports also implies an unworkable ratio.

5 Morris (1946B, p. 57).

6 Shurtleff (1853–1854B, vol. 1, pp. 74, 76).

7 Winthrop (1908B, vol. 1, p. 112).

8 Morris (1946B, p. 56).

9 Shurtleff (1853–1854B, vol. 1, p. 111) quoted in Morris (1946B, p. 59).

10 Shurtleff (1853–1854B, vol. 1, p. 110).

11 Thompson (1971J) has described an analogous phenomenon: the preservation in the English food riots of the eighteenth century of behaviors sanctioned by the emergency price-fixing orders employed during the Elizabethan period.

12 Morris (1946B, p. 74).

13 Ibid., pp. 61–3.

14 Winthrop (1908B, p. 24) quoted in Morris (1946B, p. 56).

15 Morris (1946B, pp. 70, 75–7).

16 Winthrop (1908B, vol. 1, pp. 315–18).

17 Shurtleff (1853–4B, vol. 1, p. 331).

18 Bailyn (1955B).

19 There is a clear parallel between the decline of regulation in New England and the transition from "traditional" economics (paternalistic interference with the market) to the classical economics of Adam Smith in eighteenth-century England. See the paper by Thompson (1971J) and the responses by Coats (1972J) and Genovese (1973J) for a discussion of this issue.

20 Shurtleff (1853–4B, vol. 5, pp. 62–3).

21 Morris (1946B, p. 76).

22 Davisson's (1967J) price indexes for Salem start in 1641, which is somewhat late to form an opinion concerning the first experiment, and they show, moreover, such year-to-year variability that little can be deduced about the effects of the second experiment. Anderson's (1975J) estimates are decade averages, too long to be of use here. McCusker's (1978B) series of exchange rates of Massachusetts on London has a small but distinct fillip in 1676; it rises from 123.89 in 1675 to 129.17 in 1676. But the increase might have been limited by the export of silver, even if inflationary pressures were strong. McCusker (1978B, p. 139).

23 There were a number of other factors which led to the zoot-suit riots, including racism. See Blum (1976B, pp. 205–6).

24 David and Solar (1977B) present annual specie-equivalent indexes of the consumer price index for the years 1774 onward. These are based on Bezanson's estimates. I preferred Bezanson's because an index in continental dollars reveals the full extent of the inflation, and also because this was the series that had to be used in Table 2.3.

25 Lerner (1956B, p. 173).

26 Franklin, *Writings* (1905–7B, vol. 1, pp. 306–7; vol. 2, pp. 133–155).

27 Ibid., vol. 7, pp. 292–4; vol. 8, pp. 151–52.

28 Ibid., vol. 9, p. 234.

29 *Journals of the Continental Congress*, vol. 1, pp. 78–9.

30 Morris (1946B, pp. 94–97).

31 Ibid. pp. 97–99 gives an account of the debate. He concentrates on the legal and political arguments, while I have confined myself to the economic side. Scott (1946J, pp. 456–458) also gives a brief account of the debate. All of the quotations which follow are from Burnett, *Letters*, vol. 2, pp. 250–253.

32 *Journals of the Continental Congress* (1904–37G, vol. 7, pp. 124–5).

33 Morris (1946B, p. 100).

34 Ibid., p. 102 quoting the *Providence Gazette*, June 21, 1777.

35 *Public Records of Connecticut* (1894G, vol. I, pp. 603–4).

36 Ibid., p. 603.

37 Ibid., pp. 605–6.

38 Morris (1946B, p. 103).

39 Burnett, *Letters* (1921–36B, vol. 2, pp. 568–9) quoted in Morris (1946B, p. 104).

40 Chitwood (1967B, pp. 136–42).

41 *Public Records of Connecticut* (1894G, vol. I, pp. 614–15) quoted in Morris (1946B, pp. 104–5).

42 *Public Records of Connecticut* (1894G, vol. I, pp. 615–17).

43 Scott (1946J, p. 463).

44 Washington, *Writings* (1893B, vol. VI, pp. 417–18).

45 Burnett, *Letters* (1921–36B, vol. 4, pp. 232–3).

46 Phillips (1866B, vol. 2, pp. 121–8 and 130).

47 Bezanson (1951B, p. 232).

48 Ibid., p. 150.

49 Phillips (1866B, vol. II, p. 128).

50 Gross (1976B, p. 145). Handlin and Handlin (1947J) *passim* also emphasize the conflicts among various interest groups.

51 Morris (1946B, pp. 112–13).

52 Shattuck (1835B, p. 123).

53 Morris (1946B, p. 121).

54 Gross (1976B, p. 144).

55 Morris (1946B, pp. 122–3).

56 Ibid., pp. 124–5.

57 The English-speaking colonies were not the only ones to introduce controls during this period. In October 1777 the governor of New Orleans published a set of maximum prices (Don Bernardo De Galvez, 1777U). And while controls were being abandoned on the East Coast, they were being adopted in California. What appears to be the first set of maximum prices for Spanish

California was issued in January 1781. This is discussed by Mosk (1938J). The prices set in California were, in terms of nominal units, extraordinarily low by modern standards. An "ordinary sound horse" was not to be sold for more than nine pesos, and a "bull for slaughtering," three to four years old, was not to be sold for more than four pesos. These efforts may have been connected with the events in the English-speaking parts of the continent. The Revolutionary inflation may have produced an outflow of specie that generated rising money supplies and rising prices in New Orleans and California. It is not clear how long controls were applied in California. But Mosk has an interesting hypothesis about what caused their ultimate demise. Controls were effective, he argues, as long as most agricultural commodities were produced by the missions, but when nonmission production became important, controls became unenforceable. The core of this hypothesis is that the more competitive a market, the more buyers and sellers in it, the harder it is to enforce controls. This point was made frequently by observers of controls in World Wars I and II, and was given special emphasis by John Kenneth Galbraith. I will examine this thesis in some more detail in Chapter 5.

58 Hicks (1969B, pp. 99, 162).

3. World War I

1 Coit (1957B), a detailed biography of Baruch, covers these years particularly well.
2 Cuff (1973B, pp. 58–60).
3 Garrett (1920G, p. 204).
4 Ibid., p. 223.
5 Baruch (1960B, p. 61).
6 Cuff (1973B, pp. 204–19).
7 Ibid., pp. 225–6 describes the entire process in these terms.
8 The classic discussion of bulkline pricing is Taussig (1919J).
9 The United States Sugar Equalization Board, discussed below in the text, worked on this principle.
10 Chairman Colver of the Federal Trade Commission suggested nationalizing Bethlehem Steel because of its high costs (Garrett, 1920B, p. 392).
11 This device was suggested by a committee of engineers. It is quite similar to the supply curve drawn by economists, but differs in several ways. It excludes normal profits from costs and makes a number of assumptions about the relationship between a firm's average costs at one moment and its marginal costs at other times. See Stein (1939B, pp. 105–6) for a discussion of the nature of the bulkline cost curves, and a comparison with the supply curves of economic theory.
12 Cuff (1973B, pp. 233–9) describes the attempt to develop the liberty shoe.
13 Hardy (1940B, pp. 178–80).
14 Willoughby (1934B).
15 Senate speech of February 27, 1918, quoted in Blakey (1918J, p. 589).
16 Blakey (1918J, pp. 590–1).
17 Warren (1919J, pp. 239–43).
18 Surface (1928B, pp. 123–24); Eldred (1918J, p. 34). Hoover (1920G, p. 28), not surprisingly, thought that without controls the price of flour would

have risen dramatically and that an epidemic of strikes significantly reducing industrial output would have resulted.

19 Surface (1928B, p. 145).

20 Eldred (1918J, pp. 47–8); Surface (1928B, p. 384); and Anderson (1918J, pp. 246–7).

21 Warren (1919J, p. 244).

22 Garrett (1920G, pp. 101–2).

23 U.S. Food Administration, "Official Statement," November 1918, p. 2.

24 Merritt (1920B, pp. 113–14).

25 Needham (1942G, pp. 39–53).

26 Garrett (1920G, pp. 145–6).

27 Hoover (1920G, p. 20).

28 Garrett (1920G, p. 227).

29 Ibid., pp. 640–1.

30 Hardy (1940B, p. 190).

31 Galbraith (1952B, p. 22).

32 *The Commercial and Financial Chronicle*, January 19, 1918, pp. 212–13.

33 U.S. Fuel Administration, *Report of the Distribution Division, 1918–1919*, (1919G) "Part II: The Zone System," p. 7.

34 U.S. Fuel Administration, *Report of the Distribution Division, 1918–1919*, "Part I: The Distribution of Coal and Coke," (1919G, p. 9).

35 The railroads sometimes confiscated coal on their own initiative.

36 U.S. Fuel Administration, *Final Report* (1919G, p. 252).

37 The zone system is described in U.S. Fuel Administration, *Report of the Distribution Division, 1918–1919*, "Part II: The Zone System" (1919G).

38 U.S. Fuel Administration, *Final Report*, (1919G, pp. 223, and 230–1).

39 *The Commercial and Financial Chronicle*, July 13, 1918, pp. 142–43.

40 U.S. Fuel Administration, *Report of the Administrative Division, 1917–1919*, "Report of the Bureau of State Organizations . . ." (1919G p. 14).

41 Garrett (1920G, p. 656).

42 Galbraith (1975B, p. 243) suggested that certain commodities, coal among them, could not be reduced in quality for technical reasons. Coal was simply too simple to reduce its quality. As we have seen, however, it was technically feasible. The reason for the high level of compliance in this market was probably that controls reduced fears of further price increases. This reduced the current demand for coal, so that the gap between the equilibrium price and the price the authorities were aiming at was not very large.

43 Lesher's procedure (for bituminous coal) was to take as the price in a given month the average realization for the year multiplied by one plus one-fourth of the percentage deviation of that month's spot price from the yearly average of spot prices. The average realization was simply the total value of coal mined divided by the number of tons mined. The major potential bias is the change in the quality of coal mined. Since, if anything, the average quality declined, it is likely that Lescher's procedure understates the postcontrol price increases. Lesher's results are discussed in Lesher (1919G) and Garrett (1920G, pp. 169–71, 175–7).

44 U.S. Fuel Administration, *Final Report* (1919G, p. 8).

45 Schaub (1920J, p. 14).

46 Ibid., p. 33; Hardy (1940B, p. 201). Hardy, however, mistakenly attributed the total to 78 committees.

47 There are certain limitations to the data that should be kept in mind. One was mentioned in the discussion of coal prices: The available data are too heavily weighted toward spot prices. The price of a weighted average of contract and spot prices might behave differently. It is also possible that even during a period as brief as World War I, evasion of controls, through quality deterioration (again the case of coal comes to mind), tie-in sales, and other means, may have led to some understatement in the rate of inflation in the controlled sector. A third problem is that the indexes of controlled and uncontrolled prices are for the wholesale level. In some cases prices controlled at the wholesale level rose, as we have seen, at the retail level. This tended to weaken spillover effects, since the nominally controlled sector was not, in fact, completely controlled.

48 The equation was

$$p = -0.32 + 1.21D_1 - 3.06D_2 + 1.50M + 2.21L ,$$
$$\quad (.69) \quad (1.01) \quad (2.53) \quad (3.42) \quad (1.01)$$

where p was the monthly percentage change in uncontrolled prices, D_1 was a dummy variable for the month in which the United States entered the war, D_2 was a dummy for the month in which the war ended, M was the stock of money (M_2), and L was the percentage of prices under control. The numbers in parentheses are the absolute values of the "t" statistics. The coefficients on M and L are the sum of the coefficients for an eight-period lag. These lags were estimated using the Almon method applied to a quadratic polynomial constrained at both ends. The Cochrane–Orcutt method was used to estimate the equations. The coefficient of determination was .38. The sources for the data are given in Tables 3.3 and 3.4. A few experiments were made with other lag structures, but the results were similar.

49 Cagan (1958J).

50 Friedman and Schwartz (1963B, pp. 218–19). They do not, however, specifically mention black marketeering as a factor in World War I and it is unlikely that it was important in this context.

51 Mullendore (1941B, p. 355). Hoover (1920G, p. 9) mentions an additional 750,000 people who gave part-time service on committees. But, as we will see in connection with the Office of Price Administration in World War II, the full-time equivalent service of part-time volunteers can be surprisingly small. On the other hand, Hoover argued that the profits of the grain corporation should be subtracted from the expenditures in Table 3.5 to get the true monetary costs of administration. But these profits are not resource savings, rather transfers from grain sellers to the government.

52 Fabricant and Lipsey (1952B, Table 4, column 16, p. 176).

53 This paragraph is based primarily on Blackman (1967B), *passim*.

54 Ibid., pp. 290–1.

55 Taussig (1919J, p. 209).

56 Garrett (1920G, p. 364); U.S. Bureau of the Census (1960G, series Y351, p. 718). I calculated total wartime expenditures as the sum of expenditures in 1917, 1918, and 1919. It is likely, however, that much commandeering simply represented an attempt to save out-of-pocket expenses. The extent to which it influenced compliance with price controls, though doubtless important, cannot be determined with any precision.

57 Baruch (1960B, p. 61). Urofsky (1969B, pp. 213–15) quotes this passage and credits its general accuracy. But Cuff and Urofsky (1970J, p. 299) refer

merely to a "stormy session" and then remark that "despite the general emotional hostility, however, each side followed its natural instincts in a bargaining situation and set about to make some kind of deal." But if the threat is taken seriously, this clearly was not an ordinary bargaining session, it was bargaining under duress.

58 Litman (1920B, p. 293).

59 U.S. Senate, Special Committee (1935G, pp. 50–2); Baruch (1921G, p. 100).

60 See Cuff (1971B); Cuff (1973B); Cuff and Urofsky (1970J); and Urofsky (1969B), *passim*, on this point.

61 Hoover (1920G, p. 37). This point is also made repeatedly in Hoover's *Memoirs*. Hoover (1951B, pp. 240–80).

62 Compare this argument with Clark (1917J).

63 U.S. Fuel Administration, *The Report of the Distribution Division*, 1918–1919, "Part II " (1919G, p. 6).

4. World War II: Attacking inflation directly

1 In preparing this chapter, I made extensive use of the remarkable series of histories of the war agencies, and of the programs and policies they carried out, written by former administrators under the aegis of the Committee on Records of War Administration. The Committee was organized with considerable foresight at the suggestion of President Roosevelt in March 1942. Studies were carried out not only of agencies as a whole, but also of individual programs and policies within those agencies. To be sure, these studies tend to be partisan accounts, minimizing failures or, perhaps just as frequently, blaming them on other agencies. But without these studies, our picture of wartime administration would have to remain far more uncertain than it is. See the U.S. Bureau of the Budget, *The United States at War* (1946G, pp. vii–xii) for a more detailed description of the project.

2 Wilson et al. (1947G, pp. 113–14).

3 Mansfield (1947G, p. 14).

4 Wilson et al. (1947G, pp. 21–2).

5 See, for example, Friedman and Schwartz (1963B, pp. 543, 545), and the references cited there.

6 Wilson et al. (1947G, p. 153).

7 Ibid., pp. 154–5 and 170–1.

8 Ibid., p. 156.

9 Ibid., p. 171.

10 Cantril (1951B, p. 654).

11 *Modern Industry*, September 15, 1941, p. 48.

12 Wilson et al. (1947G, pp. 46–7).

13 It was also in August 1941 that OPACS became OPA.

14 Wilson et al. (1947G, p. 128).

15 U.S. Bureau of the Budget, *The United States at War* (1947G, p. 247).

16 Wilson et al. (1947G, pp. 90–1).

17 Galbraith (1971B, p. 97).

18 Gallup (1972B, p. 305).

19 Ibid., p. 311.

20 Ibid., p. 328.

21 Cantril (1951B, p. 655).

22 Galbraith (1975B, p. 242).
23 See, for example, the speech by Chester Bowles, *New York Times*, March 1, 1944, p. 13.
24 Ibid., May 25, 1943, section 1, p. 1.
25 Ibid., July 15, 1943, section 2, p. 1.
26 Ibid., p. 15.
27 Katona (1945B, pp. 159–60).
28 Mansfield (1947G, pp. 68–9).
29 *New York Times*, April 7, 1944, p. 18.
30 Ibid., April 29, 1944, p. 14.
31 Ulman and Flanagan (1971B, p. 219).
32 Mansfield (1947G, p. 85).
33 Bernstein and Matusow (1966B, p. 65).
34 Blackman (1967B, p. 276).
35 *New York Times*, February 15, 1946, p. 1 and related stories.
36 Mansfield (1947G, p. 87).
37 Bernstein and Matusow (1966B p. 60).
38 Mansfield (1947G, p. 81).
39 Gallup (1972B, pp. 522–3).
40 Ibid., p. 535.
41 Ibid., p. 561.
42 A National Research Opinion Center survey in March 1946 showed 82 percent of the public thought controls would be "necessary" after the war; Cantril (1951B, p. 662). And a *Fortune* survey published in June 1946 showed 67 percent of the public favored continuation of controls; *Fortune*, June 1946, p. 8.
43 *New York Times*, April 9, 1946, p. 26.
44 *New York Times*, April 18, 1946, p. 1.
45 *New York Times*, August 9, 1944, p. 21. The poll was conducted by a trade association representing life insurance companies.
46 Krooss (1970B, p. 237).
47 Taft (1941J).
48 Cheney Boone, Director of the Bureau of Price Regulation, was murdered just before he was to address a dinner meeting of the National Industrial Association. Indeed, the murder weapon was a wrench that Boone had intended to exhibit during his lecture. The police were at a loss. Fortunately, detective Nero Wolfe took an interest in the case. He ferreted out the killer: Alger Kates, a weak-willed economist from the Bureau of Price Regulation, who was accepting bribes from a member of the National Industrial Association. See Stout (1946B).
49 *New York Times*, June 30, 1946, p. 1 and related stories.
50 *Monthly Labor Review*, September 1946, p. 427.
51 The Bureau argued, on stronger grounds, that the 29.6 percent increase was applicable if the base were moved back to April. Ibid., p. 424. Also see Bronfenbrenner (1947J) for a contrary view of events.
52 *New York Times*, July 17, 1946, p. 1.
53 Ibid., July 26, 1946, p. 1.
54 Here I am following the excellent summary in the *Nineteenth Quarterly Report of the Office of Price Administration*, February 18, 1947, pp. 1–10.
55 See Young (1956B, pp. 90–122) for a discussion of the Congressional politics of economic legislation in general.

56 *New York Times,* July 28, 1946, p. 1.
57 Ibid., September 25, 1946, p. 14.
58 Cantril (1951B, p. 663).
59 *New York Times,* October 15, 1946, p. 3.
60 Ibid., November 10, 1946, p. 1.
61 Ibid., November 11, 1946, p. 32.
62 By April 1942, 51.9 percent of the wholesale index was under formal controls. From September 1939 to April 1942 the average percentage under controls was 17.6 percent.
63 Wilson et al. (1947G, p. 332).
64 OPA, *First Quarterly Report,* p. 77.
65 Some evidence for this was obtained by regressing the monthly percentage change in uncontrolled prices (*P*) on lagged values of the monthly percentage change in the money supply (*M*) and the current size of the controlled sector (*L*). This regression was

$$P = \begin{matrix} -3.57 \\ (3.33) \end{matrix} + \begin{matrix} 3.70D \\ (3.23) \end{matrix} + \begin{matrix} 3.32M \\ (3.46) \end{matrix} + \begin{matrix} 8.50L \\ (3.92) \end{matrix},$$

where *D* is a dummy variable for American entry into the war. The numbers in parentheses are the *t* statistics; the R^2 was .59. The coefficients on *M* and *L* are the sum of the coefficients for an eight-period lag estimated by the Almon method applied to a quadratic polynomial constrained at both ends. The Cochrane Orcut method was used to estimate the equations. The large coefficients on *M* and *L* both suggest spillover effects. The source for *P* and *L* was the same as for Table 4.4 and for *M* it was Friedman and Schwartz (1970B, Table 1, column 9).
66 Friedman (1969B).
67 Toribio (1970D) found a similar pattern for Great Britain. His explanation, however, differs from mine. He stresses the increased sensitivity of money demanded to interest rates in a controlled economy rather than to reduced fear of inflation.
68 Wages are from U.S. Bureau of the Census, *Historical Statistics* (1975G), series D740 and D763. The adjustments to the price index are from Rockoff (1978J, p. 417).
69 Its first chairman was Donald Nelson, a former Sears executive. He has written an excellent account of the Board during his tenure, emphasizing his struggles with the military. Nelson (1946B).
70 See Novick, Anshen, and Truppner (1949B, pp. 163–93), for a detailed description of the Controlled Material Plan.
71 See Harris (1945B, pp. 176–286) for a discussion emphasizing the role of the plan in the effective prosecution of the war. It is easy, however, to exaggerate the role of these controls. By the time the Controlled Materials Plan was fully in place (July 1941), monthly war production had already reached 85 percent of the wartime peak. During the preceding months the price system, in the form of tremendously profitable war contracts, had been the mechanism relied upon to reallocate resources to the war sector.
72 This office was the successor to the Office of Civilian Supply originally associated with the OPA.
73 The OCR said much the same thing concerning the absence of a price adjustment in a memorandum on consumer surveys, Jones (1946G, pp. 247–8).

74 Ibid., pp. 222–3.
75 Ibid., pp. 321–5. One particularly ambitious scheme to deal with the shortages of low-quality textiles will be dealt with in greater detail below.
76 Fesler (1947G, pp. 324–31).
77 See Caplan (1947G) for a discussion of relations between the agencies from the OPA's point of view.
78 Marcus (1974B, p. 115).
79 Blum (1976B p. 95).
80 These and the following data on seizures are from Blackman (1967B, Appendix A, pp. 259–78).
81 Ibid., pp. 68–9.
82 For a time the two agencies were combined.
83 U.S. Bureau of the Budget, *The United States at War* (1946G, pp. 429–55).
84 Harris (1945B, p. 288).
85 *New York Times*, March 3, 1943, p. 29.
86 The ratio was formed by dividing the total civilian labor force in 1948; U.S. Bureau of the Census, *Historical Statistics* (1975G, series D14, p. 126); by the paid employment of the 3040 largest firms in 1948; Kaplan (1964B, p. 67).
87 It is also likely that certain biases exist in the data on volunteers. The estimate is based on the reported number of hours put in by volunteers, and the natural human tendency is to exaggerate. On the other hand, the estimate excludes the volunteers on certain advisory groups and in certain private sector enforcement efforts.
88 The total civilian labor force in 1943 was 55,540,000; U.S. Bureau of the Census, *Historical Statistics* (1975G, series 4, p. 126).
89 Rockoff (1981b,J, 389–92).

5. World War II: The market under controls

1 Nelson (1946B, p. 191).
2 See the section on evasion for a discussion of some of the problems of relying on rationing to allocate gasoline supplies in the Northeast.
3 U.S. Bureau of the Census, *Historical Statistics* (1960G, p. 462).
4 One of the mysteries of Table 5.2 is why the supply of edible fats was so low. The red point rationing program, which included meats and fats, was aimed primarily at providing a standard ration of edible fats rather than of protein, as someone who is familiar with today's health concerns might assume. No convincing explanation has yet been given. It was alleged at the time that there was a fat shortage because more fat was being sold with the meat during the war as a way of evading price controls. But this argument was effectively rebutted by the Mitchell Committee (1945G, p. 318). Lard consumption separately, moreover, was actually up somewhat during the war.
5 Galbraith (1952B, p. 34).
6 Tobin (1952J, pp. 538–40).
7 Bowles (1971B, pp. 80–3).
8 A more moderate step, temporary invalidation, was not tried simply because no one thought of it. Ibid., pp. 80–3.
9 U.S. Bureau of the Census, *Historical Statistics* (1960G, p. 187).
10 Russell and Crowe (1947G, p. 270).

11 Mansfield (1947G p. 176); Brinser (1951U, pp. 102–15).
12 U.S. War Production Board (1945G, p. 3).
13 Some rather limited attempts were made to achieve consumer level rationing through the voluntary cooperation of retailers (Alexander, 1946J).
14 Galbraith (1952B, p. 62).
15 A more serious problem may be the undercounting of capital produced with government financial assistance and used by the private sector. This problem does not appear to have been fully resolved as yet. Robert J. Gordon first stressed this issue. But Edward Denison suggests that taking this problem into account would not seriously affect the tenor of his conclusions. See Gordon (1969J), Denison (1974B, pp. 275–7), and the references cited in the latter source for a full discussion of the issue.
16 Gody and Searle (1946J).
17 Kuznets (1945B, pp. 50–1, 70–1).
18 Milward (1977B, pp. 66–7, 228–32) and *passim*, makes some of the same points, contrasts the American experience with that in the other belligerents, and relates productivity to the overall process of mobilization.
19 Much of this section is based on Duhl (1947U), an unpublished study which had been intended for the War Records series of administrative studies.
20 Mansfield (1947G, p. 224).
21 Duhl (1947U, p. 56).
22 George Stigler, a distinguished conservative economist, has argued that the licensing of businesses is one of the main aspects of economic life in which an unjustified diminution of freedom has taken place. See Stigler (1975B, pp. 18–19).
23 Duhl (1947U, p. 65).
24 The dilemma of a grocer who wanted to remain honest in a world of black marketeering is described in Farvish (1946J).
25 Lochridge (1944J) and (1946J).
26 OPA, *Fifth Quarterly Report*, pp. 57–8.
27 Emerson (1944U, p. 17).
28 Rothwell (1946G), *passim*.
29 Emerson (1944U, p. 17).
30 Rothwell (1946G, p. 33).
31 OPA, *Seventh Quarterly Report*, pp. 85–86; *Eighth Quarterly Report*, pp. 63–64.
32 *New York Times*, April 11, 1945, p. 16.
33 See Fantin and Madigan (1947G).
34 This section is based primarily on Caplan (1947G), and Carsel (1947G), the official histories of the Apparel Branch of OPA.
35 Carsel (1947G, p. 104).
36 Mitchell (1945G, pp. 332–5); U.S. War Production Board Textile Shortage in the First Quarter of 1945 (1945G, pp. 21–2); Katona and Leavens (1944J).
37 U.S. OPA, *NRDGA "Horror Exhibit"* (1946G).
38 Carsel (1947G, p. 134).
39 Ibid., p. 49.
40 Ibid., p. 56.
41 Ibid., p. 67.
42 MAP was eventually declared unlawful by the Emergency Court of Appeals, but by the time the decision was rendered, price controls were a dead issue.
43 Friedman and Stigler (1972B).

44 Mansfield (1947G, p. 119).
45 Gage (1947J, p. 56).
46 *Wall Street Journal*, June 21, 1946, p. 6.
47 Henderson (1946J, p. 47); quoted in Clinard (1952B, p. 196).
48 Mansfield (1947J, p. 139).
49 *New York Times*, April 23, 1946, p. 23.
50 Clinard (1952B, p. 192).
51 Ibid., p. 193.
52 Ibid., p. 201.
53 Emerson (1944U, p. 26).
54 *New York Times*, March 1, 1944, p. 1.
55 Clinard (1952B, p. 165).
56 Tobin (1952J, pp. 540–2).
57 The pleasure-driving ban is discussed in Mansfield (1947G, pp. 176–9).
58 *New York Times*, June 27, 1943, p. 3.
59 Galbraith (1975B, p. 243).
60 OPA, *Twelfth Quarterly Report*, p. 71.
61 Mitchell (1945G, pp. 366–7).
62 Ibid, p. 366.
63 Emerson (1944U, pp. 30–1).
64 Mitchell (1945G, p. 352).
65 OPA, *Seventeenth Quarterly Report*, p. 100.
66 OPA, *Eleventh Quarterly Report*, pp. 78–79.
67 Galbraith (1952B, pp. 10–27). I have also discussed this hypothesis in Rockoff (1981a,J).
68 OPA, *Seventeenth Quarterly Report*, p. 100.
69 See, for example, "Autos: The Blacker Market," "Autos: Operation Circus," "Black Market: Its Shady Dealings Involve All Kinds of Americans," Coffin (1946J), and Downs (1946J).
70 Galbraith (1975B, p. 243).
71 *Historical Statistics* (1960G, p. 570).
72 *New York Times*, February 29, 1944, p. 1.
73 See Arnow (1951B) for a complete history of the controversy.
74 Mitchell (1945G, p. 295).
75 *New York Times*, May 14, 1944, p. 40.
76 Galbraith (1975B, p. 244).
77 Galbraith (1952B, p. 21) conceded shortly after the war that the dominant memory was then of shortages.
78 Hoopes (1977B, pp. 281–307).
79 Clinard (1952B, p. vii).

6. The Korean War

1 Flash (1965B, p. 68).
2 Gallup (1972B, pp. 933, 948). Thirty-six percent thought a freeze was only a fair or poor idea, while 9 percent fell in the no opinion category.
3 *New York Times*, July 27, 1950, section 1, p. 1.
4 Ibid., July 16, 1950, section 3, p. 1.
5 Ibid., January 25, 1951, p. 15.
6 Johnson (1952J, pp. 293–4).

7 U.S. Office of Price Stabilization, *A Summary of Operations by the Director*, Second Report, p. 6.
8 Gallup (1972B, p. 992).
9 Ibid., p. 993.
10 Ackley (1953U, p. 423).
11 Ibid., pp. 425–30.
12 Defense Production Act Amendments of 1951, 65 Stat., 134.
13 Ibid., 65 Stat., 131.
14 U.S. Office of Price Stabilization, *Livestock and Meat Distribution Regulations*, section 1, p. 5, section 2, pp. 60–65; "Meat Black Market Mushrooms," *Newsweek* (1951J, p. 67).
15 Defense Production Act Amendments of 1951, 65 Stat., 135.
16 Ibid., 65 Stat., 136.
17 Letzler (1954J), *passim*.
18 Defense Production Act Amendments of 1952, 66 Stat., 298; "Case of the Simple Potato," *Consumer Reports* (1952J, pp. 393–396).
19 U.S. Economic Stabilization Agency, *ESA Under Eric Johnson* (n.d. U, p. 159).
20 *New York Times*, January 8, 1952, section 1, p. 16.
21 Ibid., January 24, 1952, section 1, p. 1.
22 Friedman and Schwartz (1963B, p. 598).
23 Hickman (1955J), *passim*.
24 In Chapter 4, I focused on the number of bureaucrats, because it is easier to examine the role of volunteers with that figure. Since this is less of an issue in this case, I have turned to the more general measure – total expenditures. For our purposes, however, the two measures of the size of the bureaucracy give roughly the same results in each case.
25 To avoid an excessively long discussion, I have omitted an explicit exploration of labor productivity in this chapter, concentrating instead on the supplementary information available with Denison's total productivity measures for the postwar period. The labor productivity numbers, however, lead to similar conclusions.
26 Marcus's *Truman and the Steel Seizure* (1977B) appears to be the best treatment for our purposes. I have relied on it considerably in this section.
27 Truman (1955–6B, volume 2, pp. 477–8).
28 Marcus (1977B, pp. 254–2).
29 U.S. Congress, Senate Select Committee on Small Business, *Steel Gray Market* (1951B, G), is the main source for the following paragraphs.
30 Friedman (1974B, pp. 86–7).

7. The Vietnam War

1 Wheeler (1976B, p. 28).
2 De Marchi (1975B, pp. 339–40).
3 *Business Week*, September 8, 1973, p. 18.
4 Nixon (1978B, p. 674).
5 Ibid., p. 518.
6 Weber (1973B, pp. 67–8). See also Cox (1980J) for a related argument.
7 The Cost of Living Council consisted of John B. Connally, Secretary of the Treasury (Chairman); Paul W. McCracken, Chairman of the Council of Economic Advisors (Vice Chairman); George P. Schultz, Director of the

Office of Management and Budget; George A. Lincoln, Director of the Office of Emergency Preparedness; Virginia H. Knauer, Special Assistant to the President for Consumer Affairs; Clifford M. Hardin, Secretary of Agriculture; James D. Hodgson, Secretary of Labor; Maurice H. Stans, Secretary of Commerce; George Romney, Secretary of Housing and Urban Development; and Arthur F. Burns, Chairman of the Board of Governors of the Federal Reserve System (special advisor to the council).

8 Gallup (1972B, p. 2321).
9 Harris (1971B, p. 175).
10 Barton (1974J, p. 512).
11 Weber (1973B, pp. 68–9).
12 Ibid, pp. 73–4.
13 Ibid, p. 121.
14 The members of the Price Commission were C. Jackson Grayson (Chairman), William Coleman, Robert Lanzilotti, J. Wilson Newman, John Queenan, William Scranton, and Marina Whitman. Mary Hamilton replaced Marina Whitman when the latter moved to the Council of Economic Advisors. The initial members of the Pay Board were George Meany, I. W. Abel, Floyd E. Smith, Frank E. Fitzsimmons, and Leonard F. Woodcock, representing labor; Leonard F. McCollum, Benjamin F. Biaggini, Rocco C. Siciliano, Virgil Day, and Robert C. Bassett, representing industry; and William G. Caples, Neil H. Jacoby, Kermit Gordon, Arnold R. Weber, and George H. Boldt (Chairman), representing the public. A number of the labor members later resigned claiming that the Pay Board was biased toward management.
15 Grayson and Neeb (1974B, p. 7).
16 The most natural way of using this data might be to introduce dummy variables for the control period. Oi (1976B, p. 43), however, argues that dummy variables would not be appropriate. He concentrates on the effects of dummies on the constant term, and argues that controls might influence other parameters of the model. Presumably he feels that introducing slope dummies is impractical because of the large number that would be needed, at least in the models he examines.
17 In part the differences might be explained by the choice of dependent variables. But it would be surprising if all of the differences between, say, Gordon's recent findings and Darby's could be explained by this choice.
18 Blinder (1979B, p. 211).
19 Nixon (1978B, pp. 26, 986).
20 Harris (1973B, pp. 341, 349, 350).
21 *Gallup Poll*, July 1973, Rept. No. 97, p. 22; October 1974, Rept. No. 112, p. 8.
22 Dunlop (1974G, pp. A121–A122).
23 Ibid., pp. A111–A113.
24 See the similar section in Chapter 6 for additional details concerning this calculation.
25 Grayson and Neeb (1974B, p. 40).
26 Kosters (1975B, p. 87).
27 Ibid., p. 79.
28 Ibid., pp. 76–7.
29 Economic Stabilization Program, *Eighth Quarterly Report*, p. 41.
30 Economic Stabilization Program, *Fifth Quarterly Report*, p. 34; *Seventh Quarterly Report*, p. 44.

31 Economic Stabilization Program, *Ninth Quarterly Report*, pp. 154–55, 163–64.
32 Economic Stabilization Program, *Eighth Quarterly Report*, pp. 19–20.
33 Mitchell (1975B, pp. 60–1); *Business Week*, September 22, 1973, pp. 20–21.
34 *Business Week*, September 22, 1973, pp. 20–21.
35 Brock and Winsby (1974G, p. 893).
36 McCracken (1980J pp. 582–3).
37 It has also been suggested that a failure to take the lags in the effect of monetary policy into account played a role.

8. Lessons for the recent crisis

1 Rockoff (1978J).
2 Galbraith (1952B, p. 74).
3 See Friedman and Schwartz (1963B, pp. 623–7) for a more detailed description of the Accord.
4 When the war began Keynes (1975B, Chapter 8), as the quotation at the head of the chapter shows, was skeptical of the value of across-the-board controls. He thought that controls would need to be limited to a small basket of wage goods. But he was apparently surprised during the war by the ease with which the cost of living was stabilized with subsidies. See Keynes (1978B, p. 357).
5 It is significant, I believe, that Daniel Quinn Mills (1975B, *passim* and pp. 269–82) reaches similar conclusions, even though he is concerned primarily with wage controls, has in mind a different set of questions, and approaches the problem of inflation from a different theoretical perspective.
6 After this chapter was first written – the title was then "Lessons for the Present Crisis" – the Federal Reserve adopted a restrictive monetary policy. But controls were not used to ease the transition to a less inflationary economy, and the result was one of the worst recessions in the postwar period. With luck the economy will return to a stable noninflationary path. But should we again face a similar situation, I hope that we will apply the lessons of history and use controls to ease the pain of extricating ourselves from the trap of runaway inflation.

Bibliography

The following bibliography lists the references cited in the notes when they are of interest beyond the particular fact I extracted, and certain additional sources that were particularly helpful, presented a unique point of view, or might be missed in a conventional search.

Books

Adams, George P., Jr. *Wartime Price Control*. Washington, D.C.: American Council on Public Affairs, 1942.

Adams, John and Abigail. *Familiar Letters of John Adams and His Wife Abigail Adams, During the Revolution*. With a memoir of Mrs. Adams by Charles Francis Adams. New York: Hurd and Houghton, 1876.

Alchian, Armen A. and William R. Allen. "Stabilization Policy, Full Employment, Inflation, and Free Markets." In *University Economics*. Second Edition, Belmont, Calif.: Wadsworth, 1967.

Arnow, Kathryn Smul. "The Attack on the Cost of Living." In *Inter-university Case Program, Cases in Public Administration*. vol 1. Washington, D.C.: Committee on Public Administration Cases, 1951.

Askin, A. Bradley. "Wage–Price Controls in Administrative and Political Perspective: The Case of the Price Commission During Phase II. In *Wage and Price Controls: The U.S. Experiment* (John Kraft and Blaine Roberts, eds.). New York: Praeger, 1975.

Backman, Jules. *Government Price Fixing*. New York: Pitman, 1938.

Wartime Price Control. New York: NYU School of Law, 1940.

Backman, Jules and Abraham Kaufman. "Price Control." In *1946 Annual Survey of American Law*. New York: NYU School of Law, 1947.

Bailyn, Bernard. *The New England Merchants in the Seventeenth Century*. Cambridge, Mass.: Harvard University Press, 1955.

Baruch, Bernard M. *Baruch: The Public Years*. Volume 2 of his autobiography. New York: Holt, Rinehart & Winston, 1960.

Bezanson, Anne assisted by Blanch Daley, Marjorie C. Denison, and Miriam Hussey. *Prices and Inflation During the American Revolution: Pennsylvania, 1770–1790*. Philadelphia: University of Pennsylvania Press, 1951.

Bezanson, Anne, Robert D. Gray, and Miriam Hussey. *Prices in Colonial Pennsylvania*. Philadelphia: University of Pennsylvania Press, 1935.

Behrens, Kathryn L. *Paper Money in Maryland 1727–1789*. The Johns Hopkins University Studies in Historical and Political Science, Series 41, No. 1. Baltimore: Johns Hopkins Press, 1923.

Bernstein, Barton J. and Allen J. Matusow. *The Truman Administration: A Documentary History*. New York: Harper & Row, 1966.

Blackman, John L. *Presidential Seizure in Labor Disputes*. Cambridge, Mass.: Harvard University Press, 1967.

Blinder, Alan S. *Economic Policy and the Great Stagflation*. New York: Academic Press, 1979.

Blum, John Morton. *V Was for Victory: Politics and American Culture During World War II*. New York and London: Harvest/HBJ, 1976.

Bogart, Earnest L. *War Costs and Their Financing: A Study of the Financing of the War and the After War Problems of Debt and Taxation*. New York: D. Appleton and Company, 1921.

Bolles, Albert Sidney. *Financial History of the United States*. 3 Vols. New York: D. Appleton, 1885.

Bonn, Moritz Julius. "Price Regulation." In *Encyclopedia of the Social Sciences* (Edwin Seligman, ed.), vol. 11, pp. 355–62. New York: Macmillan, 1933.

Bowles, Chester. *Promises to Keep*. New York: Harper & Row, 1971.

Breck, Samuel. *Historical Sketch of Continental Paper Money*. Philadelphia: J. C. Clark, 1843.

Bridenbaugh, Carl. *Cities in the Wilderness*. New York: Knopf, 1960.

Bruce, Philip A. *Economic History of Virginia in the Seventeenth Century*. 2 Vols. New York: Peter Smith, 1935.

Burnett, Edmund C., Editor. *Letters of Members of the Continental Congress*. 8 Vols. Washington, D.C.: The Carnegie Institution, 1921–36.

Byrnes, James Francis. *Speaking Frankly, All in a Lifetime*. New York: Harper & Brothers, 1958.

Campbell, Colin Dearborn, Editor. *Wage–Price Controls in World War II, United States and Germany: Reports by Persons Who Observed and Participated in the Programs*. Washington, D.C.: American Enterprise Institute, 1971.

Cantril, Hadley. *Public Opinion 1935–1946*. Princeton, N.J.: Princeton University Press, 1951.

Caridi, Ronald J. *The Korean War and American Politics: The Republican Party as a Case Study*. Philadelphia: University of Pennsylvania Press, 1969.

Chandler, Lester Vernon. *Inflation in the United States, 1940–1948*. New York: Harper & Brothers, 1951.

Chandler, Lester V. and Donald H. Wallace. *Economic Mobilization and Stabilization: Selected Materials on the Economics of War and Defense*. New York: Henry Holt and Company, 1951.

Chen, Huan-Chang. *The Economic Principles of Confucius and His School*. London: Longmans, Green & Co., 1911. Also in Columbia University Studies in History, Economics and Public Law, Volumes 44 and 45.

Chitwood, Oliver Perry. *Richard Henry Lee: Statesman of the Revolution*. Morgantown: West Virginia University Foundation, 1967.

Clark, John Maurice. *The Costs of the World War to the American People*. New Haven, Conn.: Yale University Press, 1931.

Clarkson, Grosvenor B. *Industrial America in the World War: The Strategy Behind the Line, 1917–1918*. Boston: Houghton Mifflin, 1923.

Clinard, Marshall Barron. *The Black Market: A Study of White Collar Crime*. New York: Rinehart, 1952.

Coit, Margaret L. *Mr. Baruch*. Boston: Houghton Mifflin, 1957.

Collins, Joseph Lawton. *War in Peacetime: The History and Lessons of Korea*. Boston: Houghton Mifflin, 1969.

Crowell, Benedict and Robert Forrest Wilson. *How America Went to War*. 6 Vols. New Haven, Conn.: Yale University Press, 1921.

Cuff, Robert D. "Business, the State, and World War I: The American Experience." In *War and Society in North America* (J. L. Granalstein and R. D. Cuff, eds.). Toronto: Thomas Nelson, 1971.

Cuff, Robert D. *The War Industries Board*. Baltimore: The Johns Hopkins University Press, 1973.

Darby, Michael R. "Price and Wage Controls: The First Two Years." In *The Economics of Price and Wage Controls* (K. Brunner and A. H. Meltzer, eds.), vol. 2, pp. 235–63. Amsterdam: North-Holland, 1976.

Del Mar, Alexander. *The History of Money in America*. New York: The Cambridge Encyclopedia Company, 1899.

De Marchi, Neil. "The First Nixon Administration: Prelude to Controls." In *Exhortation and Controls* (Crawford D. Goodwin, ed.). Washington, D.C.: The Brookings Institution, 1975.

Denison, Edward F. *The Sources of Economic Growth in the United States and the Alternatives Before Us*. New York: Committee for Economic Development. Supplementary Paper 13, 1962.

　Accounting for United States Economic Growth, 1929–1969. Washington, D.C.: The Brookings Institution, 1974.

　Accounting for Slower Economic Growth: The United States in the 1970's. Washington, D.C.: The Brookings Institution, 1979.

Dunlop, John T. and Arthur D. Hill. *The Wage Adjustment Board: Wartime Stabilization in the Building and Construction Industry*. Cambridge, Mass.: Harvard University Press, 1950.

East, Robert A. *Business Enterprise in the American Revolutionary Era*. Columbia University Studies in History, Economics and Public Law, Number 439. New York: Columbia University Press, 1938.

Edelman, Murray and R. W. Fleming. *The Politics of Wage-Price Decisions: A Four-Country Analysis*. Champaign: University of Illinois Press, 1965.

Fabricant, Solomon assisted by Robert E. Lipsey. *The Trend of Government Activity in the United States Since 1900*. New York: National Bureau of Economic Research, 1952.

Feige, Edgar L. and Douglas K. Pearce. "Inflation and Incomes Policy. An Application of Time Series Models." In *The Economics of Price and Wage Controls* (K. Brunner and A. Meltzer, eds.), vol. 2. Amsterdam: North-Holland, 1976.

Fite, Emerson David. *Social and Industrial Conditions in the North During the Civil War*. New York: The Macmillan Company, 1910.

Flash, Edward S., Jr. *Economic Advice and Presidential Leadership: The Council of Economic Advisors*. New York: Columbia University Press, 1965.

Franklin, Benjamin. *The Writings of Benjamin Franklin*. Edited by Albert Henry Smyth. New York: Macmillan, 1905–7.

Friedman, Milton. "The Lag in Effect of Monetary Policies in the United States." In *The Optimum Quantity of Money and Other Essays*. Chicago: Aldine, 1969. (Reprinted from *The Journal of Political Economy* 69 (1961): 447–66.)

　"Price, Income, and Monetary Changes in Three Wartime Periods." In *The Optimum Quantity of Money and Other Essays*. Chicago: Aldine, 1969. (Reprinted from *American Economic Review* 42 (1952): 612–25.)

　"What Price Guideposts?" In *Guidelines: Informal Controls and the Market Place* (G. P. Schultz and R. Z. Aliber, eds.). Chicago: University of Chicago Press, 1966.

　"Inflation, Taxation, Indexation." In *Inflation: Causes, Consequences, Cures*. London: The Institute of Economic Affairs, 1974.

Friedman, Milton and Rose Friedman. "The Cure for Inflation." In *Free to Choose: A Personal Statement*. New York: Harcourt Brace Jovanovich, 1979.

Friedman, Milton and Anna Jacobson Schwartz. *A Monetary History of the United States*. Princeton, N.J.: Princeton University Press, 1963.

Monetary Statistics of the United States: Estimates, Sources, Methods. Princeton N.J.: Princeton University Press, 1970.

Friedman, Milton and George J. Stigler. "Roofs or Ceilings? The Current Housing Problem." In *Verdict on Rent Control*. Institute of Economic Affairs Reading No. 7. Sussex, England: Cormorant Press, 1972.

Galbraith, John Kenneth. *A Theory of Price Control*. Cambridge, Mass.: Harvard University Press, 1952.

The New Industrial State. Boston: Houghton Mifflin, 1967.

The Affluent Society, second edition, revised. Boston: Houghton Mifflin, 1969.

"Inflation, Recession, or Controls." In *A Contemporary Guide to Economics Peace and Laughter*. Edited by Andrea D. Williams. Boston: Houghton Mifflin, 1971.

Money: Whence It Came, Where It Went. Boston: Houghton Mifflin, 1975.

Gallup, George H. *The Gallup Poll: Public Opinion 1935–1971*. New York: Random House, 1972.

Gold, Bela. *Wartime Economic Planning in Agriculture*. New York: Columbia University Press, 1949.

Goodwin, Crawford D., Editor. *Exhortation & Controls: The Search for a Wage–Price Policy, 1945–1971*. Washington, D.C.: The Brookings Institution, 1975.

Grayson, C. Jackson, Jr. "Controls Are Not the Answer." In *The Challenge of Economics: Readings from Challenge Magazine* (M. E. Sharpe and B. R. Schiller, eds.), pp. 134–8. New York: Random House, 1977.

Grayson, C. Jackson, Jr. and Louis Neeb. *Confessions of a Price Controller*. Homewood, Ill.: Dow Jones–Irwin, Inc., 1974.

Gross, Robert A. *The Minutemen and Their World*. New York: Hill & Wang, 1976.

Hamby, Alonzo, L. *Beyond the New Deal: Harry S. Truman and American Liberalism*. New York: Columbia University Press, 1973.

Hamilton, Alexander. *The Works of Alexander Hamilton*. Edited by John C. Hamilton. 7 Vols. New York: John F. Crow, 1850–51.

Hardy, Charles O. *Wartime Control of Prices*. Washington, D.C.: The Brookings Institution, 1940.

Harris, Louis. *The Harris Survey Yearbook of Public Opinion, 1970–1973*. New York: Louis Harris and Associates, Inc., 1971–1974.

Harris, Seymour E. *Price and Related Controls in the United States*. New York: McGraw-Hill, 1945.

The Economics of Mobilization and Inflation. New York: Norton, 1951.

Hibbard, Benjamin H. *Effects of the Great War Upon Agriculture in the United States and Great Britain. Preliminary Economic Studies of the War, No. 11*. Edited by David Kinley. New York: Oxford University Press, 1919.

Hicks, Sir John. *A Theory of Economic History*. London: Oxford University Press, 1969.

Hoopes, Roy. *The Steel Crisis*. New York: John Day, 1963.

Americans Remember the Home Front: An Oral Narrative. New York: Hawthorn Books, 1977.

Hoover, Herbert Clark. *Memoirs*. 2 vols. New York: Macmillan, 1951–52.

Hughes, J. R. T. *Social Control in the Colonial Economy*. Charlottesville: University Press of Virginia, 1976.

Kaplan, A. D. H. *Big Business in a Competitive System*. Washington, D.C.: The Brookings Institution, 1964.

Katona, George. *Price Control and Business: Field Studies Among Producers and Distributors of Consumer Goods in the Chicago Area, 1942–44*. Bloomington, Ind. The Principia Press, Inc., 1945.

Kendrick, John W. assisted by Maude R. Pech. *Productivity Trends in the United States*. Princeton, N.J.: Princeton University Press for the National Bureau of Economic Research, 1961.

Kendrick, John W. and Elliot Grossman. *Productivity in the United States; Trends and Cycles*. Baltimore: Johns Hopkins University Press, 1980.

Keynes, John Maynard. How to Pay for the War. In *The Collected Writings of John Maynard Keynes*. Edited by Donald Moggridge. Vol. 9. London: Macmillan, 1975.

    "Activities 1939–1945." In *The Collected Writings of John Maynard Keynes*. (Donald Moggridge, ed.), vol. 22. London: Macmillan, 1978.

Kosters, Marvin H. in association with J. Dawson Ahalt. *Controls and Inflation: Stabilization Program in Retrospect*. American Enterprise Institute for Public Policy Research, Domestic Affairs Study 37. Washington, D.C., 1975.

Kraft, John and Blaine Roberts, editors. *Wage and Price Controls: The U.S. Experiment*. New York: Praeger, 1975.

Krooss, Herman E. *Executive Opinion*. Garden City, N.Y.: Doubleday, 1970.

Kuznets, Simon. *National Product in Wartime*. New York: National Bureau of Economic Research, Inc., 1945.

Lanzillotti, Robert F. and Mary Hamilton. *Phase II in Review: The Lessons and Legacy of Price Control*. Washington, D.C., 1974.

Lanzillotti, Robert F., Mary T. Hamilton, and Blaine R. Roberts. *Phase II in Review. The Price Commission Experience*. Washington, D.C.: The Brookings Institute, 1975.

Lekachman, Robert. "The Inevitability of Controls." In *The Challenge of Economics: Readings from Challenge Magazine* (M. E. Sharpe and B. R. Schiller, eds.), pp. 131–3. New York: Random House, 1977.

Lerner, Eugene. "Inflation in the Confederacy." In *Studies in the Quantity Theory of Money* (M. Freidman, ed.). Chicago: University of Chicago Press, 1956.

Levitan, S. A. *Ingrade Wage–Rate Progression in War and Peace*. Plattsburg, N.Y.: Clinton Press, 1950.

Lingeman, Richard R. *Don't You Know There's a War On? The American Home Front, 1941–1945*. New York: Putnam, 1970.

Litman, Simon. *Prices and Price Control in Great Britain and the United States During the World War*. Preliminary Economic Studies of the War, No. 19. Edited by David Kinley. New York: Oxford University Press, 1920.

Manning, Thomas G. *The Office of Price Administration: A World War II Agency of Control*. New York: Holt, 1960.

Marcus, Maeva. *Truman and the Steel Seizure: The Limits of Presidential Power*. New York: Columbia University Press, 1977.

Marcus, Stanley. *Minding the Store: A Memoir*. Boston: Little, Brown, 1974.

McCusker, John J. *Money and Exchange in Europe and America, 1600–1775: A Handbook*. Chapel Hill: University of North Carolina Press, 1978.

McGuire, Timothy W. "On Estimating the Effects of Controls." In *The Economics of Price and Wage Controls* (K. Brunner and A. Meltzer, eds.). Carnegie–Rochester Conference Series, vol. 2. Amsterdam: North-Holland, 1976.

Merritt, Albert N. *War Time Control of Distribution of Foods*. New York: The Macmillan Company, 1920.

Mills, Daniel Quinn. *Government, Labor, and Inflation*. Chicago: University of Chicago Press, 1975.

Milward, Alan S. *War, Economy and Society, 1939–1945*. Berkeley: University of California Press, 1977.

Mitchell, Daniel J. B. "The Impact and Administration of Wage Controls." In *Wage and Price Controls: The U.S. Experiment* (J. Kraft and B. Roberts, eds.). New York: Praeger, 1975.

Morris, Richard B. *Government and Labor in Early America*. New York: Columbia University Press, 1946.

Mueller, John E. *War, Presidents, and Public Opinion*. New York: Wiley, 1973.

Mullendore, William Clinton. *History of the United States Food Administration, 1917–1919*. Stanford, Calif.: Stanford University Press, 1941.

Nelson, Donald. *Arsenal of Democracy: The Story of American War Production*. New York: Harcourt, Brace, 1946.

Nixon, Richard. *R. N.: The Memoirs of Richard Nixon*. New York: Grosset & Dunlap, 1978.

Novick, David, Melvin Anshen and W. C. Truppner. *Wartime Production Controls*. New York: Columbia University Press, 1949.

Oi, Walter Y. "On Measuring the Impact of Wage–Price Controls: A Critical Appraisal." In *The Economics of Price and Wage Controls* (K. Brunner and A Meltzer, eds.), vol. 2. Amsterdam: North-Holland, 1976.

Okun, Arthur M. and George L. Perry, editors. *Curing Chronic Inflation*. Washington, D.C.: The Brookings Institution, 1978.

Phillips, Henry, Jr. *Historical Sketches of the Paper Currency of the American Colonies*. 2 Vols. Roxbury, Mass.: W. Elliot Woodward, 1865–6.

Pohlman, Jerry E. *Inflation Under Control?* Reston, Va.: Reston Publishing Company, Inc., 1976.

Roberts, D. C. *National Wages Policy in War and Peace*. London: Allen & Unwin, 1958.

Schuckers, Jacob W. *A Brief Account of the Finances and Paper Money of the Revolutionary War*. Philadelphia: John Campbell & Son, 1874.

Schuettinger, Robert L. and Eamonn F. Butler. *Forty Centuries of Wage and Price Controls: How Not to Fight Inflation*. Washington, D.C.: The Heritage Foundation, 1979.

Shattuck, Lemuel. *A History of the Town of Concord*. Boston: Russell, Odiorne, and Company, 1835.

Shultz, George P. and Kenneth W. Dam. *Economic Policy Beyond the Headlines*. New York: Norton, 1977.

Shurtleff, Nathaniel B., Editor. *Records of the Governor and Company of the Massachusetts Bay in New England*. 5 Vols. Boston: William White, 1853–4. Reprinted in New York: AMS Press, 1968.

Solow, Robert M. "The Case Against the Case Against Guidelines." In *Guidelines: Informal Controls and the Market Place* (G. Schultz and R. Aliber, eds.). Chicago: University of Chicago Press, 1966.

Stein, Herbert. *Government Price Policy in the United States During the World War*. Williamstown, Mass.: Williams College, 1939.

Stigler, George J. *The Citizen and the State: Essays on Regulation*. Chicago: University of Chicago Press, 1975.

Stout, Rex. *The Silent Speaker*. New York: Viking Press, 1946.

Sumner, William G. *The Financier and Finances of the American Revolution*. New York: Dodd, Mead, 1892.

Surface, Frank Macy. *American Pork Production in the World War: A Story of Stabilized Prices and of the Contribution of American Farmers to the Allied Cause and the Post Armistice Famine*. Chicago: A. W. Shaw Company, 1926.

   The Grain Trade During the World War, Being a History of the Food Administration Grain Corporation and the United States Grain Corporation. New York: The Macmillan Company, 1928.

Truman, Harry S. *Memoirs*. 2 Vols. Garden City, N.Y.: Doubleday, 1955–6.

Ulman, Lloyd and Robert J. Flanagan. *Wage Restraint: A Study of Incomes Policies in Western Europe*. Berkeley: University of California Press, 1971.

Urofsky, Melvin. *Big Steel and the Wilson Administration*. Columbus: Ohio State University Press, 1969.

Vatter, Harold G. *The U.S. Economy in the 1950's: An Economic History*. New York: Norton, 1963.

Wallace, Donald and Marver H. Bernstein. "Direct Controls in a Stabilization Program." In *American Assembly Papers on Inflation*, vol. 2. New York: American Assembly, Columbia University Press, 1951–2.

Walsh, Richard. *The Charleston Sons of Liberty*. Columbia: University of South Carolina Press, 1959.

Warren, George F. and Frank A. Pearson. *Prices*. New York: Wiley, 1933.

Washington, George. *The Writings of George Washington*. Edited by Chauncey Ford. 14 Volumes. New York: Putnam, 1893.

Weber, Arnold R. *In Pursuit of Price Stability: The Wage–Price Freeze of 1971*. Washington, D.C.: The Brookings Institute, 1973.

Weber, Arnold R. and Daniel J. B. Mitchell. *The Pay Board's Progress: Wage Controls in Phase II*. Washington, D.C.: The Brookings Institute, 1978.

Webster, Pelatiah. *Political Essays*. Philadelphia: Joseph Crukshank, 1791. Reprinted in New York, B. Franklin, 1969.

Weeden, William B. *Economic and Social History of New England 1620–1789*. 2 Vols. New York: Hillary House Publishers, 1963.

Wheeler, Michael. *Lies, Damn Lies, and Statistics*. New York: Dell, 1976.

Wilcox, Walter. *Farmers in the Second World War*. Ames: Iowa State College Press, 1947.

Willoughby, Woodbury. *The Capital Issues Committee and War Finance Corporation. The Johns Hopkins University Studies in Historical and Political Science*, Series 52, No. 2. Baltimore: Johns Hopkins Press, 1934.

Winthrop, John. *Winthrop's Journal: History of New England, 1630–1649*. 2 vols. Edited by James Kendall Hosmer. New York: Scribner, 1908.

Wooddy, Carroll H. *The Growth of the Federal Government, 1915–1932*. New York: McGraw-Hill Book Company, Inc., 1934.

Young, Roland. *Congressional Politics in the Second World War*. New York: Columbia University Press, 1956.

Journal Articles

Ackley, Gardner. "Relation of Price and Production Controls." *American Economic Review* 41 (1951): 70–3.

   "Roles and Limits of Incomes Policy." *Oriental Economist* 42 (1974): 18–24.

Alexander, Robert S. "Wartime Adventure in Equitable Distribution Short of Rationing: Special Orders and Ratings." *The Journal of Marketing* 11 (1946): 159–173.

"A Wartime Adventure in Business Self-Regulation: The Retail Declaration of Policy." *The Journal of Marketing* 11 (1947): 394–98.

Anderson, B. M., Jr. "Value and Price Theory in Relation to Price Fixing and War Finance." *American Economic Review* 8 Supplement (1918): 239–56.

Anderson, Karl L. "The Pricing of Copper Alloy Scrap and of Brass and Bronze Ingot." *American Economic Review* 33 (1943), Part 2: 295–302.

Anderson, Terry L. "Wealth Estimates for the New England Colonies, 1650–1709." *Explorations in Economic History* 12 (1975): 151–76.

"Autos: The Blacker Market." *Newsweek* 27 (1946): 68.

"Autos: Operation Circus." *Newsweek* 28 (1946): 81–2.

Baldwin, Simeon E. "The New Haven Convention of 1778." *New Haven Colony Historical Society Papers* 3 (1882): 33–62.

Bancroft, George. Communicator. "A Hartford Convention in 1780." *The Magazine of American History* 8 (1882): 688–98.

Barro, Robert J. and Herschell I. Grossman. "Suppressed Inflation and the Supply Multiplier." *The Review of Economic Studies* 41(1974): 87–104.

Barton, Allen H. "Consensus and Conflict Among American Leaders." *Public Opinion Quarterly* 38 (1974–75): 507–30.

Berglund, Abraham. "Price-Fixing in the Iron and Steel Industry." *Quarterly Journal of Economics* 32 (1918): 597–620.

Bernhardt, Joshua. "Government Control of Sugar during the War." *Quarterly Journal of Economics* 33 (1919): 672–713.

"Transition from Government Control of Sugar to Competitive Conditions." *Quarterly Journal of Economics* 34 (1920): 720–36.

Bernstein, Barton J. "The Postwar Famine and Price Control, 1946." *Agricultural History* 38 (1964): 235–40.

"The Removal of War Production Board Controls on Business, 1944–1946." *Business History Review* 39 (1965): 243–60.

Bezanson, Anne. "Inflation and Controls, Pennsylvania, 1774–1779." *Journal of Economic History*, Supplement, 8 (1948): 1–20.

"Black Market; Its Shady Dealings Involve All Kinds of Americans." *Life* 20 (1946): 15–21.

Blakey, Roy G. "Sugar Prices and Distribution under Food Control." *Quarterly Journal of Economics* 32 (1918): 567–96.

Borders, Karl. "The Problems of Determining Fair Rents." *Journal of the American Statistical Association* 37 (1942): 34–40.

Bosworth, Barry. "Phase II: the U.S. Experiment with an Incomes Policy." *Brookings Papers on Economic Activity* 2 (1972): 343–83.

"The Inflation Problem During Phase III." *American Economic Review* 64 (1974): 93–9.

Bourne, Henry E. "Food Control and Price-Fixing in Revolutionary France." *Journal of Political Economy* 27 (1919): 73–94, 108–209.

Bowles, Chester. "Crisis in Clothes." *Collier's* 117 (1946): 14–15.

Bronfenbrenner, Martin. "A Theory of Price Control-Review." *Journal of Political Economy* 62 (1954): 68–70.

Bronson, Henry. "Historical Account of Connecticut Currency, Etc." *New Haven Colony Historical Society Papers* I (1865).

Brown, H. G. "Cost of Production, Price Control and Subsidies: an Economic Nightmare." *American Economic Review* 42 (1952): 126–34.

Cagan, Phillip. "The Demand for Currency Relative to the Total Money Supply." *Journal of Political Economy* 66 (1958): 303–28. Reprinted as *National Bureau of Economic Research*, Occasional Paper 62, 1958.

Carlson, Keith M. "The Lag from Money to Prices." *Federal Reserve Bank of St. Louis Review* 62 (1980): 3–10.

Carney, James J., Jr. "The Legal Theory of Forced Labor in the Spanish Colonies." *University of Miami Hispanic-American Studies* 3 (1942): 23–34.

"Case of the Simple Potato." *Consumer Reports* 17 (1952): 393–6.

Chandler, Lester V. "Direct Controls over the Prices of Non-Cost-of-Living Items." *American Economic Review* 41 (1951): 67–70.

Cheung, Steven N. S. "A Theory of Price Control." *The Journal of Law and Economics* 2 (1974): 53–72.

Clark, J. M. "The Basis of War-Time Collectivism." *American Economic Review* 7 (1917): 772–90.

Coats, A. W. "Contrary Moralities: Plebs, Paternalists and Political Economists." *Past and Present* 54 (1972): 130–3.

Coffin, Tris. "So You Want a New Car." *Nation* 163 (1946): 258–60.

"Confessions of a Black Market Butcher." *Saturday Evening Post* 219 (1946): 17+.

Cooke, Jay. "The Work of the Federal Food Administration." *Annals of the American Academy of Political and Social Science* 78 (1918): 175–84.

Count, Jerome. "Enforcement Aspects of Price and Rent Controls." *Administrative Law Service* (1945): 585–621.

Cox, Charles. "The Enforcement of Public Price Controls." *Journal of Political Economy* 88(1980): 887–915.

Cuff, Robert D. and Melvin I. Urofsky. "The Steel Industry and Price Fixing during World War I." *Business History Review* 44 (1970): 291–306.

David, Paul A. and Peter Solar. "A Bicentenary Contribution to The History of the Cost of Living in America." *Research in Economic History.* 2 (1977): 1–80.

Davis, Andrew McFarland. "The Limitation of Prices in Massachusetts, 1776–1779." *Publications of the Colonial Society of Massachusetts* 10 (1905): 119–34.

Davisson, William. "Essex County Price Trends: Money and Markets in 17th Century Massachusetts." *Essex Institute Historical Collection* 103 (1967): 144–88.

Derber, Milton. "The Wage Stabilization in Historical Perspective." *Labor Law Journal* 23 (1972): 453–61.

Downs, K. T. "Rocket on Wheels, Black-Market in New and Used Automobiles." *Collier's* 118 (1946): 20+.

Drapkin, Michael K. "Steel Concrete-Reinforcing Bar Shortage May Severely Hurt Nonresidential Building." *Wall Street Journal* 21 (1974): 24.

Duffus, W. M. "Government Control of the Wheat Trade in the United States." *American Economic Review* 8 (1918): 62–87.

Eldred, W. "The Wheat and Flour Trade under Food Administration Controls." *Quarterly Journal of Economics* 33 (1918): 1–70.

Faragher, Robert V. and Fritz F. Heimann. "Price Controls, Antitrust Laws, and Minimum Price Laws: The Relation Between Emergency and Normal Economic Controls." *Law and Contemporary Problems* 19 (1954): 648–84.

Farvish, Celia. "The Black Market Broke Us." *Saturday Evening Post* 219 (1946): 17 + .

Feige, Edgar L. and Douglas K. Pearce. "The Wage–Price Control Experiment – Did it Work?" *Challenge* 16 (1973): 40–44.

Fisher, I. "Some Contributions of the War to our Knowledge of Money and Prices." *American Economic Review* 8 Supplement (1918): 257–8.

Flory, Anne P. "Field Administration in OPS." *Law and Contemporary Problems* 19 (1954): 604–24.

Fortune, Peter. "An Evaluation of Anti-Inflation Policies in the United States." *New England Economic Review* (1974): 3–27.

Friedman, Milton. "A Theoretical Framework for Monetary Analysis." NBER Occasional Paper 112. New York: Columbia University Press, 1971.

Gage, Daniel D. "Wartime Experiment in Federal Rent Control." *Journal of Land and Public Utility Economics* 23 (February 1947): 50–7.

Galbraith, John Kenneth. "The Selection and Timing of Inflation Controls." *Review of Economic Statistics* 23 (1941): 82–5.

"Price Control: Some Lessons from the First Phase." *American Economic Review* 33 (1943): Part 2, 253–9.

Genovese, Elizabeth Fox. "The Many Faces of Moral Economy: A Contribution to a Debate." *Past and Present* 58 (1973): 161–8.

Gephart, W. F. "Perishable Produce Under Food Regulation." *Quarterly Journal of Economics* 32 (1918): 621–34.

"Provisions of the Food Act and Activities Which Should be Made Permanent: With Discussion." *American Economic Review* 9, Supplement (1919): 61–78.

Gettell, Richard Glenn. "Rationing: A Pragmatic Problem for the Economist." *American Economic Review* 33 (1943): part 2, 260–71.

Gody, Celia Star, and Allan D. Searle. "Productivity Changes Since 1939." *Monthly Labor Review* 63 (1946): 893–917.

Gordon, Robert J. "$5 Billion of U.S. Private Investment Has Been Mislaid." *American Economic Review* 59 (1969): 221–38.

"Inflation in Recession and Recovery." *Brookings Papers on Economic Activity* (1971): 105–58.

"Wage-Price Controls and the Shifting Phillips Curve." *Brookings Papers on Economic Activity* 2 (1972): 385–421.

"The Response of Wages and Prices to the First Two Years of Controls." *Brookings Papers on Economic Activity* 3 (1973): 765–79.

"The Impact of Aggregate Demand on Prices." *Brookings Papers on Economic Activity* 3 (1975): 613–62.

"Can the Inflation of the 1970's Be Explained?" *Brookings Papers on Economic Activity* 1 (1977): 253–77.

Gorter, W. and G. H. Hildebrand. "Is Price Control Really Necessary." *American Economic Review* 41 (1951): 77–81.

Gray, L. C. "Price Fixing Policies of the Food Administration." *American Economic Review* 9, Supplement (1919): 252–71.

"Gray and Black Markets." *Life* 20 (1946): 32.

"Gray Market Returns." *Fortune* 43 (1951): 14–15 + .

Hadary, Gideon. "Effectiveness of Price Control in the Dairy Industry." *The Journal of Business* 19 (1946): 76–81.

Hamilton, Mary T. "Price Controls in 1973: Strategies and Problems." *American Economic Review* 64 (1974): 100–2.

Hamilton, Walton H. "The Requisites of a National Food Policy." *Journal of Political Economy* 26 (1918): 612–38.

Handlin, Oscar and Mary F. "Revolutionary Economic Policy in Massachusetts." *William and Mary Quarterly*, 3d ser. 4 (1947): 3–26.

Haney, L. H. "Price Fixing in the United States During the War." *Political Science Quarterly* 34 (1918): 104–26.

Harlow, Ralph V. "Economic Conditions in Massachusetts During the American Revolution." *Publications of the Colonial Society of Massachusetts* 20 (1918): 163–92.

"Aspects of Revolutionary Finance, 1775–1783." *American Historical Review* 35 (1929): 46–68.

Henderson, Leon. "How Black Is Our Market?" *Atlantic Monthly* 178 (1946): 46–53.

Henig, Harry and S. Herbert Unterberger. "Wage Control in Wartime and Transition." *American Economic Review* 35 (1945): 319–36.

Hickman, Bert G. "The Korean War and United States Economic Activity, 1950–1952." New York: National Bureau of Economic Research, Occasional Paper 49, 1955.

Hitchcock, Curtice N. "The War Industries Board: Its Development, Organization and Functions." *Journal of Political Economy* 26 (1918): 545–66.

Holt, Byron W. "Continental Currency." *Sound Currency* 5 (1898): 81–112.

Horowitz, Morris A. "Administrative Problems of the Wage Stabilization Board." *Industrial and Labor Relations Review* 7 (1954): 390–403.

Humes, Helen and Bruno Schiro. "The Rent Index: Part 1 – Concept and Measurement." *Monthly Labor Review* 67 (1948): 631–7.

"The Rent Index: Part 2 – Methodology and Measurement." *Monthly Labor Review* 68 (1949): 60–68.

Hurwitz, Abner. "Consumer's Price Index: Relative Importance of Components." *Monthly Labor Review* 67 (1948): 156–60.

Hynd, A. "Joe, the Black Marketeer, is Back." *Nation's Business* 39 (1951): 56–9.

Johnson, George and Bruno Schiro. "Correction of New Unit Bias in Rent Component of CPI." *Monthly Labor Review* 72 (1951): 437–44.

Johnson, G. Griffith. "Reflections on a Year of Price Controls." *American Economic Review* 42 (1952): 289–300.

Jones, Eliot. "Report on Anthracite and Bituminous Coal." *American Economic Review* 42 (1952): 289–300.

Kaldor, Nicholas. "Rationing and the Cost of Living Index." *Review of Economic Studies* 8 (1941): 185–7.

Katona, George and Dickson H. Leavens. "Price Increases and Uptrading: The Change in Advertised Prices of Apparel and House Furnishings." *The Journal of Business* 17 (1944): 231–43.

Keezer, Dexter Meriam. "Observations on the Operations of the National War Labor Board." *American Economic Review* 36 (1946): 234–57.

Kobler, J. "Black Marketeers' Best Friend." *Saturday Evening Post* 225 (1953): 28+.

Koshetz, Herbert. "Black Market in Textile Yarns Is Seen." *New York Times*, January 15, 1974, p. 49.

Kuznets, Simon. "National Product War and Prewar." New York: National Bureau of Economic Research, Occasional Paper 17, 1944.

Lacy, M. G. "Food Control during Forty-six Centuries." *Scientific Monthly* 16 (1923): 623–37.

Lang, D. "Menus, Nylons, Wiping Cloths, and Abdullahs." *New Yorker* 21 (1945): 36+.

Lanzillotti, Robert F. and Blaine Roberts. "Experiments with an Incomes Policy." Paper presented at the Tulane Conference on Incomes Policy, April 1973. "The Legacy of Phase II Price Controls." *American Economic Review* 64 (1974): 82–7.

Letzler, Alfred. "The General Ceiling Price Regulation: Problems of Coverage and Exclusion." *Law and Contemporary Problems* 19 (1954): 486–521.

Lewis, Ben W. "Price Control and Rationing." *International Encyclopedia of the Social Sciences*. Vol. 12, pp. 464–70. Macmillan, 1968.

Lewis, David and Myron E. Sharpe. "The Great Debate on Wage–Price Controls." *Challenge* 17 (1975): 26–32.

Lipsey, Richard G., and Michael J. Parkin. "Incomes Policy: A Reappraisal." *Economica* 37 (1970): 1–31.

Lloyd, E. M. H. "Price Control and Control of Inflation." *Review of Economic Statistics* 27 (1945): 149–55.

Lochridge, Patricia. "I Shopped the Black Market." *Woman's Home Companion* 71 (1944): 20–21+.

"I Shop the Black Market Again." *Woman's Home Companion* 73 (1946): 4+.

"Lumber: Black Market Is a National Specter." *Newsweek* 27 (1946): 68+.

Mack, Louise J. "Postwar Changes in the Quality of Apparel." *Monthly Labor Review* 67 (1948): 34–9.

Martin, Frances H. "Effect of Price Controls on Retail Food Prices." *Monthly Labor Review* 73 (1951): 424–8.

McCracken, Paul W. "Reflections of an Economic Policy Maker." *Journal of Economic Literature* 18 (1980): 579–85.

"Meat Black Market Mushrooms: Control Muddle Nears Climax." *Newsweek* 38 (1951): 67.

Mehren, G. L. "Direct Price Control in Food and Agriculture" (with discussion by E. J. Working). *Journal of Farm Economics* 34 (1952): 698–712.

Miller, John Perry. "The Tactics of Retail Price Control." *Quarterly Journal of Economics* 57 (1943): 497–521.

Mills, D. Quinn. "Some Lessons of Price Controls in 1971–1973." *Bell Journal of Economics* 6 (1975): 3–49.

Mills, Frederick C., Chairman. "An Appraisal of the U.S. Bureau of Labor Statistics Cost-of-Living Index, by a Special Committee of the American Statistical Association." *Journal of the American Statistical Association* 38 (1943): 387–405; "Appendix," 39 (1944): 57–95. Reprinted in *Report of the President's Committee on the Cost of Living*. Washington: Government Printing Office, 1945.

Mitchell, Wesley Claire. "War Prices in the United States." *Economic Journal* 28 (1918): 460–3.

Moore, Geoffrey H. "Production of Industrial Materials in World Wars I and II." New York: National Bureau of Economic Research, Occasional Paper 18, 1944.

"More and More Scarcities: Who is Feeling the Pinch." *U.S. News & World Report* 3 (1973): 15.

Morris, Richard B. and Jonathan Grossman. "The Regulation of Wages in

Early Massachusetts." *New England Quarterly* 11 (1938): 470–500. Reprinted in *American Economic History: Essays in Interpretation*. Edited by Robert F. Byrnes and Robert D. Cross. Philadelphia: J. Lippincott, 1966, pp. 18–39.

Morse, L. K. "The Price-Fixing of Copper." *Quarterly Journal of Economics* 33 (1918): 71–106.

Mosk, Sanford A. "Price-Fixing in Spanish California." *California Historical Society Quarterly* 17 (1938): 118–22.

Neiswanger, William A. "Price Control in the Machinery Industries." *American Economic Review* 33 (1943): part 2, 287–94.

Nelson, Saul. "OPS Price Control Standards." *Law and Contemporary Problems* 19 (1954): 554–80.

Nicholson, J. L. "Rationing and Index Numbers." *The Review of Economic Studies* 10 (1943): 68–72.

"Nickel Profits." *Time* 58 (1951): 102–4.

Niskanen, William and Robert Berry. "The 1973 Economic Report of the President." *Journal of Money, Credit, and Banking* 5 (1973): 693–703.

Notz, William. "World's Coal Situation During the War." *Journal of Political Economy* 26 (1918): 567–612.

Okun, Arthur, M. "Upward Mobility in a High-Pressure Economy." *Brookings Papers on Economic Activity* 4 (1973): 207–52.

Olson, Robert E. "Adjustments and Other Special Problems Under the General Ceiling Price Regulation." *Law and Contemporary Problems* 19 (1954): 539–53.

Paarlberg, D. "Production and Distribution Problems Under Direct Price Controls." *Journal of Farm Economics* 33 (1951): 676–84.

Paul, A. B. "Food Price Controls Reconsidered." *Journal of Farm Economics* 40 (1958): 30–46.

Pearson, F. A. "Principles Involved in Fixing the Price of Milk." *Journal of Farm Economics* 1 (1919): 89–96.

Perry, George L. "The Success of Anti-Inflation Policies in the United States." *Journal of Money, Credit, and Banking* 5 (1973): 567–93.

Popkin, Joel. "Prices in 1972: An Analysis of Changes During Phase II." *Monthly Labor Review* 96 (1973): 16–23.

"Price Control in a Cold War." *Law and Contemporary Problems* 19 (1954): 477–684.

Record, Jane Cassels. "The War Labor Board: An Experiment In Wage Stabilization." *American Economic Review* 34 (1944): 98–110.

Ripley, Frank C. and Lydia Segal. "Price Determination in 395 Manufacturing Industries." *Review of Economics and Statistics* (1973): 263–71.

Robison, Jesse. "OPS and the Problem of Small Business." *Law and Contemporary Problems* 19 (1954): 625–47.

Rockoff, Hugh. "Indirect Price Increases and Real Wages in World War II." *Explorations in Economic History* 15 (1978): 407–20.

"The Response of Giant Corporations to Wage and Price Controls in World War II." *Journal of Economic History* 41 (1981): 123–8.

"Price and Wage Controls in Four Wartime Periods." *Journal of Economic History* 41 (1981): 381–401.

Rothbarth, E. "The Measurement of Changes in Real Income Under Conditions of Rationing." *The Review of Economic Studies* 8 (1941): 100–7.

Ruderman, Armand Peter. "Wartime Food-Consumption Patterns and the Cost of Living." *The Journal of Business* 17 (1944): 244–9.

Saville, L. "A Problem in the Economics of Price Control." *Southern Economic Journal* 16 (1951): 187–91.

Schaub, Edward L. "The Regulation of Rentals During the War Period." *Journal of Political Economy* 28 (1920): 1–36.

Scott, Kenneth. "Price Control in New England During the Revolution." *New England Quarterly* 19 (1946): 453–73.

Shultz, George P. and Kenneth W. Dam. "Reflections on Wage and Price Controls." *Industrial and Labor Relations Review* 30 (1977): 139–51.

Sumner, John D. "Differential Pricing in Nonferrous Metals." *American Economic Review* 33 (1943): part 2, 279–86.

Taft, Robert A. "Price Fixing – A Necessary Evil." *American Bar Association Journal* 27 (1941): 527–38.

Taussig, F. W. "Price-Fixing as Seen by a Price Fixer." *Quarterly Journal of Economics* 33 (1919): 205–41.

"Is Market Price Determinate?" *Quarterly Journal of Economics* 35 (1921): 394–411.

Teper, Lazare. "Observations on the Cost of Living Index of the Bureau of Labor Statistics." *Journal of the American Statistical Association* 38 (1943): 271–84.

Thompson, E. P. "The Moral Economy of the English Crowd in the Eighteenth Century." *Past and Present* 50 (1971): 76–136.

Tobin, James. "A Survey of the Theory of Rationing." *Econometrica* 20 (1952): 521–53.

Wachter, Michael L. "Phase II, Cost-Push Inflation, and Relative Wages." *American Economic Review* 64 (1974): 482–91.

"Cyclical Variation in the Interindustry Wage Structure." *American Economic Review* 60 (1970): 75–84.

Wallace, D. H. "Price Control and Rationing." *American Economic Review* 41 (1951): 60–2.

Wallich, Henry C. and Sidney Weintraub. "A Tax-Based Incomes Policy." *Journal of Economic Issues* (1971): 1–19. Reprinted in *Keynes, Keynesians and Monetarists* by Sidney Weintraub. Philadelphia: University of Pennsylvania Press, 1978, pp. 259–280.

Warne, Colston E. "Price Control Under Attack." *Current History 9* (1945): 87–93.

"Should Price Control Be Retained?" *Current History 10* (1946): 496–502.

Warren, G. F. "Some Purposes and Results of Price Fixing." *American Economic Review* 9, Supplement (1919): 233–245.

Williams, Faith M. "Bureau of Labor Statistics Cost-of-Living Index in Wartime." *Monthly Labor Review* 62 (1943): 82–95.

Wilson, C. E. "I Hate Controls, But We Need Them Now." *New York Times Magazine* (1951): 9+.

Wolf, Franz B. and Forrest E. Keller. "Problems of the Industry Earnings Standard." *Law and Contemporary Problems* 19 (1954): 581–603.

Worsley, Thomas B. "Economic Stabilization." *Annals of the American Academy of Political and Social Science* 278 (1951): 98–109.

"Wyatt Manuscripts." Fourth Installment. *William and Mary Quarterly*, Series 2, 7 (1927): 246–54.

Youngman, Anna. "The Federal Reserve System in Wartime." New York: National Bureau of Economic Research, Occasional Paper No. 21, January 1945.

Zwerdling, Joseph. "Pricing Techniques." *Law and Contemporary Problems* 19 (1954): 522–38.

Government documents

Baruch, Bernard. *American Industry in the War.* A Report of the War Industries Board. Washington, D.C.: U.S. Government Printing Office, 1921.

Benes, Robert J. "Iron and Steel Scrap," "Pig Iron," and "Iron Ore." *Studies in Industrial Price Control.* General Publication No. 6. *Historical Reports on War Administration: Office of Price Administration.* Washington, D.C.: U.S. Government Printing Office, 1947.

Brock, Jonathan and Roger Winsby assisted by Mark Kramer. "Removing Controls: The Policy of Selective Decontrol." U.S. Office of Economic Stabilization. *Historical Working Papers on the Economic Stabilization Program, Aug. 15, 1971 to April 30, 1974.* Washington, D.C.: U.S. Government Printing Office, 1974.

Caplan, Benjamin. "Price Policy and Production Controls in Textiles and Apparel: OPA and WPB." *Problems in Price Control: Changing Production Patterns.* General Publication No. 9. *Historical Reports on War Administration: Office of Price Administration.* Washington, D.C.: U.S. Government Printing Office, 1947.

Carsel, Wilfred. *Wartime Apparel Price Control.* General Publication No. 3. *Historical Reports on War Administration: Office of Price Administration.* Washington, D.C.: U.S. Government Printing Office, 1947.

Clark, J. Reuben. *Emergency Legislation Passed Prior to December* 1917. Washington, D.C.: U.S. Government Printing Office, 1918.

Cutler, Addison T. "Price Control in Steel." *Studies in Industrial Price Control.* General Publication No. 6. *Historical Reports on War Administration: Office of Price Administration.* Washington, D.C.: U.S. Government Printing Office, 1947.

Defense Production Act of 1950. *Statutes at Large,* Vol. 64 (1950).

Defense Production Act Amendments of 1951. *Statutes at Large,* Vol. 65 (1951).

Defense Production Act Amendments of 1952. *Statutes at Large,* Vol. 66 (1952).

Dunlop, John T. *"Statement Before the Subcommittee on Production and Stabilization of the Senate Banking, Housing and Urban Affairs Committee on the Economic Stabilization Act."* February 6, 1974.

Economic Stabilization Program. *Quarterly Reports.* August 15, 1971–April 4, 1974.

Fantin, Renee. "Fats and Oils and Dairy Products Rationing," *Studies in Food Rationing.* General Publication No. 13. *Historical Reports on War Administration: Office of Price Administration.* Washington, D.C.: U.S. Government Printing Office, 1947.

Fantin, Renee and John J. Madigan. "Livestock Slaughter Controls." *Studies in Food Rationing.* General Publication No. 13. *Historical Reports on War Administration: Office of Price Administration.* Washington, D.C.: U.S. Government Printing Office, 1947.

Fesler, James W. et al. *Industrial Mobilization for War: History of the War Production Board and Predecessor Agencies, 1940–1945.* General Study No. 1. *Historical Re-*

ports on War Administration: War Production Board. Washington, D.C.: U.S. Government Printing Office, 1947.

Garrett, Paul Willard assisted by Isador Lubin. *Government Control over Prices*. Bulletin No. 3. *History of Prices During the War*. Wesley C. Mitchell, Editor in Chief. Washington, D.C.: U.S. Government Printing Office, 1920.

Historical Working Papers on the Economic Stabilization Program, Aug. 15 1971 to April 30, 1974. U.S. Office of Economic Stabilization. Washington, D.C.: U.S. Government Printing Office, 1974.

Hoover, Herbert. *Preface to a Report of the United States Food Administration*. Washington, D.C.: U.S. Government Printing Office, 1920.

Jones, Drummond. *The Role of the Office of Civilian Requirements in the Office of Production Management and War Production Board, January 1941 to November 1945*. Special study No. 20, *Historical Reports on War Administration: War Production Board*. Washington, D.C.: U.S. Government Printing Office, 1946.

Journals of the Continental Congress, 1774–1789. Washington, D.C.: U.S. Government Printing Office, 1904–1937.

Krug, J. A. *Wartime Production Achievements and the Reconversion Outlook*. Final Report of the Chairman of the War Production Board. Washington, D.C.: U.S. Government Printing Office, October 9, 1945.

Lesher, C. E. "Prices of Coal and Coke." War Industries Board Price Bulletin No. 35. Washington, D.C.: U.S. Government Printing Office, 1919.

Mansfield, Harvey C. and Associates. *A Short History of OPA*. General Publication No. 15. *Historical Reports on War Administration: Office of Price Administration*. Washington, D.C.: U.S. Government Printing Office, 1947.

Mitchell, Wesley C. *History of Prices During the War: Summary*. War Industries Board Price Bulletin No. 1. Washington, D.C.: U.S. Government Printing Office, 1919.

Chairman. "Prices and the Cost of Living in Wartime – An Appraisal of the Bureau of Labor Statistics Index of the Cost of Living in 1941–44: Report of the Technical Committee Appointed by the Chairman of the President's Committee on the Cost of Living." *Report of the President's Committee on the Cost of Living*. Chaired by William H. Davis. Washington, D.C.: U.S. Government Printing Office, 1945.

Needham, Enoch. "The Enforcement of the Food Control Law." U.S. Bureau of Labor Statistics. Historical Studies of Wartime Problems, Historical Study No. 42. Washington, D.C.: U.S. Government Printing Office, 1942.

The Public Records of the State of Connecticut, from October 1776 to February 1778, Inclusive. Vol. 1. Hartford: The Case, Lockwood & Brainard Company, 1894.

Putnam, Imogene H. *Volunteers in OPA*. General Publication No. 14. *Historical Reports on War Administration: Office of Price Administration*. Washington, D.C.: U.S. Government Printing Office, 1946.

Redford, Emmette C. *Field Administration of Wartime Rationing*. General Publication No. 4. *Historical Reports on War Administration: Office of Price Administration*. Washington, D.C.: U.S. Government Printing Office, 1947.

Ritz, Philip. "Wartime Subsidies and Food Price Stabilization." *Problems in Price Controls: Stabilization Subsidies*. General Publication No. 10. *Historical Reports on War Administration: Office of Price Administration*. Washington, D.C.: U.S. Government Printing Office, 1947.

Rothwell, Doris P. *The General Maximum Price Regulation*. United States Department of Labor, Bureau of Labor Statistics, Bulletin No. 879. Washington, D.C.: U.S. Government Printing Office, 1946.

Russell, Judith. "Coffee Rationing," "The Fat Salvage Campaign," and "Processed Food Rationing." *Studies in Food Rationing*. General Publication No. 13. *Historical Reports on War Administration: Office of Price Administration*. Washington, D.C.: U.S. Government Printing Office, 1947.

Russell, Judith assisted by Hobart Crowe. "Plans for Fluid Milk Rationing." *Studies in Food Rationing*. General Publication No. 13. *Historical Reports on War Administration: Office of Price Administration*. Washington, D.C.: U.S. Government Printing Office, 1946.

Shaw, Carroll K. *Field Organization and Administration of the War Production Board and Predecessor Agencies, May 1940 to November 1945*. Special Study No. 25. *Historical Reports on War Administration: War Production Board*. Washington, D.C.: U.S. Government Printing Office, 1946.

Sitterson, J. Carlyle. *Aircraft Production Policies Under the National Defense Advisory Commission and Office of Production Management, May 1940 to December 1941*. Special study No. 21. *Historical Reports on War Administration: War Production Board*. Washington, D.C.: U.S. Government Printing Office, 1946.

Surface, Frank Macy. *The Stabilization of the Price of Wheat During the War and its Effect Upon the Returns to the Producer*. Washington, D.C.: United States Grain Corporation, 1925.

U.S. Administrative Office of the United States Courts. *Annual Report of the Administrative Office of the United States Courts*. Washington, D.C.: U.S. Government Printing Office, 1953–75.

U.S. Bureau of Agricultural Economics. *Price Fixing by Governments 424 B.C.–1926 A.D., a Selected Bibliography*. Compiled by M. G. Lacy, A. M. Hannay and E. L. Day. Washington, D.C.: U.S. Government Printing Office, 1926.

U.S. Bureau of the Budget. Committee on Records of War Administration. *The United States at War*. Washington, D.C.: U.S. Government Printing Office, 1946.

Budget of the United States. Washington, D.C.: U.S. Government Printing Office, 1953–55.

U.S. Bureau of the Census. *Historical Statistics of the United States, Colonial Times to 1957*. Washington, D.C.: U.S. Government Printing Office, 1960.

U.S. Bureau of Economic Analysis. *Long Term Economic Growth, 1860–1970*. Washington, D.C.: U.S. Government Printing Office, 1973.

U.S. Bureau of Labor Statistics. Bulletin 287. *National War Labor Board*. Washington, D.C.: U.S. Government Printing Office, 1922.

U.S. Congress. House. Committee on Banking and Currency. *Extension of the Emergency Price Control Act, Hearings*. 78th Cong., 2nd Sess., 1944.

Defense Production Act of 1950. H. Rept. 2759, 81st Cong., 2nd Sess., 1950.

Defense Production Act of 1950. Hearings, on H. R. 9176, 81st Cong., 2nd Sess., 1950.

Defense Production Act Amendments of 1951. H. R. 639, 82nd Cong., 1st Sess., 1951.

Defense Production Act Amendments of 1951. Hearings, on H. R. 3871. 82nd Cong., 1st Sess., 1951.

Defense Production Act Amendments of 1952. Hearings. 82nd Cong., 2nd Sess., 1952.

Defense Production Act Amendments of 1953. Hearings, on S. 1081. 83rd Cong., 1st Sess., 1953.

U.S. Congress. House. Committee on Conference. *Defense Production Act of 1950.* Conference Report. H. R. 3042, 81st Cong., 2nd Sess., 1950.

U.S. Congress. House. Committee on Education and Labor. *Investigation of the Wage Stabilization Board Hearings*, pursuant to H. R. 532. 82nd Cong., 2nd Sess., 1952.

Investigation of the Wage Stabilization Board. H. R. 2190, 82nd Cong., 2nd Sess., 1952.

U.S. Congress. House. Special Committee to Investigate Food Shortages for the House of Representatives. *Food Shortages, Hearings.* 79th Congr., 1st Sess., 1945.

U.S. Congress. House. *The Steel Seizure Case.* H. Doc. 534, 82nd Cong., 2nd Sess., 1952.

U.S. Congress. Joint Committee on the Economic Report. *The Consumer's Price Index: Report of the Joint Committee on the Economic Report.* 80th Cong., 2nd Sess., 1949.

U.S. Congress. Senate. Committee on Banking and Currency. *Emergency Price Control Act, Hearings.* 77th Cong., 1st Sess., 1941.

Extension of the Emergency Price Control Act of 1942, Hearings. 78th Cong., 2nd Sess., 1944.

Inflation Control Program of OPA, Hearings. 79th Cong., 1st Sess., 1945.

1946 Extension of the Emergency Price Control and Stabilization Acts of 1942, as Amended. 79th Cong., 2nd Sess., 1946.

Defense Production Act of 1950. S. Rept. 2250, 81st Cong., 2nd Sess., 1950.

Defense Production Act of 1950. Hearings, on S. 3936, 81st Cong., 2nd Sess., 1950.

A Bill To Amend and Extend the Defense Production Act of 1950 and the Housing and Rent Act of 1947, as Amended. S. Rept. 470, 82nd Cong., 1st Sess., 1951.

Defense Production Act Amendments of 1951. Hearings. 82nd Cong., 1st Sess., 1951.

Defense Production Act Amendments of 1952. Hearings. 82nd Cong., 2nd Sess., 1952.

U.S. Congress. Senate. Committee on Labor and Public Welfare. *Staff Report on WSB Recommendations in Steel Dispute.* S. Doc. 122, 82nd Cong., 2nd Sess., 1952.

U.S. Congress. Senate. Select Committee on Small Business. *Nickel Gray Market. Hearings* before a subcommittee of the Select Committee on Small Business, 82nd Cong., 1st Sess., 1951.

Steel Gray Market. Hearings before a subcommittee of the Select Committee on Small Business, 82nd Cong., 1st Sess., 1951.

U.S. Congress. Senate. Special Committee Investigating the National Defense Program. *Investigation of the National Defense Program.* Senate Report 10. 78th Cong., 1st Sess., 1943.

Investigation of the National Defense Program. Senate Report 110. 79th Cong., 1st Sess., 1945.

Investigation of the National Defense Program. Senate Report 440. 80th Cong., 2nd Sess., 1948.

U.S. Congress. Senate. Special Committee to Investigate the Munitions Industry. *Final Report of the Chairman of the United States War Industries Board to the*

President of the United States, February 1919. Committee Print No. 3, 74th Cong., 1st Sess., 1935.

Minutes of the Price Fixing Committee of the War Industries Board.. Committee Print No. 5. 74th Cong., 2nd Sess., 1935.

U.S. Department of Commerce, Bureau of the Census. *Statistical Abstract of the United States, 1972.* Washington, D.C.: U.S. Government Printing Office, 1972.

U.S. Department of Labor, Bureau of Labor Statistics. *Employment and Earnings in the U.S., 1909–1975.* Bulletin No. 1312 (10). Washington, D.C.: U.S. Government Printing Office, 1976.

U.S. Food Administration. *Official Statement of the United States Food Administration.* No. 7. Washington, D.C.: U.S. Government Printing Office, November 15, 1918.

U.S. Food and Drug Administration. *Annual Reports, 1941–1942, 1942–1943.* Washington, D.C.: U.S. Government Printing Office, 1943.

U.S. Fuel Administration. *Final Report of the United States Fuel Administrator, 1917–1919.* H. A. Garfield. Washington, D.C.: U.S. Government Printing Office, 1919.

Report of the Administrative Division, 1917–1919. "Reports of the Bureau of State Organizations and of the Federal Fuel Administrators for the Various States and Districts." Edited by George Edwin Howes. Washington, D.C.: U.S. Government Printing Office, 1919.

The Report of the Distribution Division, 1918–1919. "Part 1: The Distribution of Coal and Coke." C. E. Lesher. Washington, D.C.: U.S. Government Printing Office, 1919.

Report of the Distribution Division, 1918–1919. "Part II: The Zone System." Wayne P. Ellis. Washington, D.C.: U.S. Government Printing Office, 1919.

U.S. National Archives. *Handbook of Federal World War Agencies and their Records, 1917–1921.* Washington, D.C.: U.S. Government Printing Office, 1943.

Federal Records of World War II. Washington, D.C.: U.S. Government Printing Office, 1951.

U.S. Office of Economic Stabilization. *Historical Working Papers on the Economic Stabilization Program, August 15, 1971 to April 30, 1974.* Washington, D.C.: U.S. Government Printing Office.

U.S. Office of Price Administration. *NRDGA "Horror Exhibit."* Washington, D.C.: U.S. Government Printing Office, March 1946.

Quarterly Reports (1-22). Washington, D.C.: U.S. Government Printing Office, March 31, 1942, through May 31, 1947.

U.S. Office of Price Stabilization. Coordinator for Government Purchases and Sales. *Economy in National Defense.* Washington, D.C.: U.S. Government Printing Office, April 1953.

"Price Stabilization to April 1953." J. H. Freehill. Washington, D.C.: U.S. Government Printing Office, 1953.

Price Stabilization: A Summary of Operations by the Director. Washington, D.C.: U.S. Government Printing Office, 1951–1953.

U.S. President. *Public Papers of the Presidents of the United States. Harry S. Truman, 1951,* and *Harry S. Truman, 1952–1953.* Washington, D.C.: U.S. Government Printing Office, 1965–66.

U.S. Treasury. *Combined Statement of Receipts, Expenditures and Balances of the United States Government.* Washington, D.C.: U.S. Government Printing Office, 1952–1954.

U.S. War Production Board. Office of Civilian Requirements. "The Textile Shortage in the First Quarter of 1945." Bulletin from Civilian Surveys Division, Series T, No. 18, Washington, D.C.: U.S. Government Printing Office, August 15, 1945.

Van Hise, Charles R. *Conservation and Regulation in the United States During the World War: An Outline for a Course of Lectures to be Given in Higher Educational Institutions.* Washington, D.C.: U.S. Government Printing Office, 1917. *Part II.* Madison, Wisconsin: Cantwell Printing Co., 1918.

Wilson, William Jerome, John A. Hart and George R. Taylor. *The Beginnings of OPA.* General Publication No. 1. *Historical Reports on War Administration: Office of Price Administration.* Washington, D.C.: U.S. Government Printing Office, 1947.

Dissertations and other unpublished manuscripts

Ackley, Gardner. "Selected Problems of Price Control Strategy, 1950–1952." Washington: Defense History Program, 1953. National Archives, Record Group 295. (Microfilm.)

Adams, George P. "The Scope and Significance of American Wartime Price Control." Dissertation. University of California, 1940.

American Meat Institute. "Meat Controls: An Objective Evaluation of the Beef Situation Today." Chicago, October 11, 1951.

Bartels, Andrew Hudson. "The Politics of Price Control: The Office of Price Administration and the Dilemmas of Economic Stabilization, 1940–1946." Ph.D. Dissertation, The Johns Hopkins University, 1980.

Bernstein, Marver H. "Enforcing Government Regulations: The Experience of the Office of Price Administration." Ph.D. Dissertation, Princeton University, 1948.

Brinser, Ayers. "A History of the Administration of Rationing in the United States in the Second World War." Harvard, April 1951. (Mimeographed.)

DeGalvez, Don Bernardo. "An Order." October 14, 1777. Unpublished manuscript, New York Public Library.

DiSalle, Michael V. "Interview with Bernard Kalb and John Hart for CBS, August 18, 1971." Encyclopedia Americana/CBS News Audio Resource.

Duhl, Ruth and other members of the enforcement staff. "Enforcement History." Spring 1947. Harvard University Law Library. (Typescript.)

Emerson, Thomas I. "Report on the Operations of the Enforcement Department, January 1–June 30, 1944." National Archives. Record Group 188, Box 910.

"First Draft of Bankhead Monograph." Henry M. Hart Papers, Box 39, file 2. Harvard University Law Library. This was probably written by Hart or one of his subordinates in 1946 for the OPA history series.

Miller, Byron S. and Marshall B. Clinard. "Regulation Coverage of Sanctions, 1944." Memorandum, March 15, 1945. National Archives Record Group 188, Box 910.

Meany, George and R. J. Thomas. "Recommended Report for the Presidential Committee on the Cost of Living." Washington, D.C., 1944.

National Opinion Research Center. "Poll #232, 1945." In the files of the Roper Institute for Public Opinion Research, Williamstown, Mass.

"Poll #236, 1945." In the files of the Roper Institute for Public Opinion Research, Williamstown, Mass.

Rodgers, Phillip Ray." Rent Control in the Emergency Price Program." Ph.D. Dissertation, American University, 1947.

Solo, Carolyn Shaw. "An Analysis of Selected Rationing Programs in the United States During World War II." Harvard, October 1950. (Mimeographed.)

Toribio, Juan J. "On the Monetary Effects of Repressed Inflation." Ph.D. dissertation. University of Chicago, 1970.

U.S. Economic Stabilization Agency. "Administrative History of the ESA under Administrator Alan Valentine, Sept. 9, 1950 to Jan. 19, 1951," by Marver H. Bernstein. (National Archives)

"Administrative History of ESA under Eric Johnston," by Herbert Kaufman. (National Archives)

"The Economic Stabilization Administrator and the Wage Stabilization Board," by Joseph P. Goldberg. (National Archives)

"Livestock and Meat Distribution Regulations." Operational History Papers (May 1953).

"The Problem of Price–Wage Coordination in 1950–1953," by John Kaufmann with assistance from Elliot Bold (June 1953).

U.S Office of Price Stabilization. "Beef at Retail: Ceiling Price Regulation 25, 1951–1953." Operational History Papers (June 1953).

"Field Administration of Price Stabilization," by Anne P. Flory. OPS History Monographs (June 1953).

"The General Ceiling Price Regulation – Problems of a Freeze," by Alfred Letzler, Joseph Zwerdling, Robert E. Olson, and Karl Schmeidler, edited by Alfred Letzer. OPS History Monographs (June 1953).

"History of Building Materials Branch, 1951–1953." Operational History Papers (June 1953).

"History of Ceiling Price Regulation 24: Beef at Wholesale, 1951–1953." Operational History Papers (June 1953).

"History of the Consumer Durables Branch, 1951–1953." Operational History Papers (June 1953).

"History of the Regulation of Automobile Prices, 1950–1953," by Horace H. Robbins. Operational History Papers (undated).

"History of Restaurant Price Control, 1951–1953." Operational History Papers (June 1953).

Weiss, Leonard W. "Import Price Control in the United States." Ph.D. Dissertation. Columbia University (Faculty of Political Science), 1954.

Name index

Subject index

accord, *see* Treasury–Federal Reserve Accord

across-the-board controls, 32, 92–4, 96, 98, 242

administrative revolution in government, 41–2

Agricultural Stabilization and Conservation Service, 205

amendments to price-control law, weakening in Korean War, *see* exemptions to price-control law

American Textile Manufacturers Institute, 225

American Vanadium Company, 82

Arab Oil Embargo, 214

army, and controlled materials plan in WWII, 116

automobiles, evasion of controls, 161–2, 229–30

black market, *see* evasion of controls

blue spruce logging, 77

Board of Overseers, 243–5

Boston, price controls in, 37–9, 105

Brest-Litovsk, Treaty of, 70

bulkline pricing, 47–50

Bureau of Industrial Housing and Transportation, 43, 63, 74

Bureau of Labor Statistics, 150, 160, 167

bureaucracy, size of, 73–5, 122–5, 188–9, 222, 236–7

business attitudes toward price controls, 103–4, 78, 202

candy bars, shrinking of in WWII, 147

catch-up inflation, 6–7, 111

Capehart Amendment, 183, 192

Capital Issues Committee, 52, 74

Chrysler Corporation, 229

Cincinnati Transit Corporation, 207

Civil War, 26, 42

clothing, evasion of controls in WWII, 150–4, 230, 240–1, 244; new program, 152–3; Maximum Average Price Regulation, 153–4

commandeering: in Revolution, 24; in WWI, 77

concentration of production, 116–7

Concord (MA) Conventions, 37–8

Construction Industry Stabilization Committee, 210

consumer durables, in WWII, 129, 160–3

Continental Currency, 26–7, 34

Controlled Materials Plan, 115, 121

copper, 44, 78, 225–6, 237

Cost of Living Council, 205–6, 208, 210

Council of Economic Advisors, 207

Council of National Defense, 43–4, 87

criminal proceedings, 58–9, 141–2; *see also* evasion of controls

decontrol of prices: WWII, 100–8; Korean War, 184–5; Vietnam War, 211–12

Defense Production Act 1950, 178, 180

Defense Production Act Amendments 1951, 182

distortions, *see* efficiency

distribution of income, effect of price controls on, 70–1, 114, 188

Department of Agriculture, 73, 205

Division of Standards and Purchases, New York State, 182

dollar-and-cents ceilings, 93

dollar-a-year employees, 46, 74, 123t

durables, consumer, evasion of controls in WWII, 160–3

Economic Stabilization Agency, Korean War, 179

efficiency, 8–9, 237–8; WWI, 55–6, 78–80; WWII, 134–9; Korean War, 189–91; Vietnam War, 222–8